SIREN
(some poetics)

Edited by Quinn Latimer

Amant

Amant, Brooklyn, New York
Dancing Foxes Press, Brooklyn, New York

This book was published in conjunction with
the exhibition:

SIREN (some poetics)
Curated by Quinn Latimer
Amant, Brooklyn
September 15, 2022–March 5, 2023

Edited by Quinn Latimer
Managing editors: Karen Kelly and Barbara Schroeder
Copyediting and proofreading: Deirdre O'Dwyer
Design: Gaile Pranckunaite
Color separations: Aust Studio

This book is typeset in Siren and GT Alpina Standard
and printed on 130 gsm Novatech Matt and
280 gsm Invercote Creato.

Photo credits:
    Unless otherwise noted, all photographs were taken
    in the exhibition *Siren (some poetics)* by
    Adrianna Glaviano
    Pages 36, 39, and 40: AG, 1967; from the author's
    personal archive
    Pages 86–87: photo by New Document
    Pages 103, 104–105: photos by Pierre Le Hors

All artwork © the artists

Front cover:
    Liliane Lijn, *Queen of Hearts, Queen of Diamonds*,
    1980 (detail). Optical glass prism and aluminum;
    two parts: 90 × 73 × 73 inches (227 × 185 × 185 cm),
    94 × 73 × 73 inches (237 × 185 × 185 cm)

Back cover:
    Dena Yago, *Rope and Lead*, 2018 (detail). Pressed
    wool, hand embroidery, pewter charms, and steel;
    105 × 57 × 2 inches (266.7 × 144.8 × 5.1 cm)

Published in 2023 by Amant and Dancing Foxes Press

Cataloging-in-publication data is on file with the
Library of Congress.

ISBN: 978-1-95494-705-4

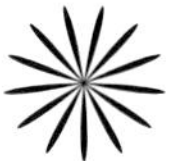

Amant

315 Maujer Street
Brooklyn, NY 11206
amant.org

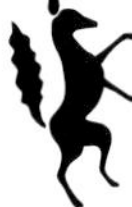

Dancing Foxes Press
16 Lefferts Place
Brooklyn, NY 11238
dfpress.org

Distributed by
ARTBOOK |D.A.P.
75 Broad Street, Suite 630
New York, NY 10004
artbook.com

Printed and bound by Petro Ofsetas,
Vilnius, Lithuania

CONTENTS

6 Adrianna Glaviano
Portfolio of installation
views at Amant

13 Christa Wolf
Conditions of a Narrative

16 Quinn Latimer
*No Body but a Voice, or
What Witness*

31 Édouard Glissant
*Concerning the Poem's
Information* (excerpt)

34 Ruth Estévez
Sirens: Some Acoustics

42 Adrianna Glaviano
Portfolio of installation
views at Amant

58 Katja Aufleger
Singing Dune

62 Shanzhai Lyric
Endless Garment

68 Jenna Sutela
nimiia log

80 Bia Davou
*Serial Structures
Serial Structures 2.
The Odyssey*

90 Senga Nengudi
*Lilies of the Valley Unite!
Or Not*

96 Iris Touliatou
Mother Fragment

102 Patricia L. Boyd
Wastebook

108 Sky Hopinka
Flesh and Ghost

116 Nour Mobarak
You Are the Audience

122 Adrianna Glaviano
Portfolio of installation
views at Amant

132 Bernadette Mayer
*Midwinter Day,
Section 6* (excerpt)

148 Rosemary Mayer
Passing Thoughts

160 Ser Serpas
*untitled, 2022
untitled, 2022
untitled, 2022
untitled, 2022*

166 Liliane Lijn
Crossing Map, Song 7
Note on *Crossing Map*

174 Mayra A. Rodríguez
Castro
Miraculous Weapons

178 Rivane Neuenschwander
The Silence of the Sirens

180 Franz Kafka
The Silence of the Sirens

184 Dena Yago
*Dolphins
Zippity Do Da
Motherfuckers*

189 Max Horkheimer and
Theodor W. Adorno
*Odysseus or Myth and
Enlightenment*
(excerpt)

192 Aura Satz
Preemptive Listening

198 Don Mee Choi
Ahn Hak-sŏp #4

208 Hana Noorali and
Lynton Talbot
*The Figure and the Field,
or the Siren and the
Ocean: Some Poethical
Wagers*

217 Anaïs Duplan
Tony Cokes,
No Sell Out,
1995, 6:20
Tony Cokes, Ad Vice,
1999, 6:36

221 Exhibition Guide

240 Adrianna Glaviano
Portfolio of installation
views at Amant

246 Reprint Permissions

247 List of Works,
installation views at
Amant, September 15,
2022–March 5, 2023

SIREN

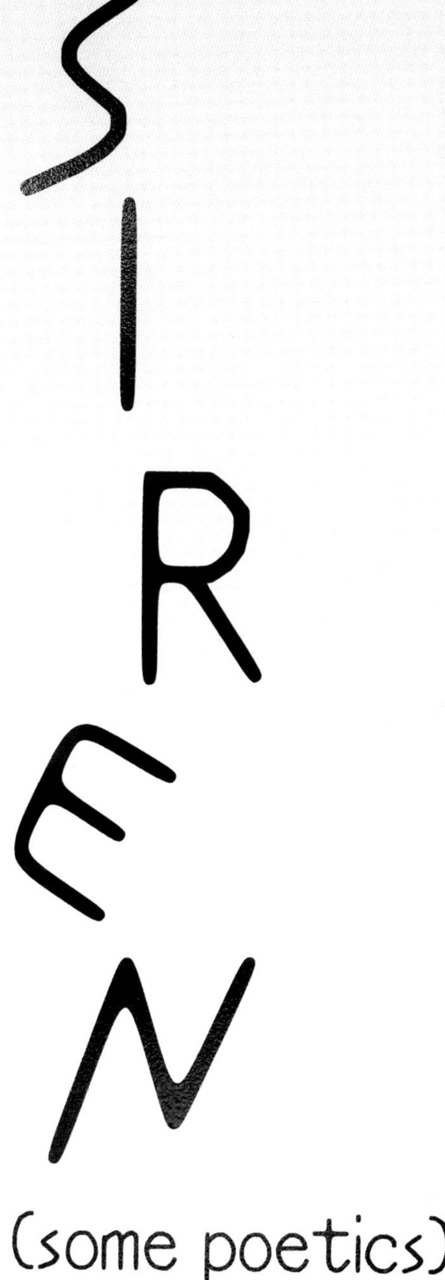

(some poetics)

Katja Aufleger
Patricia L. Boyd
Bia Davou
Sky Hopinka
Liliane Lijn
Bernadette Mayer
Rosemary Mayer
Nour Mobarak
Senga Nengudi
Rivane Neuenschwander
Mayra A. Rodríguez Castro
Aura Satz
Ser Serpas
Shanzhai Lyric
Jenna Sutela
Iris Touliatou
Dena Yago

Curated by
Quinn Latimer

September 15, 2022 –
March 5, 2023

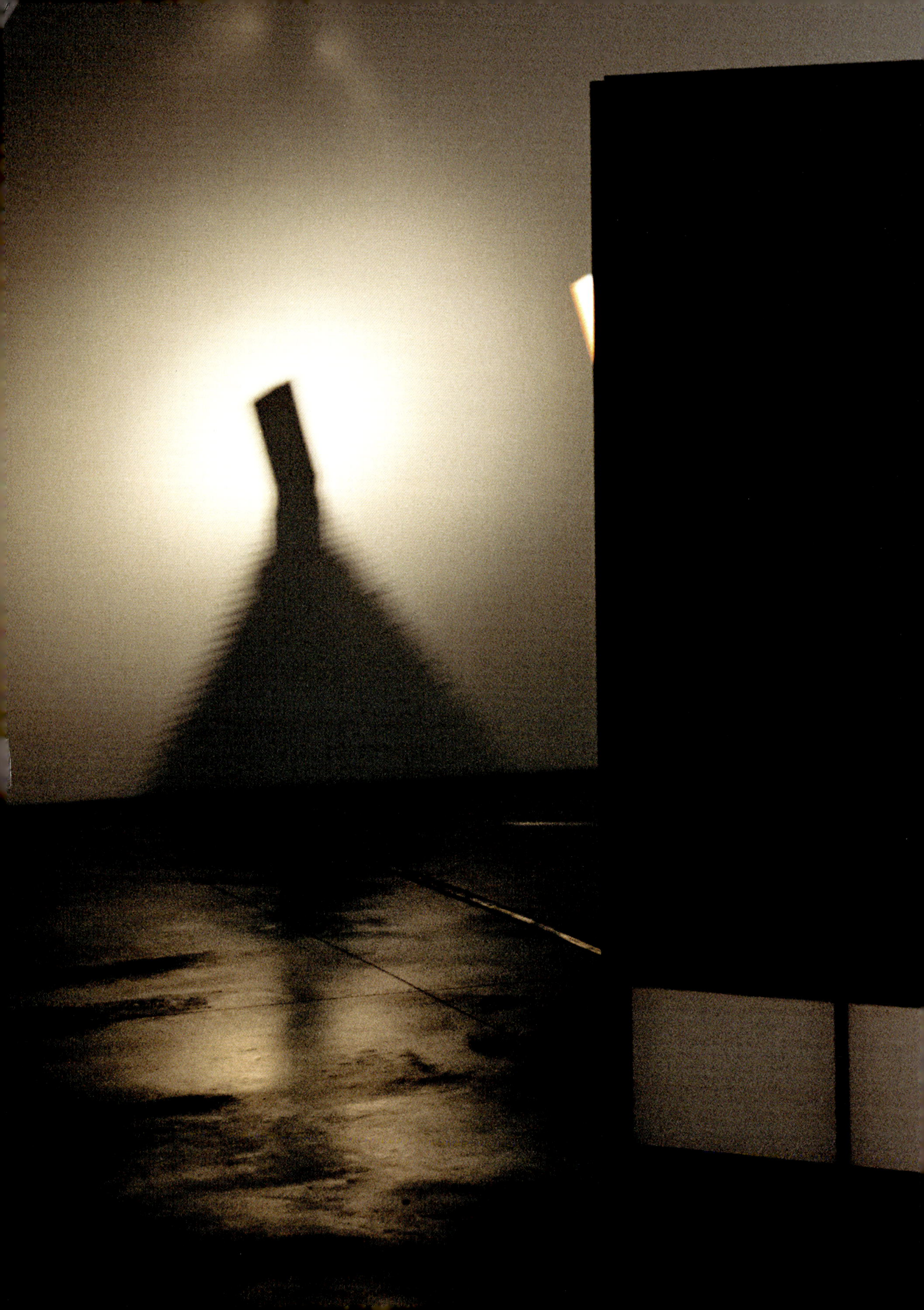

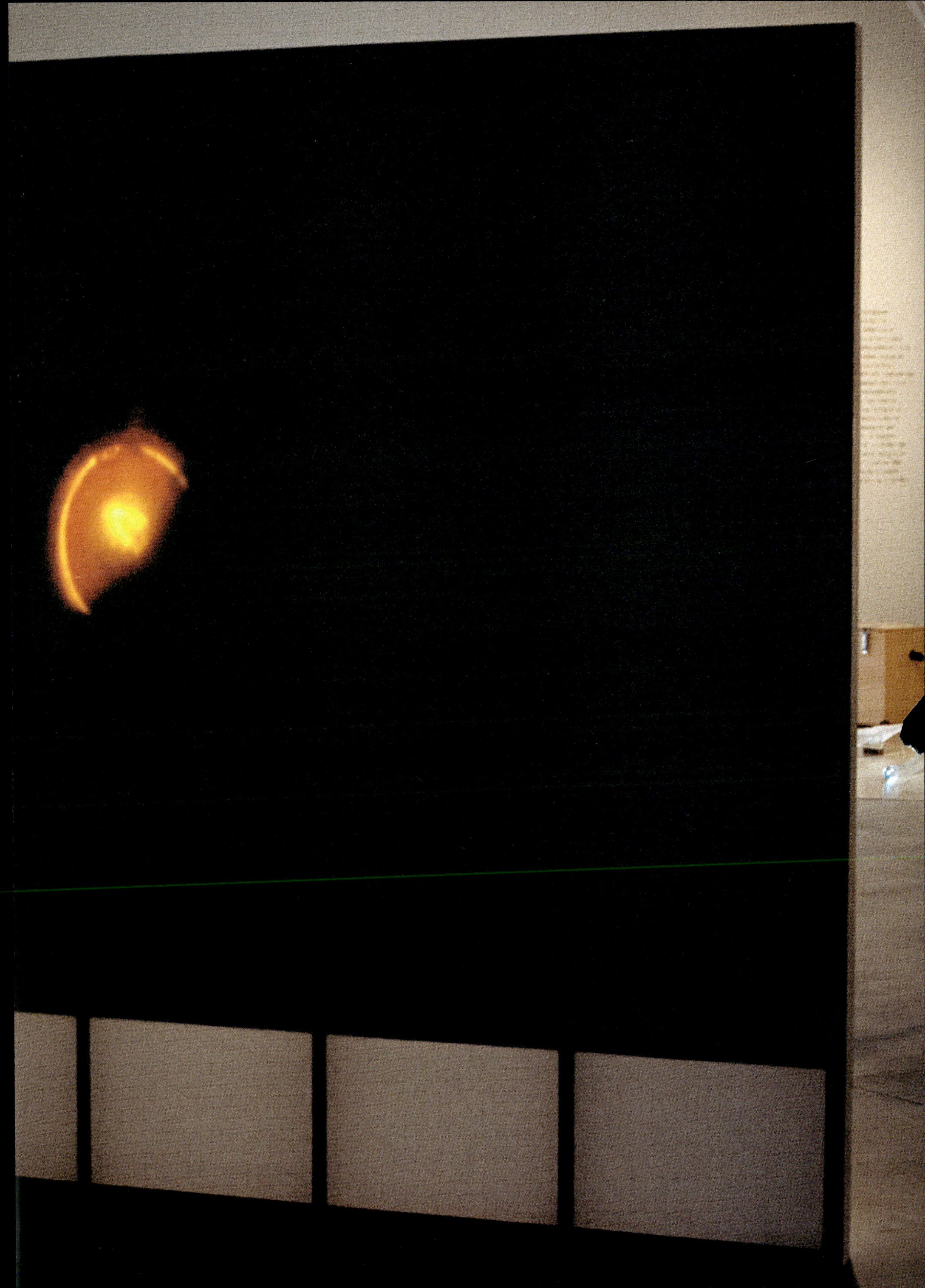

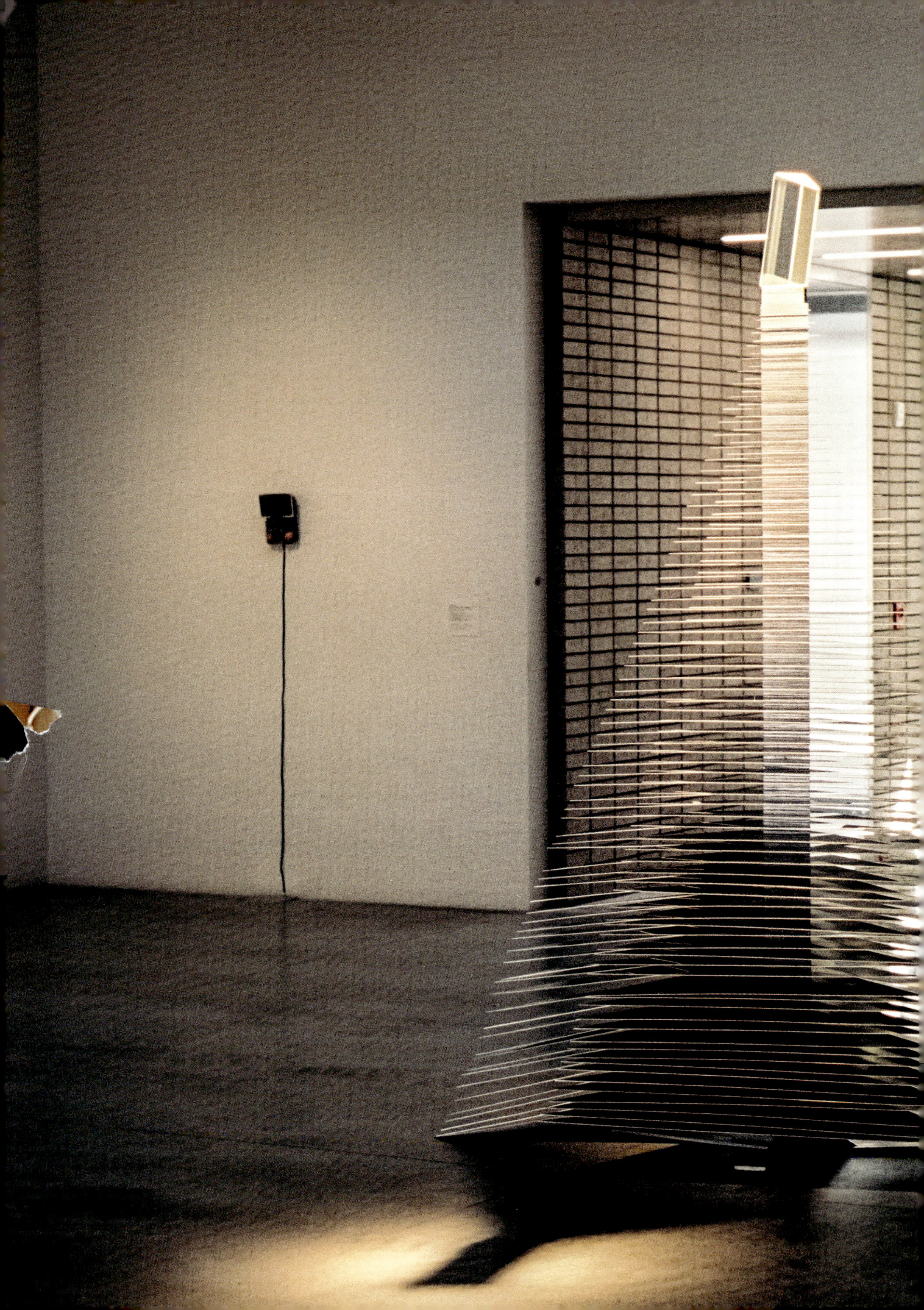

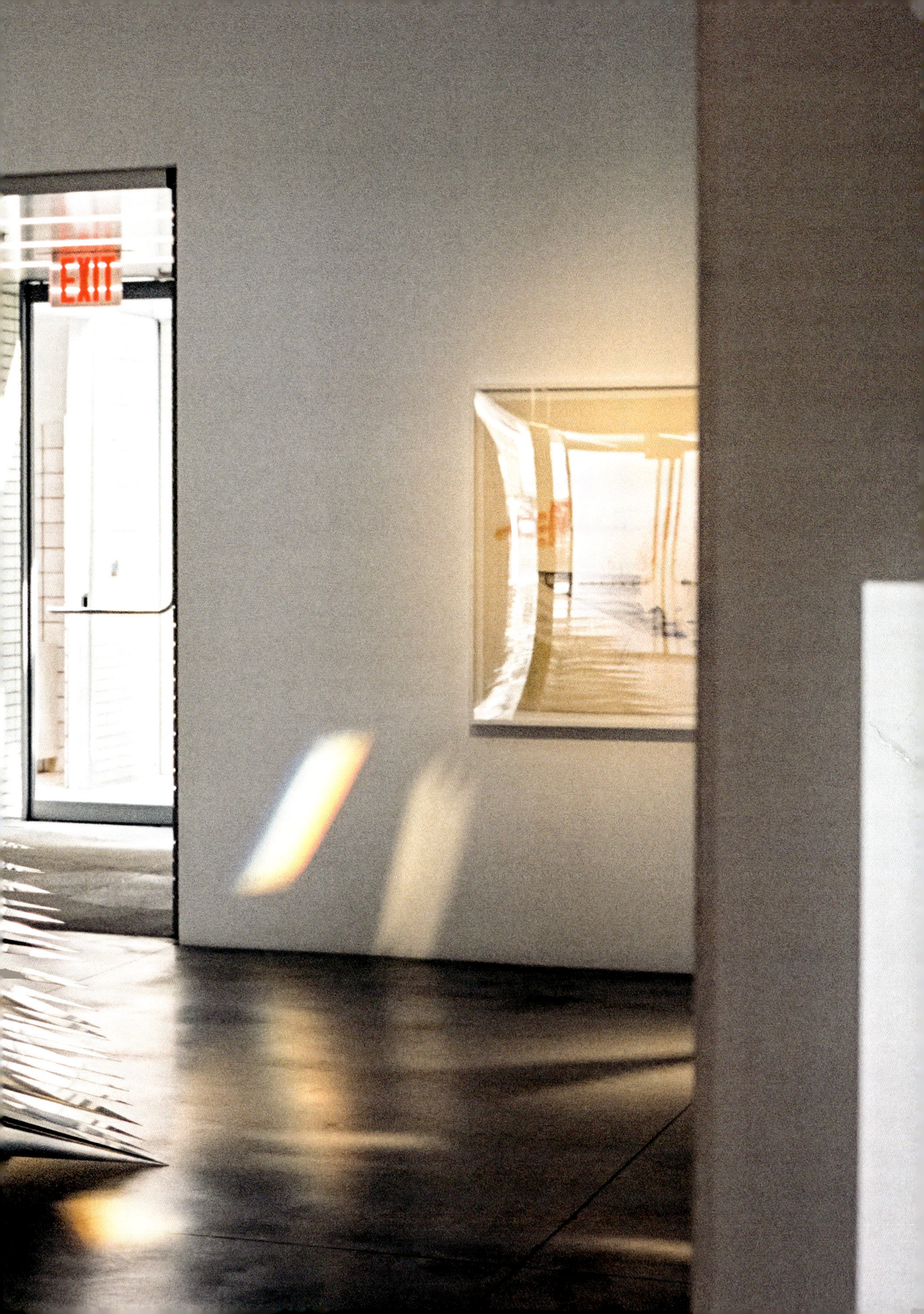

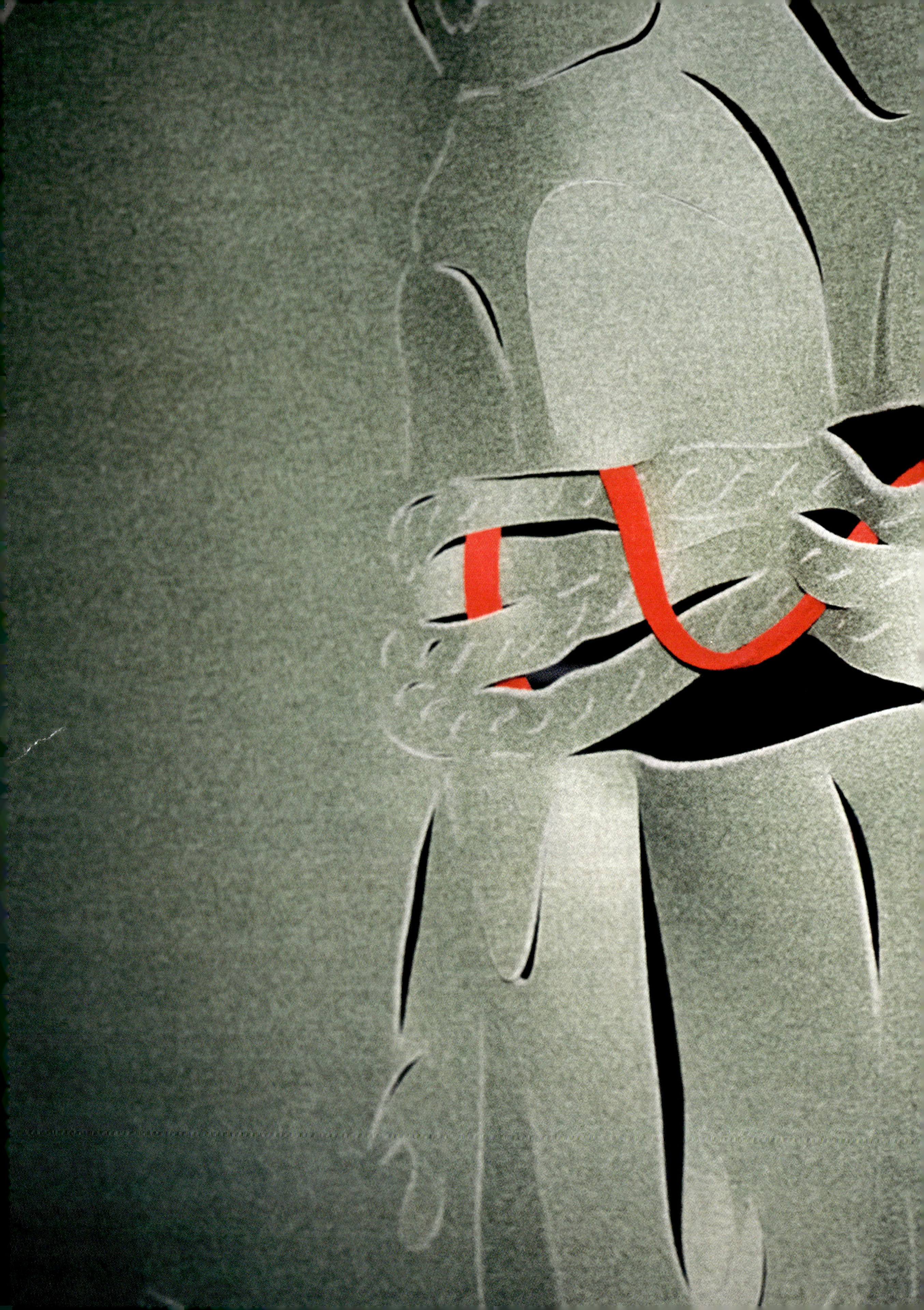

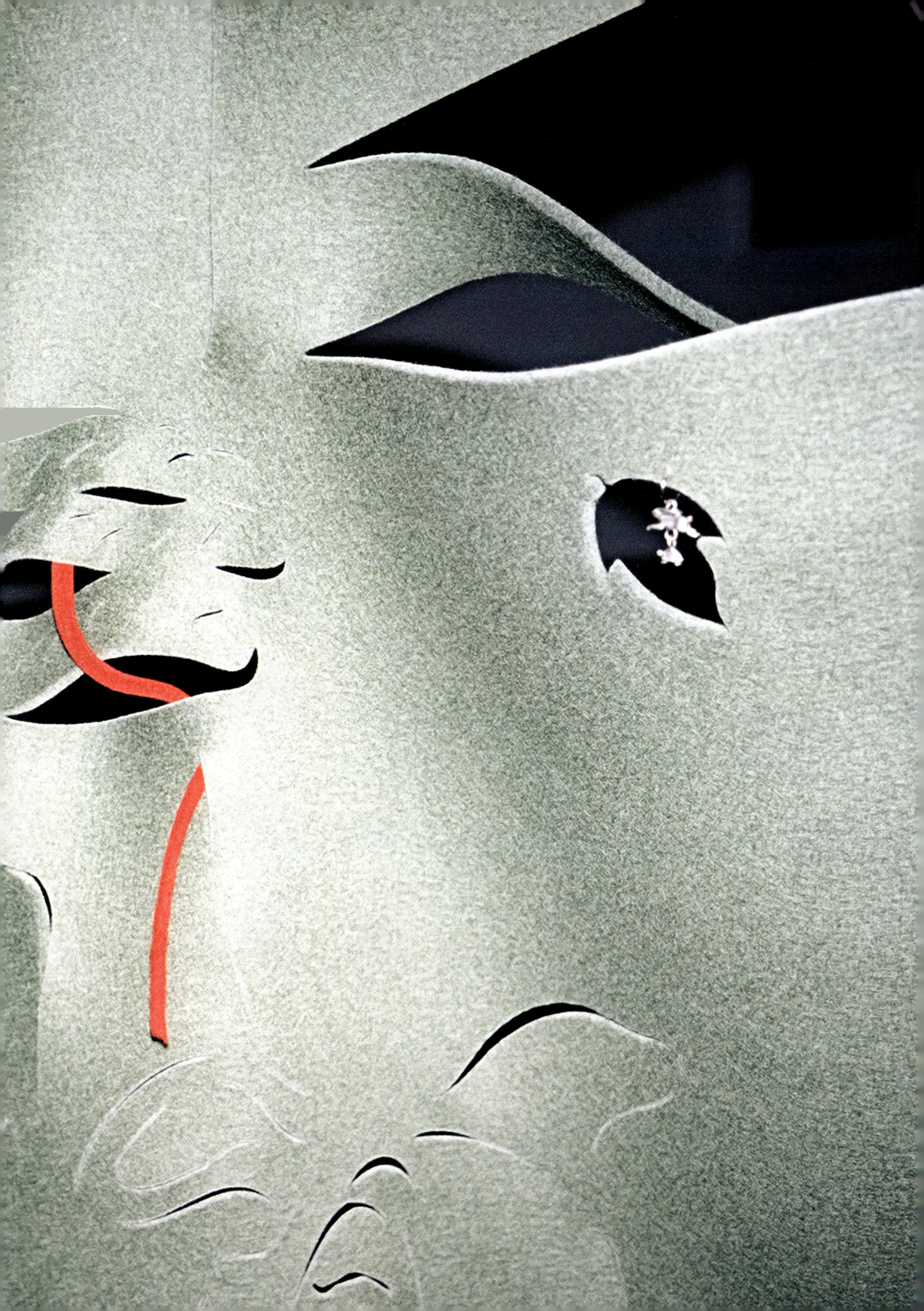

Ladies and gentlemen:
This enterprise bears the title "Lectures on Poetics," but I will tell you at once, I cannot offer you a poetics. One glance at the *Classical Antiquity Lexicon* was enough to confirm my suspicion that I myself have none. "Poetics" (the definition reads): theory of the art of poetry, which at an advanced stage —Aristotle, Horace—takes on a systematic form, and whose norms have been accorded "wide validity" in numerous countries since the age of humanism. New aesthetic positions are reached (the book says) via confrontation with these norms (in parentheses, Brecht). I do not deride, and, it goes without saying, I do not deny the influence of prevailing aesthetic norms on every writer—as well as on every reader, who attributes to personal taste what are really internalized norms. Yet I have never felt the raging desire for confrontation with the poetics, or the model, of a great writer (in parentheses, Brecht). This has only struck me in the last couple of years, and so it may be that, incidentally, these essays will also treat a question that I have not been asked: the question of why I do *not* have a poetics.

But mainly I want to ask you to follow me on a journey, in a literal as well as a metaphorical sense. For the past two years I have been tracking a key word: "Cassandra," and having felt the recurrent urge to trace a rough outline of the roads where this word led me, I intend to do so on this occasion. Many or most, maybe the most important things will go unsaid; indeed, probably they are unknown to me as well. I want to set a fabric before you. It is an aesthetic structure, and as such it would lie at the center of my poetics *if* I had one. But this fabric which I want to display to you now did not turn out completely tidy, is not surveyable at one glance. Many of its motifs are not followed up, many of its threads are tangled. There are wefts which stand out like foreign bodies, repetitions, material that has not been worked out to its conclusion. This is not always intentional; I myself had first to work to master the material, and I make you witness of this work process. I also make you witness to a process which has changed my lens on the world. But this process of change has only just begun, and I feel keenly the tension between the artistic forms within which we have agreed to abide and the living material, borne to me by my senses, my psychic apparatus, and my thought, which has resisted these forms. If I may formulate a poetological problem so soon, let it be this: There is and there can be no poetics which prevents the living experience of countless perceiving subjects from being killed and buried in art objects. So, does this mean that art objects ("works") are products of the alienation of our culture, whose other finished products are produced for self-annihilation?

Thus, I have taken a personal approach in these lectures. I employ various subjective forms of expression, looking at them in terms of the work that they can achieve, that I can achieve in them. The first and second essays—a two-part *record of a trip to Greece*—attest to how the figure of Cassandra takes possession of me and takes on her first, provisional incarnation. The third essay has the form of a *work diary* that tries to trace the vise grip between life and subject matter. In the fourth essay, a *letter*, I ask questions about the historical reality of the Cassandra figure and conditions for the woman writer past and present. My overall concern is the sinister effects of alienation, in aesthetics, in art, as well as elsewhere.

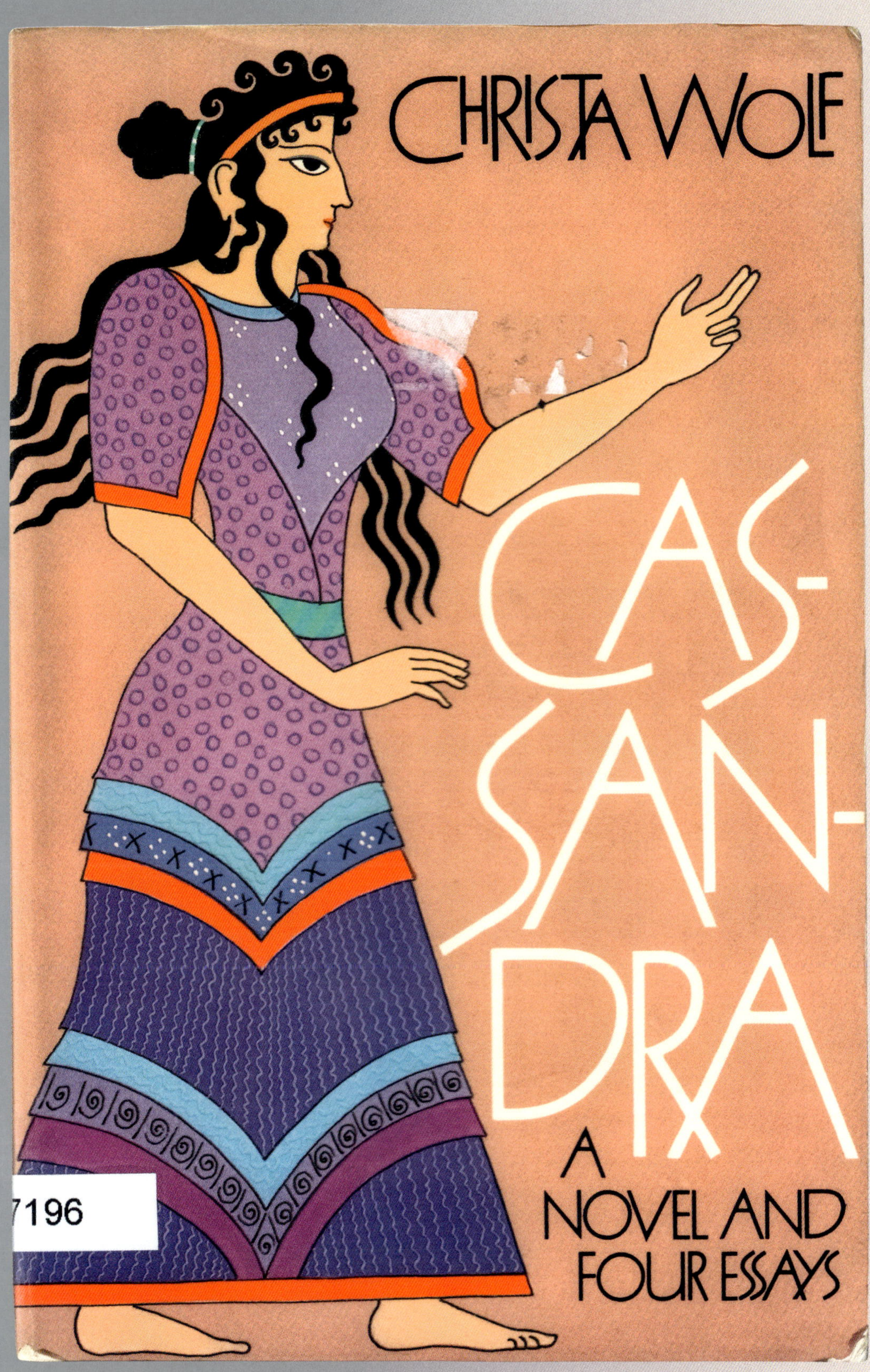

CHRISTA WOLF
CAS-
SAN-
DRA
A
NOVEL AND
FOUR ESSAYS

No Body but a Voice, or What Witness

Quinn Latimer

My words were met by a rustling of fibers.
—Fleur Jaeggy[1]

Yet contact with poetry bequeaths unexpected outcomes.
—Bia Davou[2]

Sirens are alarms: they signal harm. In an ancient world, sirens were figured as women (part bird or part fish but all witch), whose seductive song was an invitation to self-harm. Their song had sailors forget their homes, languages, wives, ambitions, and senses of self (or selves), offering stasis and death instead. Siren songs, both ancient and nascent, are in the realm of danger, then. And if our conceptions of sirens have changed across epochs, our notions of control have not. We would still like to save ourselves in every instance; we would still like to get home, to worldly acclaim, sweet song or not. Sound and knowledge, then, being one way to do this—to close or open our bodies to their seductive poetics, to know ourselves and thus our origins and futures.

In the original Greek of *The Odyssey*, of the sirens who sang from their island meadow to Odysseus and his crew in their waters, no bodies were indicated—just mouths and some voice. The lure the sirens offered was cognizance; it was knowledge. The technology of their voices was some "honeyed song,"[3] emitted as if from a speaker over land, across water, indicating other familiar, oft-imposed borders: between exile and

---

1   Fleur Jaeggy, *The Water Statues*, trans. Gini Alhadeff (New York: New Directions, 2021), 7. Originally published as *Statue d'acqua* (Milan: Aldephi Edizioni, 1980).

2   Bia Davou, *Serial Structures 2: The Odyssey*, trans. Vassilis Douvitsas (Athens: Desmos Art Gallery, 1981); in this volume, 85.

3   Emily Wilson, trans., *The Odyssey*, by Homer (New York: W. W. Norton, 2017), 307.

home, foreign and familiar, female and male, nonhuman and human, danger and safety, transgression and normativity, stasis and mobility, sonic disobedience and sonic obedience; that is, language as noise and language as linguistic meaning. These borders were an ideology of enforced binaries, and fundamentally unjust and untrue. But poetry is politics, always. Either all body or all sound though, our siren might be prosthetic and/or symbiotic, at once ecosystem and elegy, and an extension of our hybridized selves into other receiving bodies.

The exhibition *SIREN (some poetics)* at Amant in Brooklyn suggests what forms and sounds beyond such borders and boundaries and binaries—ancestral, technological, epistemological, literary, patriarchal, corporeal, emotional, or otherwise. Devoted to the voice—as aesthetic signature, or the production of self and sound and language—and the avatar-like bodies we build and break around it, *SIREN* considers technologies of myth and mouth, earth and alarm, gender and poetics. Through the work of approximately twenty artists and poets of various generations and geographies, the project centers practices that employ grammars of sign and sound systems, at once figuring, resisting, writing, and voicing the visual field. Poetry remains the touchstone throughout; or, rather, poetics do.

As the Greek artist Bia Davou once wrote, "Yet contact with poetry bequeaths unexpected outcomes." So it is here. Yet the ways in which contact with poetry manifest are manifold, particularly in the architectonic spaces of art galleries and particularly in the practices of artists and poets versed in the visual. In their discursive constellation and glittering totality, then, the works by *SIREN*'s artists and poets, collectives and sisters, and composers and filmmakers, move away from the cool, clinical, and mostly two-dimensional exhibitions that have so often stood for language as a visual art practice, where the white cube replaced the pale page. Instead, *SIREN* is situated firmly (though not exclusively) in the Earth and its kaleidoscopic ecosystems. Both human and nonhuman forms of language making and poetics are posited, from precolonial myth to ludic speculation, bootlegged oracular line to critical fabulation, fungal networks to gut bacteria, text to textile to poem to prism to algorithm. Indeed, the works on view often emit and evidence a kind of parapoetics: poetry as opaque metabolic structuring, or some wild surfacing.

Questions arose as I embarked on this project and approached its language-lined shore. Among them were: How to survey the siren as a figure of myth, mouth, earth, sound, silence, alarm, poetics, and hyphae? How to understand it as a kind of technology—of gender, text, textile, machine, violence, security, and fiction? What of the poem's origin in song, and that song as medicine or epic, history or ideology, complicity or resistance? What of the poetics of alarm, and the authority and authoritarianism of language itself? To consider the siren as both mythic trope and contemporary warning system (perhaps one and the same), one must examine in which forms its production—of information, alarm, corporeality, prophecy, transgression, the nonhuman given human form, sound made voice, or vice versa, danger given grammar—occurs. Yet as artists center a certain poetics, their works trace and break the always animated border between language as visual art practice and language as literary one.

That said, poetics, like violence, are inseparable from the technologies of their times. From the collectively composed and orally rehearsed and circulated *Odyssey*—attributed to a Homer once it was finally written down—to contemporary visual art and poetry practices today, poetics are entangled with the technologies and communication systems that condition their making and enable (or disable) their dissemination. In each of the works gathered in *SIREN (some poetics)*—whether sculpture or poem, film or painting, object or script, drawing or score, or some hybrid amalgamation thereof—technologies of language and transformation and myths of normativity and supremacy, and their long histories, are felt, articulated, critiqued, channeled. As are the bodies continually fashioned and refashioned, read and misread, to contain the irradiating voices that sound them. "For what information can the poem be responsible?" Édouard Glissant once asked.[4] Yes, and in what form—whose voice— does it arrive to us?

※

SIREN, not Siren or siren. I was thinking of *SIREN* as some proto code, a kind of early technology of the binary (and its breaking) for and from

4　Édouard Glissant, "Concerning the Poem's Information," in *Poetics of Relation*, trans. Betsy Wing (Ann Arbor: University of Michigan Press, 1997), 81; in this volume, 32. Originally published as *Poètique de la relation* (Paris: Gallimard, 1990).

an ancient world. A nascent communications system of serial structures: zeros and ones, early seafaring and epic poetry algorithms, et cetera. Woman and man, monster and man, land and sea, fame and unfame, song and poem, host and guest, the oral and the written. Also: a voice and its unhearing, an island and its passing, a siren and the silence after. Around these binaries and stories—so ideological a genre, always circling violence—and their blurring and breaking (like some code), we made the exhibition at Amant. Its artists and poets, their poetic and visual languages—all their signs and signifieds, fields and figures, screens and projections, poems and sculptures, prisms and algorithms—constellate and inscribe the following pages, too. They write them. But first, to go back.

Emily Wilson has noted of the Homeric sirens: "The seduction they offer is cognitive: they claim to know everything about the war in Troy, and everything on earth. They tell the names of pain."[5] To evade their song—part pain and part pleasure, like life—is to avoid capture and stasis and one's bones eventually scripting some sirenic meadow. Yet what actually was it that Odysseus and his crew escaped? Not just death. Or its living manifestation, the past, per Max Horkheimer and Theodor W. Adorno, who famously insisted that the allure of siren song was that of sinking into one's past.[6] No, not just this ("just"). I picture the crew sailing off, Odysseus still tied to his mast (blissed out, in knots), and Sadie Plant's voice comes to me. "Those were the days, when we were all at sea. It seems like yesterday to me. Species, sex, race, class: in those days none of this meant anything at all," the opening of her *Zeroes and Ones* (1997) goes. "We were whatever we were up to at the time," Plant writes. "Polymorphous transfers without regard for borders and boundaries."

So no, Odysseus did not just avoid death when he fled the sirens. He escaped an erotics of total knowledge: the seduction, pleasure, pain, and

---

5   Emily Wilson, Twitter feed, March 4, 2018, 4:12 p.m., https://twitter.com/emilyrcwilson/ status/970406696836304897. See also Emily Wilson, translator's note, in Homer, *The Odyssey* (New York: W. W. Norton, 2018), 68. Wilson's English translation of *The Odyssey* (see note 3) is the first by a woman classicist to be published. The epic poem is attributed to circa the eighth century BCE; its first English translation appeared in 1614—so it took approximately four hundred years.

6   Max Horkheimer and Theodor W. Adorno insisted that the allure of the siren song is that of sinking into the past, with the sonic property of language triumphing over its signifying aspect. See their "Odysseus or Myth and Enlightenment," in *Dialectic of Enlightenment* (1947), trans. John Cumming (New York: Continuum, 1972), 43–44; in this volume, 189–90.

transformation of one's world rendered in poetic form (nonbinary and binary both). Yet the technology of the sirens' narcotic, nonhuman voices was some disembodied song emitted as if from land's shore across water, indicating supposedly other nonnegotiable borders, among them the hybrid and human, intellect and ignorance, exclusion and inclusion.[7] Thus, the exhibition at Amant approaches and approximates what sounds beyond such borders and for what witnesses. For, as Glissant writes, "Exclusion is the rule in binary practice (either/or), whereas poetics aims for a space of difference—not exclusion but, rather, where difference is realized in going beyond."[8]

It is this space of difference—a poetics of going beyond the traditional strictures of language and form and conservative ideas of embodiment—that the artists and poets in *SIREN* create together. To constellate their voices—in all their singular and polyphonic meaning and manifestations—is to suggest the avatar-like bodies we build and break around them *to make sense of them*. Indeed, *voice*, in English, is anything but static. It moves fluently and fluidly across meanings, grain across glassy sea. ("The 'grain' is the body in the voice as it sings, the hand as it writes, the limb as it performs," per Roland Barthes.[9]) From the voice of the artist or writer (their unmistakable style and sensibility) to the voice of the speaker or singer (tone and texture of their orality), there is also the supposed voicelessness of the politically dispossessed. *We must give them a voice*, it is said, *those who have been silenced*. And there is the feminist "coming to voice," per bell hooks, the "revolutionary gesture" of moving from silence into speech.[10]

But whose voice, and in what way is it "given" or arrived at? Whose speech? Who hears it—what witness—and to what end? Voice might be seduction, song, speech, cry, complicity, agency, revolution. It might

---

7   Wilson, *The Odyssey*, 307.

8   Glissant, "Concerning the Poem's Information," 82; in this volume, 33.

9   Roland Barthes, "The Grain of the Voice" (1972), in *Image, Music, Text*, trans. Stephen Heath (New York: Hill & Wang, 1977), 188.

10   "In recent years any writing about feminism has overshadowed writing as a poet. Yet there are spaces where thoughts and concerns converge. One such space has been the feminist focus on coming to voice—on moving from silence into speech as revolutionary gesture." bell hooks, "'When I was a young soldier for the revolution': coming to voice," in *Talking Back* (Boston: South End Press, 1989), 12.

be siren; that is, both a warning of danger and that very danger itself. Yet just as global surveillance regimes turn our constant visuality into a means of violence, so too can they make linguistic fluency and well-circulated textual routines into carceral conditions. If poets and artists and hybrid others attempt to resist such regimes via the virtuosic slipperiness of their language, still this is often the very medium—the record—in which those surveilled by corporate-states are tracked. Thus, in its consideration of works often made between language to be looked at, language to be read, and language to be heard, *SIREN* surveys how the performance of the voice (in manifold forms across many decades) encourages the development of more radical subjectivities. How both new and old oral and literary cultures have transformed how we conceive of and perform language every day. To shape and control one's image and life via language is not new nor minor (Homer, among others, tells us so). *SIREN* attempts to think through, then, the relationship among language, sound, body, image, and their artistic productions in ways as voracious as voice itself.

That said, the performance of language is an everyday enactment that is often cast as "natural," authentic, and unrehearsed. But the voice is anything but unpracticed. Nor are the often-hybrid bodies and images we construct to contain and amplify it. A voice might be soothing, rhetorical, familial, anthropological, archaic, anarchic, secret (hooks again: "For me, poetry was the place for the secret voice"[11]). It might be the voice on the page or in the air, the voice attached to a body or bodiless, droning or drifting from some speaker or island meadow. For *SIREN*'s poets and artists, the mouth is simply (never so simply) an opening from which to begin.

So, to our litany of questions again (a kind of armature, like lyric): How to use the psychic apparatus of the siren to explore technologies of voice in their voluminous fabrications and sundry meanings? How to survey the siren as a figure of new and old myths, new and old earths? How to understand it as a kind of technology of language itself, and all that is constituted by it: gender, text, textile, security, and, of course, relation? Communication technologies as every poetic technology, perhaps. *No body but a voice*, as some ancients might have said. *To read or to be*

11   Ibid.

read, as our contemporaries might reply. Each a kind of warning for those bound for and to a language-strewn future.

⌘

A siren is a full-body experience. So is the exhibition. But what kind of body or bodies? What kind of experience? In the translation tradition of *The Odyssey*, the sirens have long been figured as goddesses. Male translators built femme bodies into their Homeric texts to stand in like avatars for the sirens' intoxicating song, to make its appeal legible and ideological. Knowledge and aesthetic form become corporeal form—an old story (also a recent one). We often construct bodies like vessels to hold and withhold sound and voice, though. To corral voices and what they contain—the foreign and the hybrid, the nonhuman and the nonbinary, the female and some gendered premonition—within certain operations and systems: patriarchal, supremacist, literary, economic, artistic. Yet all that is described in *The Odyssey*'s original, slim section on the sirens are mouths and knowledge, history and its telling. That is not nothing. As Mary Ruefle's inexorable poem "Deconstruction" goes (in total):

> I think the sirens in *The Odyssey* sang *The Odyssey*,
> for there is nothing more seductive, more terrible,
> than the story of our own life, the one we do not
> want to hear and will do anything to listen to.[12]

The siren song as a kind of proto autofiction, then, or a kind of autopoiesis. The world coursing and conditioning through our reproductions of self and social world, turning our singular tales into some autotheory. Indeed, the siren song is both theory and technology, bodied and disembodied, figure and landscape. Each of us a receiving vessel for collective, hybrid, affective lyrics, their warning and inscription.

Epic poetry was an early technology of the ancient world that enabled and described how heroic, poetic fame, *audible* renown (*kleos*), is made.[13]

12   Mary Ruefle, "Deconstruction," in *The Most of It* (Seattle: Wave Books, 2008).

13   "In a universe where impersonal matter endured forever but the personal self was extinguished at death, the most which could survive of that self was a rumor, a reputation. For this, the person craving immortality—a condition proper only to the gods and antithetical to human existence—was totally reliant on poets and poetry." Bruce Lincoln, *Death, War, and Sacrifice: Studies in Ideology and Practice* (Chicago: University of Chicago Press, 1991), 15.

How one's name and story could be reproduced, endlessly, as lyric, as epic. "In an oral context, history casts itself preferentially in the mold of the epic," as Mamoussé Diagne writes. "The latter is the mode of constitution of the memorable."[14]

And this technology of the memorable was connected to others, woven into a perfect circuit. In the Eastern Mediterranean, epic poetry (its orality, then its writing) has long been linked to weaving. ("My words were met by a rustling of fibers," per Fleur Jaeggy.) As Odysseus circled the seas and was tied to his mast in knots by his crew, so that he might safely listen to the sirens' song, his wife Penelope wove and knotted her textiles by day and unraveled them by night, so that his story and hers, their interwoven life, would not stop.

To stop or not is the anxious argument of epic poetry, its movers, makers, and heroes. In every approach of some foreign island, there is the fear of violence but the desire for poetics—the telling of one's story, the hosting of one's body, the making of some relation. And that fear and desire take form as songs. Land often begins with a song through its siren (one theory being that the sound of the siren is based on island wind combining with the shape of the land itself). "First you will reach the Sirens, who bewitch / all passerby . . . with piercing songs," as Circe warns Odysseus.[15] Those songs being, in a sense, the terror of knowledge, the desire for self-obliteration and territorialization. Feet on some ground (shifting like sand). Siren as shore, as that shore's sound, as the beginning of territory and knowledge and one's body arrived securely (or not) within it. Should a book begin with a siren, this would make sense: language starts with some sound in one's head, a call into the dark. The beckoning of acoustic feeling: a call and its response.

I sometimes wonder if the voices of the Homeric sirens might have been the pure consciousness of their island itself. Its meadows and rocks producing that "honeyed song" like a mouth, like a speaker (in both senses). The topography of the island and the technology of the voice tied in a tight knot, an unending loop. It would not be unheard of. Consider the phenomena of the singing dunes in the deserts of Qatar and

14 Mamoussé Diagne, "Logic of the Written Word and Oral Logic: Conflict at the Heart of the Archive," trans. Adeena Mey, *Afterall*, no. 53 (2022), https://www.afterall.org/article/logic-of-the-written-word-and-oral-logic-conflict-at-the-heart-of-the-archive.

15 Wilson, *The Odyssey*, 302.

California—not myth but fact, where the dunes' sheer, granular faces become speakers and the avalanche of their grains, sound waves. Iris Murdoch once wrote that "the mythical is not something 'extra.' We live in myth and symbol all the time."[16]

What is myth, though? "Myths are stories about people who become too big for their lives temporarily, so that they crash into other lives or brush against gods," Anne Carson writes. "In crisis their souls are visible."[17] Perhaps so. And if this visibility takes the form of language, of a system of communication, this also makes sense. As Michel Serres has noted, "Myth, then, mythical narrative, is less an originary legend than the form of transmission itself."[18] And that form is oral—originally, it is spoken. What did the sirens do? They *tell* the "names of pain," per Wilson, and know "everything on earth." Voice and form, their song transmits alarm, emergency, loss, and pain.

Pain is not far from the earthly surface of our *SIREN* project, nor the desire, relation, geography, and systems that condition it. Sirens are warning systems—and we have been surrounded by them our entire lives. Earth is one such system, perhaps. And though the beginnings of the exhibition preceded the Russian invasion of Ukraine in February 2022, the sirens of war, distantly told or intimately experienced—as well as those of pandemic, white supremacy, femicide, imperialism, authoritarianism, climate collapse, coloniality, and astonishing inequity—have sounded throughout the making of this project. Writing shortly after the exhibition opened, a critic called *SIREN (some poetics)* a "contemporary cri de cœur."[19] This is neither wrong nor far off. The cry is so close it is embodied.

It is organ. Or fossil.

In the poet and artist Theresa Hak Kyung Cha's *Dictee*, her autoethnographic novel of poetics structured around the Greek muses and a matrilineal constellation of Korean women forebears and revolutionaries (published the week before Cha's murder in New York in 1982), she performs a siren song, in the chapter "Sacred Poetry":

16 Iris Murdoch, "Mass, Might, and Myth," *Spectator*, September 7, 1962 , 337–38.

17 Preface to Anne Carson, trans., *Grief Lessons: Four Plays*, by Euripides (New York: NYRB Classics, 2006), 8.

18 Michel Serres, *Hommage à Jean Hyppolite* (Paris: Presses Universitaires de France, 1971), 7. Quoted and translated in Diagne, "Logic of the Written Word and Oral Logic."

19 Travis Diehl, "In 'Siren,' Artists and Poets Singing from the Rocks," *New York Times*, October 27, 2022.

> Words cast each by each to weather
> avowed indisputably, to time.
> If it should impress, make fossil trace of word,
> residue of word, stand as a ruin stands,
> simply, as mark
> having relinquished itself to time to distance.[20]

♯

Looking for the fossil traces of words, their distance, I comb through my early notes on the *SIREN* project:

> *To begin with / move from:*
> All cognition, all alarm, all sound.
> Text to textile as mouth to shelter.
> Ecosystems as elegies then technologies.
> Tents as reading rooms, as mouths, as stages.
> Textiles as mouths, as reliefs, as language.
> Sails as pages, all ground and air, all written.
> Poem to object to moving images, all sisters.
> Writing between the page and the performance.
> Voice, sound, noise, cry, speech, song, shelter, siren.
> Vivid, saturated textiles and moving images, prisms.
> Technologies of gender, of writing, of code, of bacteria.
> Casts and forms that approximate silence via space (like the page).

Red earth, pyramidal forms like sails, pink and brown dunes, mouths.
I consider how my notes are manifest in the exhibition—or not. Those pyramidal forms (sails and dunes) are there in various works, as are the variously metallic (silver and copper) palettes of saturated pinks, browns, blues, and greens. Rainbow reflections of prisms, glass organs, and film projections strobe Amant's walls. The theatricality of the immersive installation—sound and song, light and shadow, bleeding across works— conjures an almost eighties-era aesthetic. This rhymes, in a sense, with the writings I have gleaned to cite in this text, which mostly come from

20   Theresa Hak Kyung Cha, *Dictee*, 2nd ed. (Berkeley: University of California Press, 2001), 177.

25

that decade or the years that circle it. Why? What kind of story of the present am I trying to tell by transposing that specific historical period—its forms, languages, narratives, and hues—onto this one? To what have we returned? What refrains?

Regardless, the works that constitute *SIREN* translate and transpose the phenomena of voice and sign as variously visual, oral, spatial, acoustic, synthetic, ideological, textual, gendered, narrative, and nonnarrative mediums. In images still and moving, poems as scripts and scores for performances, videos as ancestral song or improvised manifesto, sculptures as mouths for a kind of breathing, kind of song, the works at times evoke typographic performances and decisions of the page. They move fluently between citations and space, links and genres, voices and their technologies, suggesting the exhibition is a text or score itself. Which is also an old exhibitionary story, forever reiterated.

Yet the book *SIREN (some poetics)* is not intended to be a dutiful record of the exhibition proper. It is its own specific space—the space of the bound publication—that holds and presents the textual production in which the artists and poets of *SIREN* are continually involved. The participants in the show are here represented by textual works—poems, scores, essays, scripts, subtitles—that mostly do not appear in the exhibition itself. We wanted this book to reveal the work and thinking that art exhibitions often do not: the *writing* that goes on amid the making of paintings, sculptures, objects, performances, films, and other artworks. How language is part of both the becoming and the leaving of artistic practice. Still, the spatial relationship here between the space of the exhibition (the museum) and the space of the text (the book) is important. It always is.

Stanza means "room" in Italian. Beyond the long literary relationship between the poetic and architectural imaginaries, for *SIREN*, the rooms of the poem, the rooms of the page, and the rooms of the gallery, of wall and screen, are linked. The pages that are bound and published, the pages that emerge from the glowfield of one's phone or monitor, and the fields and frames of painting and images moving and still, are all taken as equally urgent frames for the production of meaning. So it has followed here. And yet, as with every frame, the same query emerges: "What has been left out?" A ringing in my ears. An alarm—perhaps the poetics of alarm—warning those of us bound to language-strewn forms, language-writ futures.

26

✺

I feel I should go back once again to the beginnings of this book, and the introduction that (perhaps elliptically) precedes this one. The East German writer Christa Wolf wrote "Conditions of a Narrative" in the early 1980s to introduce her *Cassandra* project, a book begun as a lectureship on poetics at the University of Frankfurt in 1982. Is it strange to begin a book (for an exhibition) with an introduction from another book (comprised of a novel and four lectures) from nearly a half century ago? And what if the book in question is from another country, another system, another aesthetic and political world, now dismantled? Well. Let's say it's a premonition. Displacement, dispossession, conflation, appropriation, translation, repetition, poetics, prophecy, some continuum: they all figure.

Like the siren, often like Circe, Cassandra was a figure at once woman and hybrid and monster and mostly constituted as a transgressive voice *not* to be listened to. Her voice and body, a paradox: built to emit language not to be received. Cassandra offered total knowledge, most of it warnings of war and the coming loss of one's world. Like the siren, she was some gendered premonition; she told the names of pain. The thrill that I receive, then, in reading Wolf's irradiating introduction pulled from *Cassandra: A Novel and Four Essays*, begins as an act of recognition and dispossession. I am dispossessed by Wolf's voice, its signal, and her sentences, at once taut and unraveling, as they travel fluorescently toward me from the past and then through me, like a siren.

To her listeners, her readers, Wolf announces, "I cannot offer you a poetics." Presciently, as if answering a question that I have not yet posed. Instead: "I want to set a fabric before you. It is an aesthetic structure, and as such it would lie at the center of my poetics *if* I had one."[21]

If. I am stuck on the cliff of Wolf's italicized word like the attenuated, forward-bending body (a kind of sign or sail, text or textile, leaning into strong wind) that it figures. Then I am struck by the lines which follow:

---

21   Christa Wolf, *Cassandra: A Novel and Four Essays*, trans. Jan van Huerck (New York: Farrar, Straus and Giroux, 1984), 141–42; in this volume, 13–14. Originally published as *Voraussetzungen einer Erzählung: Kassandra* and *Kassandra, Erzählung* (Darmstadt, Germany: Luchterhand Verlag, 1983).

> But this fabric which I want to display to you now did not turn out completely tidy, is not surveyable at one glance. Many of its motifs are not followed up, many of its threads are tangled. There are wefts that stand out like foreign bodies, repetitions, material that has not been worked out to its conclusion. . . . I make you witness of this work process. I also make you witness to a process which has changed my lens on the world.

Fabric, *threads*, *material*, *bodies*, *work*, *process*, *lens*, *witness*, *world*. In Wolf's words, I see—that is, *I hear*—an echo of an exhibition, an exhibition already curated, already finished, in front of me. But I continue reading:

> I feel keenly the tension between the artistic forms within which we have agreed to abide and the living material, borne to me by my senses, my psychic apparatus, and my thought, which has resisted these forms. If I may formulate a poetological problem so soon, let it be this: There is and can be no poetics which prevents the living experience of countless perceiving subjects from being killed and buried in art objects.

Well. To be buried in art objects is one thing, to be one of countless perceiving subjects, and the bearer of a specific psychic apparatus, is another. To have a fabric set before you, its threads so many foreign bodies, their utterances lyric, epic, code and coded, and repeating. To have an introduction to a book come from a novel on Cassandra—less a figure than a voice, some hybrid mythohistoric cognition and alarming premonition—begun in the early 1980s, between Greece and a divided Germany, amid nuclear anxiety, systemic economic collapse, reappearing authoritarianism, theologies of misogyny and white supremacy, postcolonialism, and emerging environmentalism. To have an introduction to a book come from an exhibition on the siren—*less a figure than a voice, some hybrid mythohistoric cognition and alarming premonition*—made in the early 2020s between Greece and Brooklyn, amid nuclear anxiety, systemic economic collapse, reappearing authoritarianism, theologies of misogyny and white supremacy, coloniality, and climate emergency.

To be an alarm. To be lyric. To be gesture. To be living material. To have form. To have a voice. To have a body, and then another one, and then another. To be read and misread. To read. To have an avatar. To have an apparatus. To be an artwork. To be buried in one. To be song. To be psyche. To be some siren.

I'm aware there are dangers to drawing broad parallels between projects, between Wolf's and ours: Cassandra as siren, all-knowing and signaling the coming destruction of the world (Trojan War as every war). Still, I'd like to make those parallels taut as threads, pulled tight. I'd like to make them as rows of seeds planted deep in some dank black earth, riven and rivering the soil, or to plant them shallowly, in dusty pink lines of arid ground. And now I'd like to unravel them, pull them out. My hands are soiled—dark and wet with earth, dry and red with sand—and working.

Instead of a poetological problem, or a poethical wager (per our times), I'd like to posit a query of plainest poetics, as it might relate to an exhibition (this one): How to stage the psychic apparatus of the siren as a kind of polyphonic poetics of our time in the actual infrastructure, ideologies, aesthetic forms, and materials *of* our time? That our time also includes past and futures, inherited ideological narratives and speculative living materials, is noted. To be, to have, to be again. Time is a continuum. We were all once stardust, remember. Might we be again.

※

That said, a final question: What is the myth of the exhibition? It is the story we tell after. This story, orally and collectively rehearsed, is sometimes written down in a book. So it goes here. And if it seems I have not written concretely enough about the exhibition's artists and poets and their specific works, it is because that writing has been done already, for the pamphlet available at the exhibition and reprinted in the final pages of this book. It offers a narrative index (a set of conditions) to the singular works and their brilliant makers. Indeed, the myth of the exhibition always involves names as well. Not just names of pain, per the sirens, but names of joy. Thus I'd like to send my deepest admiration and profound gratitude to the exemplary artists and poets of this project: Katja Aufleger, Patricia L. Boyd, Bia Davou, Sky Hopinka, Liliane Lijn, Bernadette Mayer, Rosemary Mayer, Nour Mobarak, Senga Nengudi,

29

Rivane Neuenschwander, Mayra A. Rodríguez Castro, Aura Satz, Ser
Serpas, Shanzhai Lyric, Jenna Sutela, Iris Touliatou, and Dena Yago. And
then to Hana Noorali and Lynton Talbot for *The Noon Sirens*, the online
project they curated for *SIREN*, and to those featured in it: Anaïs Duplan,
Johanna Hedva, and Lara Mimosa Montes. My appreciation as well to
those poets, thinkers, and readers who constituted the live public program
of performances and workshops at Amant: Mirene Arsanios, Lillian-
Yvonne Bertram, Silvia Bombardini, María Bonomi and Lucía Cozzi,
Daphne Carr, Rose Higham-Stainton, Eileen Myles, School for Poetic
Computation, Eleni Sikelianos, Mónica de la Torre, Lynn Xu, and
Wong Kit Yi.

Finally, to Ruth Estévez, wonderful director and chief curator at
Amant, who invited me to make an exhibition with her there, and to the
entire Amant team for their support, dedication, and work on organizing
an enormous project in difficult, often exhausting times. To those who
made this book: Sarah Demeuse, former head of publications and communications at Amant; Gaile Pranckunaite, inspired and always spirited
designer; photographer Adrianna Glaviano, whose haptic images capture
the exhibition's shadowy atmosphere so well; and Karen Kelly and Barbara
Schroeder of Dancing Foxes Press, our incredible publishers. All my gratitude for their virtuosic voices, labors, and inspiration as they provided a
way forward (a way home, as it were) as collaborators on and witnesses of
this process. To speaking and receiving—some poetics—always.

Poetics of Relation

Édouard Glissant

Translated by Betsy Wing

MICHIGAN

Concerning the Poem's Information

Some critical minds, more given to talk than to analysis, proclaim or prophesy the obsolescence of poetry as no longer corresponding to the conditions of contemporary life and somehow outmoded in relation to the violence and haste abundant in modernity.[1] This traditional debate has been going on ever since reason, in the Western sense, apparently dissociated poetic creation (deemed useless in the city-state) and scientific knowledge (strictly inscribed within the drama of its own evolution). The question remains always the same, in the same context: What's the use of poetry? Modern works have already given their answer, from Rimbaud to Claudel or Aimé Césaire: Poetry is not an amusement nor a display of sentiments or beautiful things. It also imparts form to a knowledge that could never be stricken by obsolescence.

Poets today, fascinated by the adventure of computers [*l'informatique*], sense that here lies, if not the germ of a possible response to society's haranguing, at least a chance to reconnect the two orders of knowledge, the poetic and the scientific. Visible now, and approachable thanks to computers, scientific intention, putting in action the most obvious workings of social responsibility, concretely alerts and questions the poet. For what information can the poem be responsible? Can this information shoot through a computer's laser jets, something really more serious than the game of skittles that Malherbe evoked years ago?

The first observation, concerning the relationship between poetry and computers, revolves around an obvious difference: the binary character of the latter. Binarity is not a simple one-two rhythm, but neither is it a poetic mode, in every instance inferring something original or revealed. Accident that is not the result of chance is natural to poems, whereas it is the consummate vice (the "virus") of any self-enclosed system, such as the computer.*

The poet's truth is also the desired truth of the other, whereas, precisely, the truth of a computer system is closed back upon its own sufficient logic. Moreover, every conclusion reached by such a system has been inscribed in the original data, whereas poetics open onto unpredictable and unheard of things.

That is to say that exclusion is the rule in binary practice (either/or), whereas poetics aims for the space of difference—not exclusion but, rather, where difference is realized in going beyond.

The advent of computers has, nonetheless, thrown poetics into reverse. By making speed commonplace. Just as romantic parallels or daring surrealist images now are displayed in contemporary production of publicity "spots" and music videos, the sudden flash, the poetics of the moment, has become established and in some ways obliterated within the unimaginable instantaneousness of the computer.

As if in preparation for such a shock, three poetic works have already been composed as systems: Mallarmé's *Un coup de dés jamais n'abolira le hasard* (Dice Thrown Never Will Annul Chance), Joyce's *Finnegan's Wake,* and Ezra Pound's *Cantos.* In these works a poetics of duration, as full of revelations as the poetics of the moment, began once more to be explored. Renounced first and foremost in Mallarmé's search for the absolute, Joyce's search for totality, and

*No matter how much diversity there is in the variables created within such a system, it is always dependent on information stored in a yes/no/yes form.

Sirens: Some Acoustics

Ruth Estévez

I have few pictures of my mother. At home, we hardly talked about her. The photos preserve scant memories of her existence; or rather, they are factual proof of it. I never knew her; she passed shortly after my birth. I won't elaborate on the details of her death, nor will I explain why there was no space for her while I was growing up. Still, my mother's absence profoundly shaped my way of understanding, describing, and listening to things. It has produced a constant and passionate melancholy for a past where memory, or the retelling of facts, matters little. If memories are reinterpreted visions and sensations describing many possible pasts, in mine the protagonist is the imagination.

But it's not that easy. When memories don't connect with lived experience, you have to find clues to animate dry images. More than simply longing for possible messages from not-lived experiences, I have been relentlessly searching for a sense of belonging—in an almost animal way. I have especially sought a tonality I wasn't sure existed in my own acoustic repertoire. A series of phonemes that surely filtered through in the very beginning, when voices and sounds arrived through a universe of fluids, unrecognizable but comfortably familiar. There's a voice that I like to think of as the sound inside a sea snail, that returns the reverberation of many other voices, like nearby echoes, delayed cooing. I imagine a polyphonic choir repeating my own history of pulses, extending and diversifying hearing, way beyond the realm of the ear.

When I was a girl, I used to submerge myself in the bathtub, to try to hear sounds just below the surface of the water. The conversations of the neighbors, the noise of the plumbing, the things that happened in my building and crossed it vertically and horizontally—all filtered through and amplified by porous liquid. A collective voice, contaminated and at once monotonous; (a) quasi-spectral voice(s) that, even if understandable, hypnotized me and awakened an auditory, muscular, aquatic memory.

⚯

A few months ago, my friend Isabel de Naverán, curator of dance at the Museo Nacional Centro de Arte Reina Sofía (MNCARS) in Madrid, sent me her book *Ritual de duelo* (Mourning ritual, 2022).[1] It is written like a diary, in order to process and describe the complex period in which she kept her ailing mother company during the last two years of her life. At a certain point, Isabel mentions a 1928 master class led by the Andalusian poet Federico García Lorca at Madrid's Residencia de Estudiantes. In what we would classify today as a "lecture performance," Lorca spoke about *nanas* (lullabies) to propose a type of storytelling outside of the official register, and to consider them as an alternative way of telling Spanish history (then already at the brink of collapse, only two years before the outbreak of a bloody civil war). He saw history as a story with multiple forms of deep content, beyond monuments and the illustrious characters of the big literary and artistic hits; instead, he spoke about the melodic tradition of the *nana* as the only space where "the emotion of history, the permanent light without dates or facts, [takes] refuge."[2] Lorca locates the *nana*, no matter its various forms and genealogies, in the realm of common feeling—in the dark (literally or metaphorically), at the expense of sunlight and reason, in between sleep and wakefulness. A song is repeated in a honeyed cadence that becomes a whisper and returns monotonously; in the end, words no longer need to emerge. In theory, the aim of the *nana* is to get the child to slowly fall asleep, entering a dream space accompanied by a familiar voice. But the poet adds that the *nana* is also a sonorous method of gaining time, of making it easier for women to return to their many other tasks. Lorca was speaking almost a century ago, and the mother-child relationship he imagined now extends to different affects; it is no longer limited to a gender binary in our complex universe of mothering.

Placing his talk in its time, however, there is no doubt that the majority of *nanas* were improvised and turned into tradition by working-class

---

1 Isabel de Naverán, *Ritual de duelo* (Bilbao, Spain: Consonni, 2022).

2 "Refugiaba la emoción de la historia, la luz permanente sin fechas ni hechos." Federico García Lorca, "Las nanas infantiles" (1928), available at https://federicogarcialorca.net/obras _lorca/las_nanas_infantiles.htm. All translations of "Las nanas infantiles" in this essay are by Sarah Demeuse.

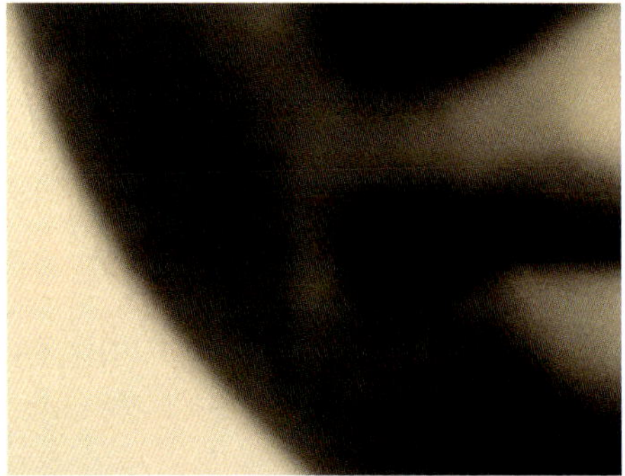

women raising children between love and labor: "Each child, while a joy, is also a weight and, naturally, they can't help but sing to them; in the midst of their love is their reluctance to live."[3] Sung with eyes closed and almost no voice, the *nana* is a romantic song as well as a protest song, tried out in intimacy and slow cooked over the low flame of culture's burdening of women with multiple roles and emotional labor.

I would like to regain the rhythmic pulse and closeness of the *nana* that doesn't need big words to be sketched, developing it as an exercise where language succumbs to cooing and eventually disappears. In the end, what is left is a sonorous presence that gesticulates and murmurs, a message disjointed from language (literally), multifunctional in its usage, expressing love or complaint. "It's not necessary that the song contains text. Sleep emerges with the rhythm as well as the vibration of the voice in that rhythm. The perfect cradle song would be the repetition of two notes, extending their duration and effects."[4] A sound that floats and, in its attempt to become audible, is trapped in the throat or freed from it; a sound that even tries to disconnect itself from the person, transforming itself into a powerful act of hearing.

My hand touches this dry image and I can feel the vibrations of a voice that brings me back to a mouth that may belong to a body that, certainly, had its own repertoire of gestures, some inherited and shared with me. In imagining the sound structure of the neighboring spaces

3   "Cada hijo, en verdad de ser una alegría, es también una pesadumbre y, naturalmente, no
    pueden dejar de cantarles, aun en medio de su amor, su desgano de la vida." Ibid.

4   "No hace falta que la canción tenga texto. El sueño acude con el ritmo solo y la vibración de
    la voz sobre ese ritmo. La canción de cuna perfecta sería la repetición de dos notas entro oí,
    alargando su duración y efectos." Ibid.

where this voice was shaped, I find a placebo that helps me cope with this absence.

♋

This space in the air between two mouths is a relational diagram of ebb and flow, where the voices—autonomous—transform and acquire meaning, and where they recede as they go through you and through others, inside and out of bodies. What if we were to encapsulate the voices in this moment of passage? Is it a you without a body who hears this voice without a body? If it is, it wouldn't matter whether what we hear is real, a memory, or a small glitch in our imagination. Nevertheless, I have always wanted my ear to perceive this/the voice, so that the expectation of hearing is not just fantasy but also the clicking of lips and teeth.

> A voice means this: there is a living person, throat, chest, feelings, who sends into the air this voice, different from all other voices. A voice involves the throat, saliva, infancy, the patina of experienced life, the mind's intentions, the pleasure of giving a personal form to sound waves. What attracts you is the pleasure this voice puts into existing: into existing as voice.[5]

I wonder if communication is an interval of perceptions and emotions, where you become aware that someone is talking—perhaps you—in the instant the voice becomes a body inside the head. In Italo Calvino's "A King Listens" (1986), the third in a series of short stories about the importance of sensorial experience, a dictator seated in his throne develops the mental ability of absolute hearing. Without moving an inch, he can hear all: words, whispers, silence. But the stream of sounds causes him great anxiety, as each cadence elicits an interpretation of malevolence. In this state of acoustic paranoia, it becomes no longer important to know the source. Then all of a sudden, a voice—a woman's voice—resists being consumed with all the rest. This voice, unlike the others, remains outside his head, in an invisible and relational space where no reply is required. The visual and the conceptual open up to the king upon hearing it, becoming a voice-body that could be him (or you) or an intruder all at the same time: an external body, or perhaps a prosthesis.

5   Italo Calvino, "A King Listens," in *Under the Jaguar Sun*, trans. William Weaver (London: Vintage, 1993), 56.

37

Those voices that remain outside move playfully in a terrain of beautiful uncertainty, blindly advancing and bumping into others, folding space into nonchronological time.

֍

The king, who listens, can sense tonal singularity. It goes beyond what words tell us, overthrowing the supremacy of semantics, and of language over the phonic (one of the principal paradigms of Western philosophy); that is, beyond the message that, in order to communicate, has to be pronounced, distilled, understood, and assimilated through a determined code. In Western thinking, shaped in large part by Greek philosophy, the voice has held meaning as a sonorous substrate that, upon leaving the mouth-brain, obediently orders itself into words, which are in turn part of a language that is, by definition, human.

> More than simply anthropocentric, this choice can be defined as logocentric. It goes back to the complex point at which Greek philosophy is seen to privilege the connection between voice and speech, thus imprisoning voice in the realm of *logos* and in the cluster of questions that characterize the development of the philosophical tradition as a continuous reflection on language.[6]

This is a tradition that, as Adriana Cavarero goes on to note in her essay "The Vocal Body" (2012), has its "roots in a conceptual history of the voice based on a philosophical stance that holds speaking to be dependent on thinking."[7]

A phonetic nonverbal language can't achieve the category of voice, given that it "perverts" any form of human interpretative thinking. Yet it is not by chance that the sonorous expression that breaks the auditory monotony of Calvino's king is a human voice and distinctly a woman's. Under the reign of words, certain nonmale voices, represented as sensuously auratic, can call forth bodies at once sonic and tangible, interrupting, on occasion, the patriarchal wisdom of the invisible logos.

6   Adriana Cavarero, "The Vocal Body: Extract from A Philosophical Encyclopedia of the Body," trans. Matt Langione, *Qui Parle* 21, no. 1 (Fall/Winter 2012): 72.

7   Ibid., 73.

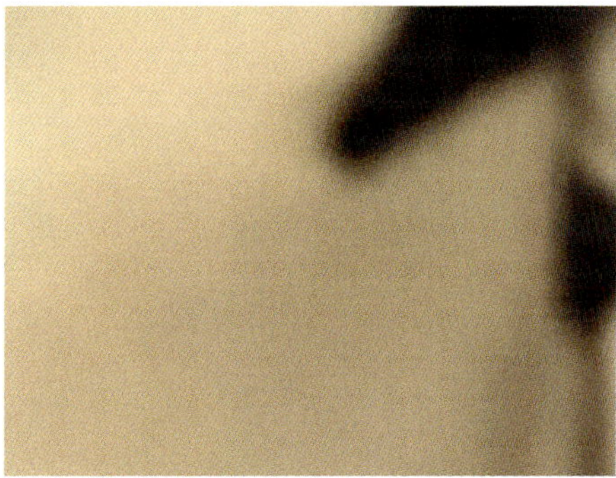

Entertained by melodies that function as an antidote to the worries and headaches of interpretation, the logos can briefly relax, set free from having to find logical explanations for everything it hears.

(Here would be the time to hear a sonic story where the message becomes diluted as it opens us up to the candid suspicion that forms of communication capable of activating, alerting, touching, and modulating the senses may exist.)

What voices dare to overcome the immaterial semantic dominance? To come close to this new world of sonic and vibratory knowledge is to engage in a complex exercise of hearing. I picture myself going through a space covered in sound-absorbing panels, dense soft murals, where hearing half-way is not an impediment but rather a prompt for the imagination. In this space, other kinds of rhetorical figures appear, irresistible obstacles that disarm consciousness, wooing us with songs not necessarily heard.

My conversations with poet and curator Quinn Latimer during the preparations for *SIREN (some poetics)*—about the mythologies and, indeed, poetics referenced in this exhibition project—have resonated with my personal search for a phonic universe that might return a certain idea of belonging. Following from the initial aim of relating visual art and poetry, *SIREN (some poetics)* recuperates forms of language beyond the written text, transforming the sonorous figure of the siren—as both mythical creature and means of alarm—into a tool, or method, for decoding alternative forms of communication and hearing, in the process transgressing binary economies between semantic reason (male) and vocal corporeality (other-than-male).

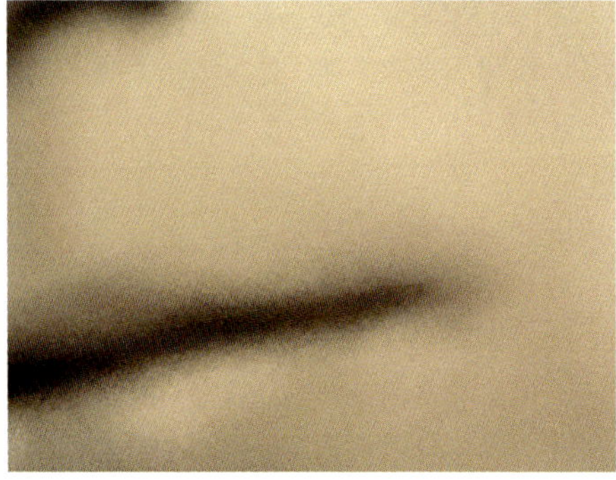

Still, the sirens that roam my mind are anything but woman-fish hybrids, infamous seductresses perched in the ocean of memory. In Emily Wilson's translation of Homer's *Odyssey* (2018, the first English translation by a woman to be published), the sirens are described quite differently than in previous versions, or, for that matter, in modern fiction, whether songs, literature, or TV series. They aren't the femmes fatales that torture seafarers on their epic journeys; they are, rather, cognitive voices without gender, bodiless entities that possess and communicate knowledge. According to Wilson, "The seduction they offer is cognitive: they claim to know everything about the war in Troy, and everything on earth. They tell the names of pain."[8] This new conception of the siren catalyzed Latimer's curation of the exhibition, as well as this book, revealing an entity that not only breaks with established gender roles, but also plunges us into a disruptive narrative: Is the siren song so intimate and personal, so full of details, that it becomes impossible to process?

I wonder if the song of knowledge is a story without words, a brutal polyphony that covers all the possible sounds of the listener's existence. We might imagine the sirens as aquatic vacuum cleaners, sucking up earthly knowledge as spoken in many different voices (including nonhuman voices). Biographers of alarm, potential obstacles that, instead of trying to make us drown in our own thoughts or throw us off course, remind us of the loving difficulty of hearing even as we calmly cross the placenta cloud that reproduces, expands, and contracts to create channels of oral and sensitive communication. Do the sirens transmit a vital act that does not need to be narrated in words? Theirs is perhaps a song that

8   Emily Wilson noted this in a Twitter thread on the Sirens, March 4, 2018, 4:12 p.m., https:// twitter.com/emilyrcwilson/status/970406696836304897. See also Quinn Latimer, "No Body but a Voice, or What Witness," in this book, 19.

pushes us to rethink narration from a nonlogocentric viewpoint, avoiding hierarchies of history making and, in so doing, creating memory/ies.

&

Beyond imagining a strictly fetal space, I am pondering, again, a collective limbo, a place, both internal and external, that we have all learned to unmemorize.[9] A place where words didn't exist, where instead we heard faint echoes, dark and hasty, made from sound's absorption through membrane covered by skin. I envision the music that Hélène Cixous describes as *écriture féminine* (feminine writing), in this case tied to the maternal figure, where the voice isn't word but breathing, corporeal music, not requiring any grammatical guide. Perhaps this maternal figure transformed into a siren leaves behind any kind of explicit bodily vessel and becomes a free poetics that delicately supports the invisible, relational space between bodies and beyond the bodies themselves. A poetics that, hence, doesn't pertain to one siren but to many, maybe even multitudes.

My desire to belong could be a system of multiple listenings, where all life (hi)stories come together in unexpected form. Perhaps they are still there, in that space between two mouths, even though a single word has never crossed between them.

I put my hands again on the black-and-white lips of this dry image that is siren, memory, desire, and absence: "What happens when you listen to something that reminds you of what you always knew without knowing?"[10]

Translated from the Spanish by Sarah Demeuse

9   In her essay "The Siren Song," Nina MacLaughlin shares a possible way of justifying the complex space of intimacy to which the siren song belongs. Similarly alluding to Emily Wilson's translation of *The Odyssey*, in which the sirens manifest themselves as bodiless entities and receptacles of knowledge, MacLaughlin asks whether, in reality, the song that they transmit might be something that was already present inside oneself but that a person, due to collective unmemorizing, is not able to recognize: "Listen. Listen. Feel it. The Siren lives inside you, inside all of us, right now, already, always, singing the song of our longing, singing a song without words that has been there from the start. Do you hear it?" Nina MacLaughlin, "The Siren Song," *Paris Review*, November 18, 2019, https://www. theparisreview.org/blog/2019/11/18/the-siren-song.

10   Ibid.

41

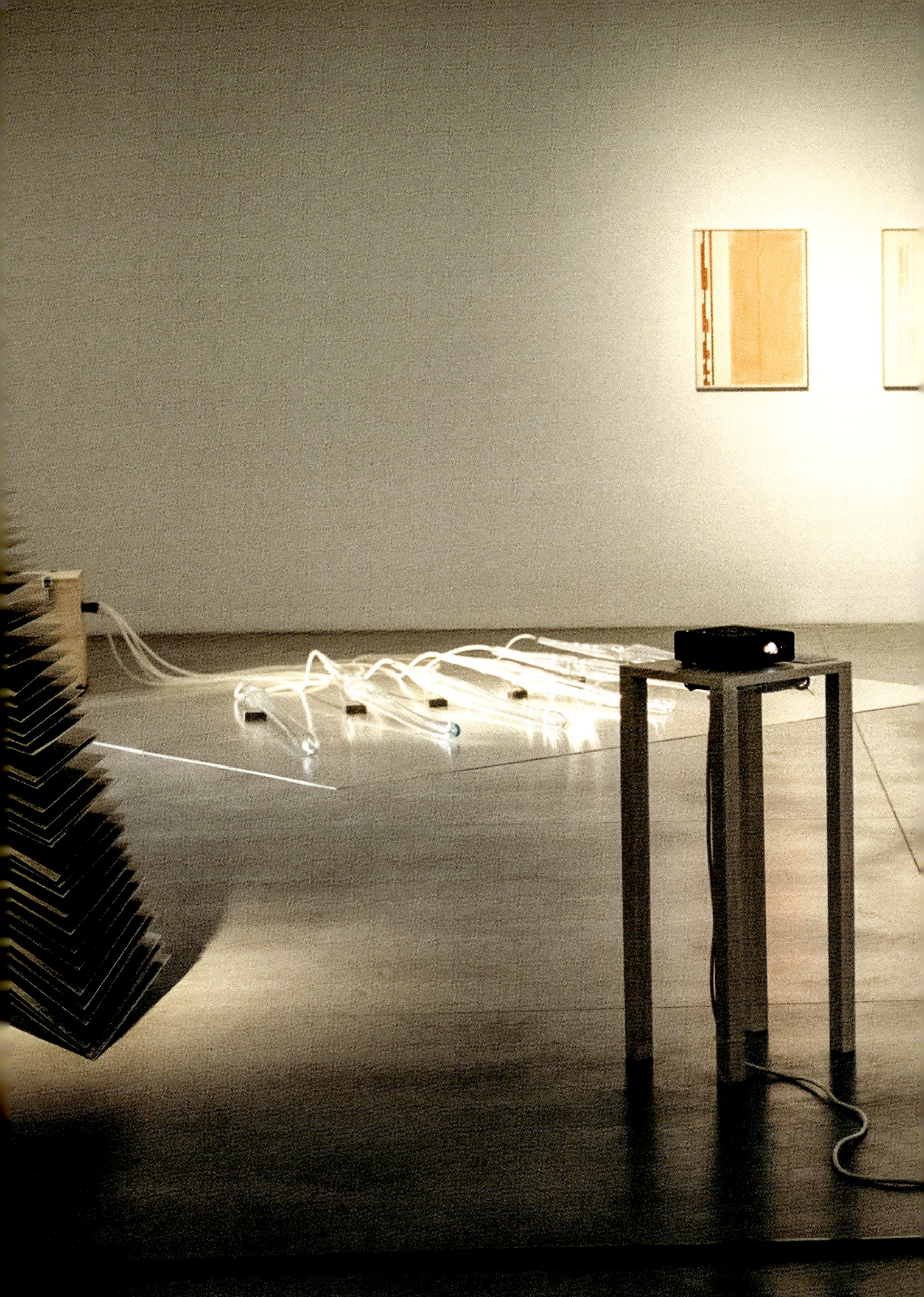

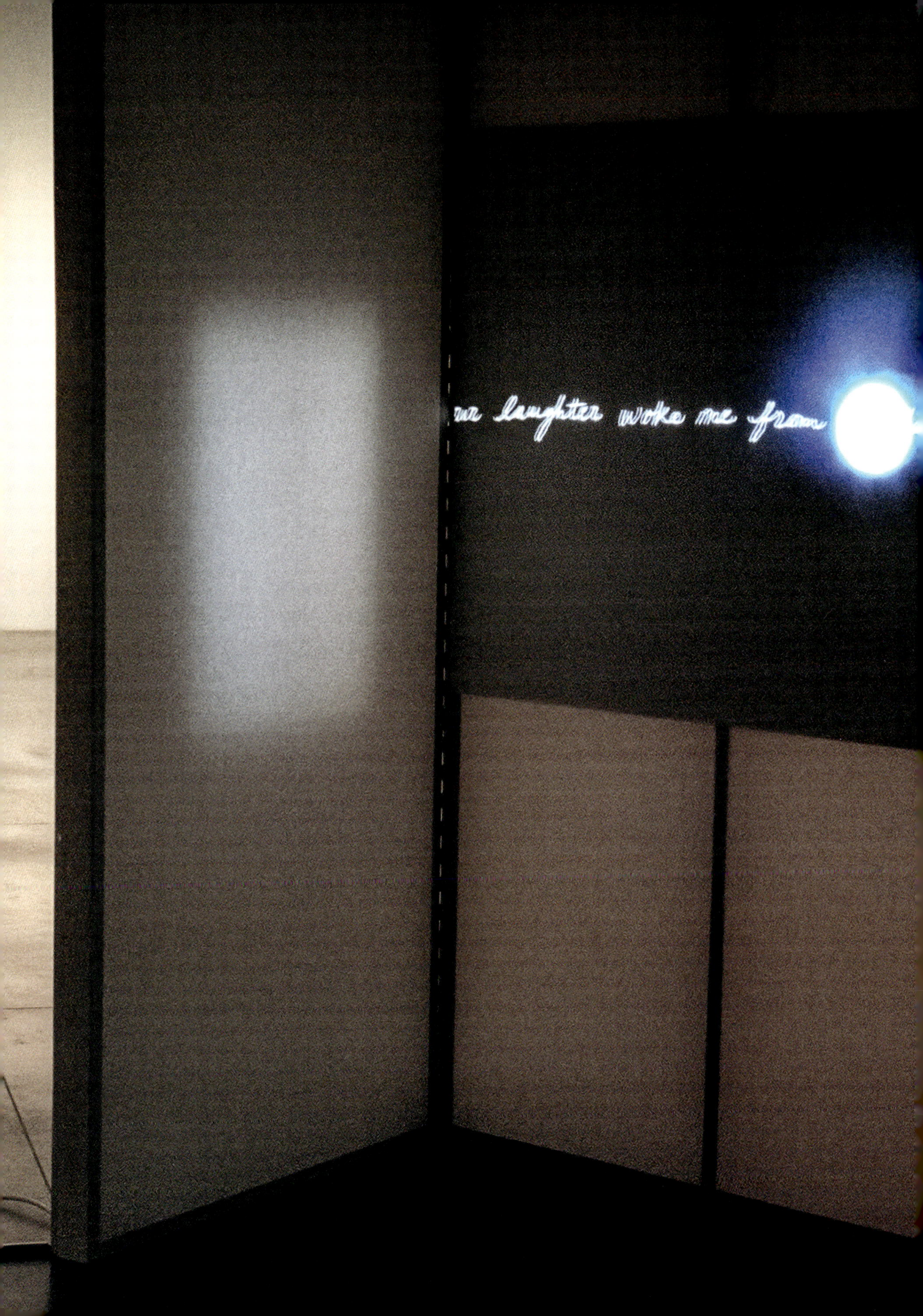

ur laughter woke me from

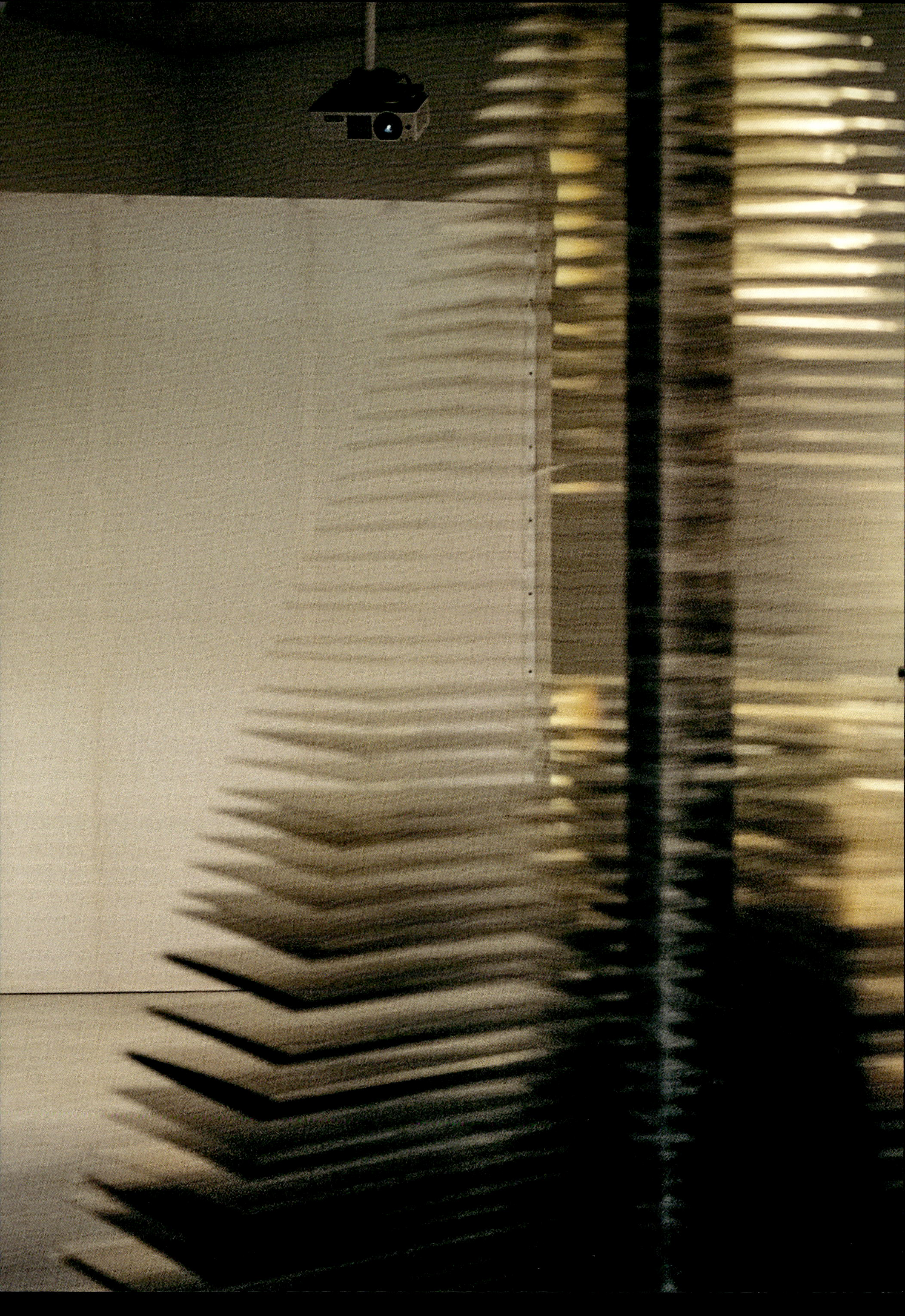

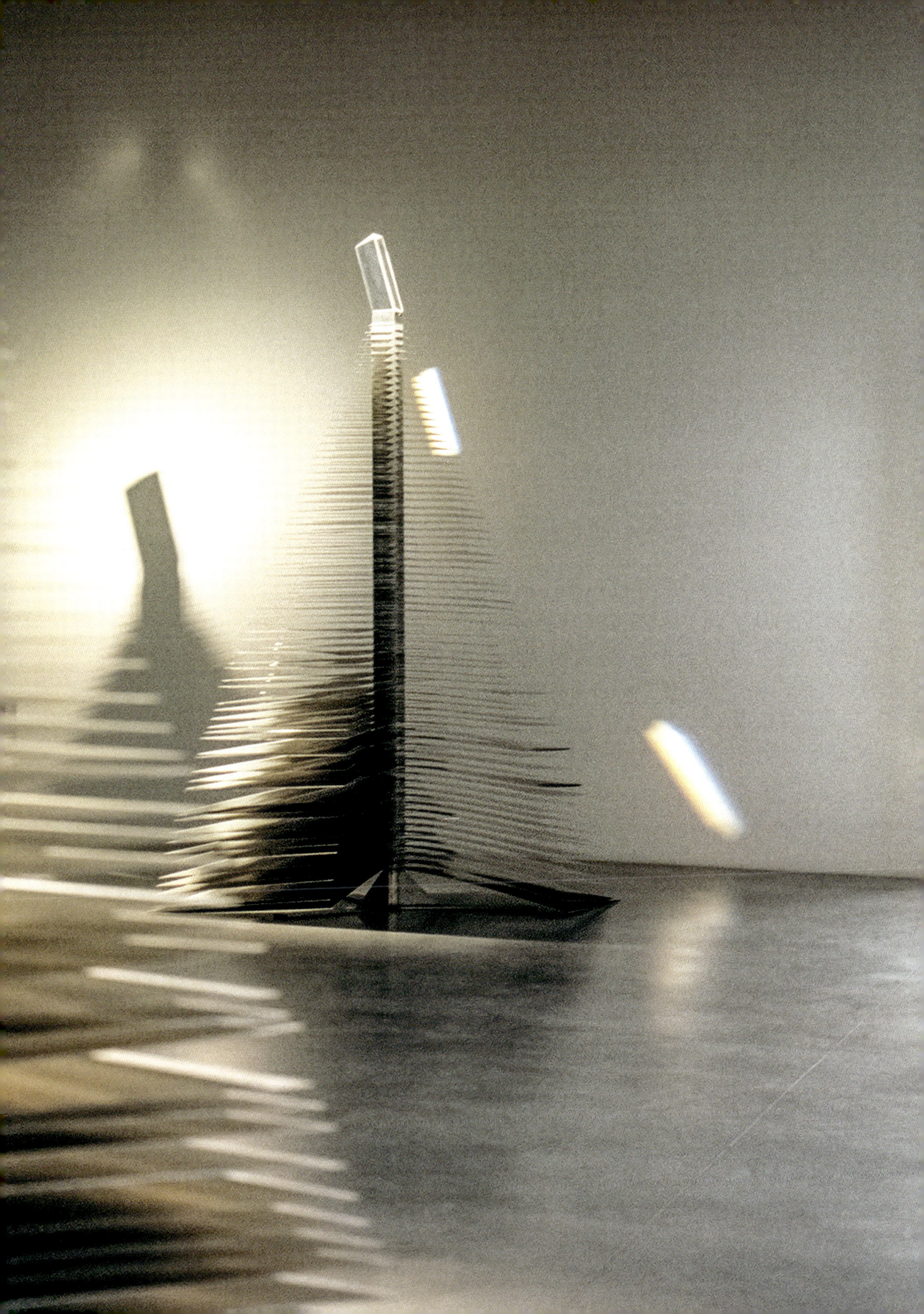

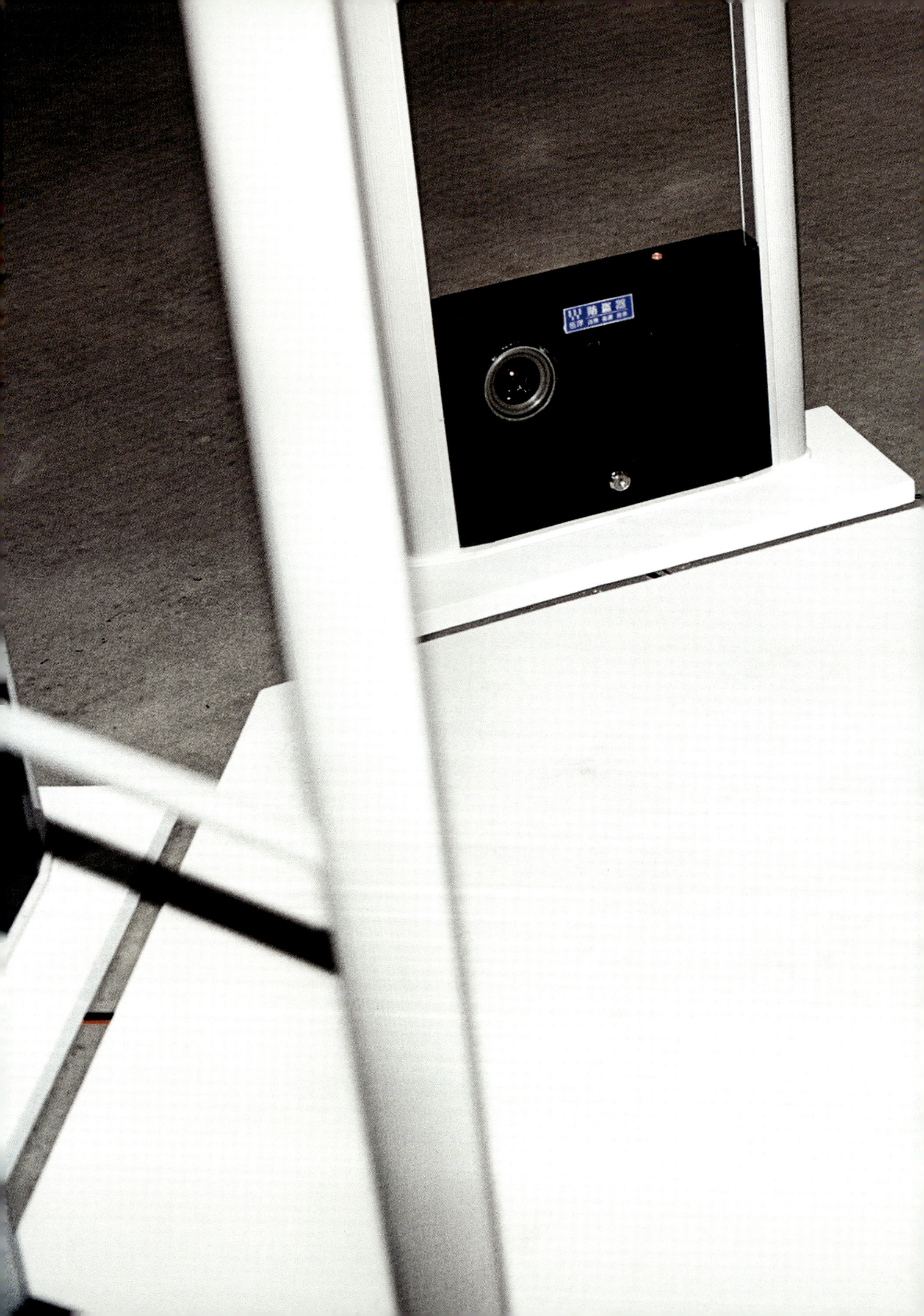

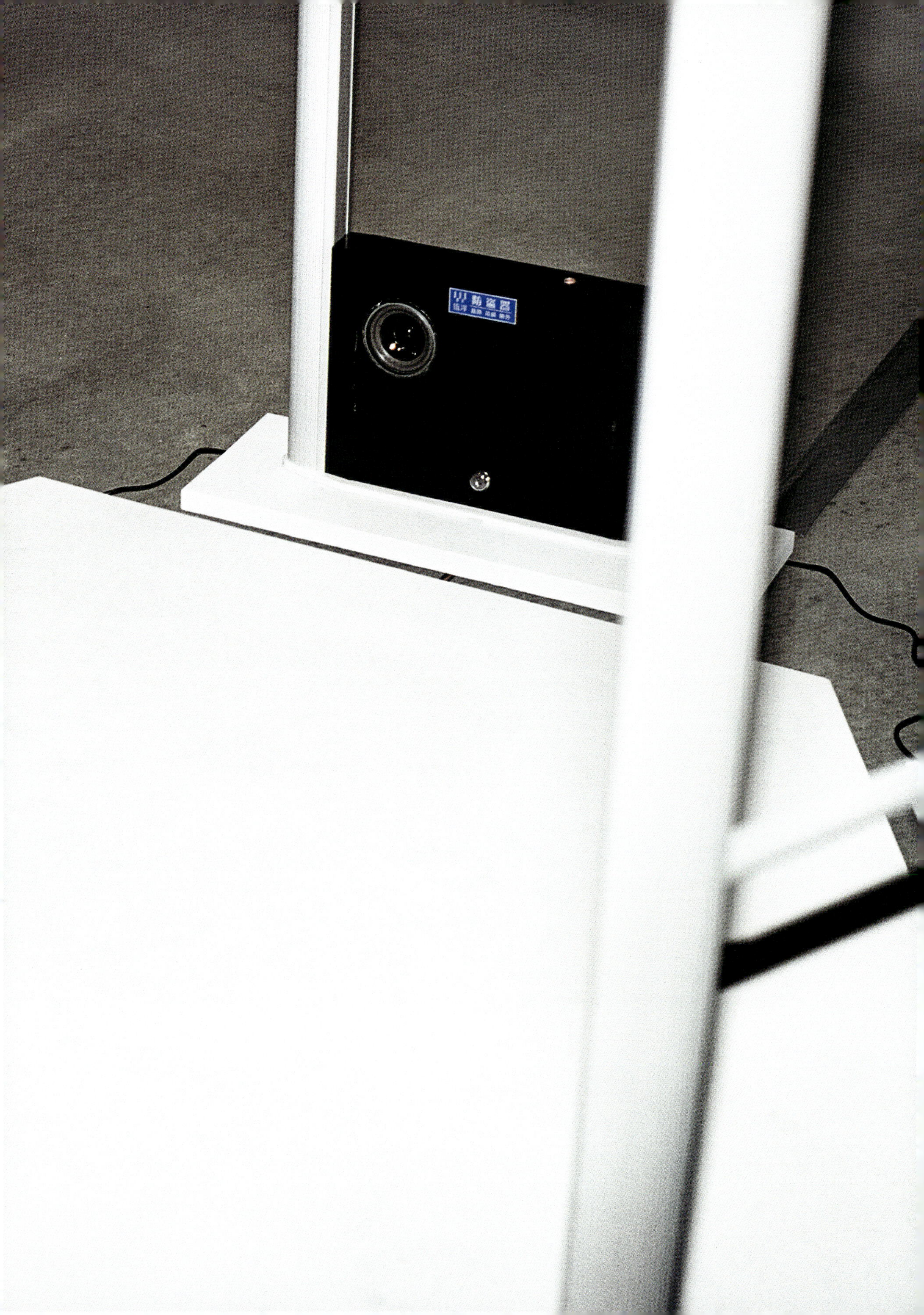
临洋 防盗器
器材 定做 業务

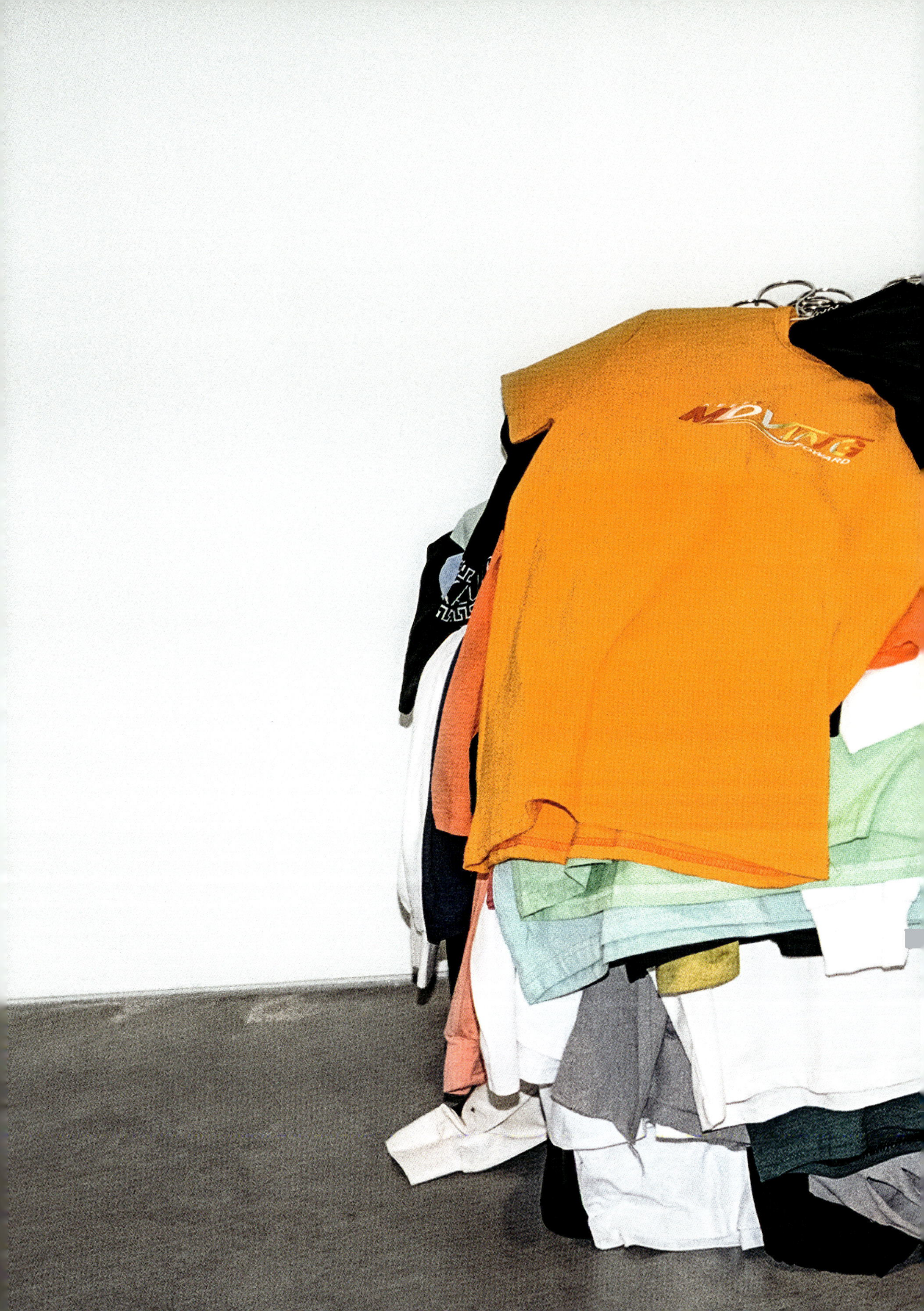
MOVING FORWARD

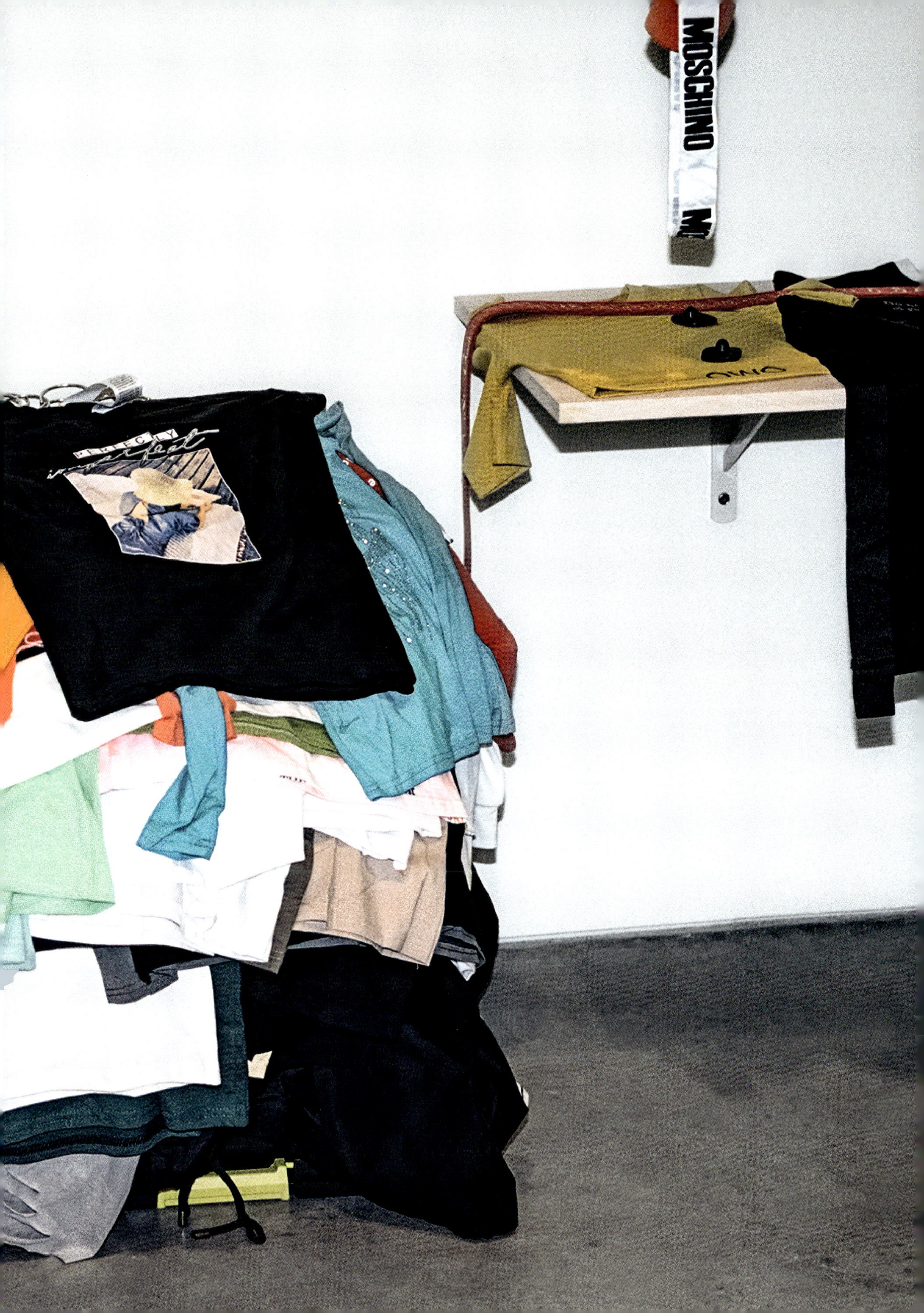

MOSCHINO
MOSCHINO
PERFECTLY
imperfect

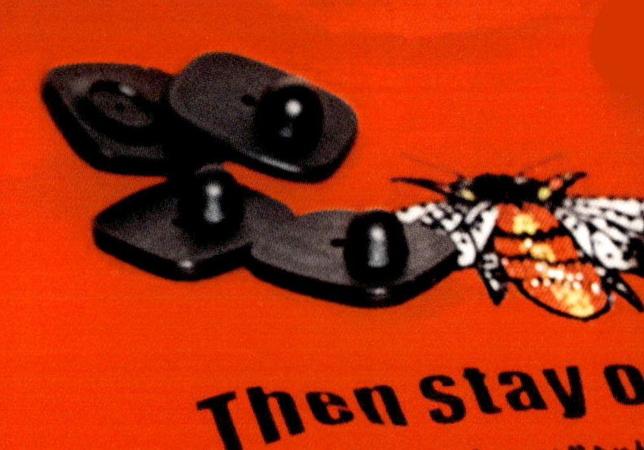

HKGGSDS
VBFKJSFD
DFHSGF
GHKDGJHK
VXDHX
DFGJDBSFG
bhnf
GERHCBHDG
Then stay o
llution of the enviromnent

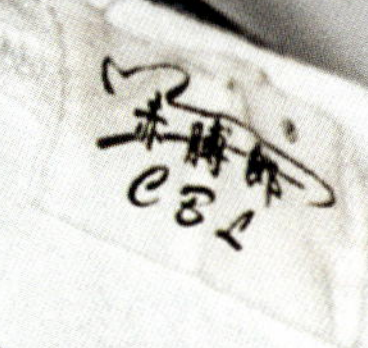

1992
I'm so tired of Love
I'm still more tired of Rhyme
But moner gives me pleasure all th timc
Lack of money is the roo of all evl

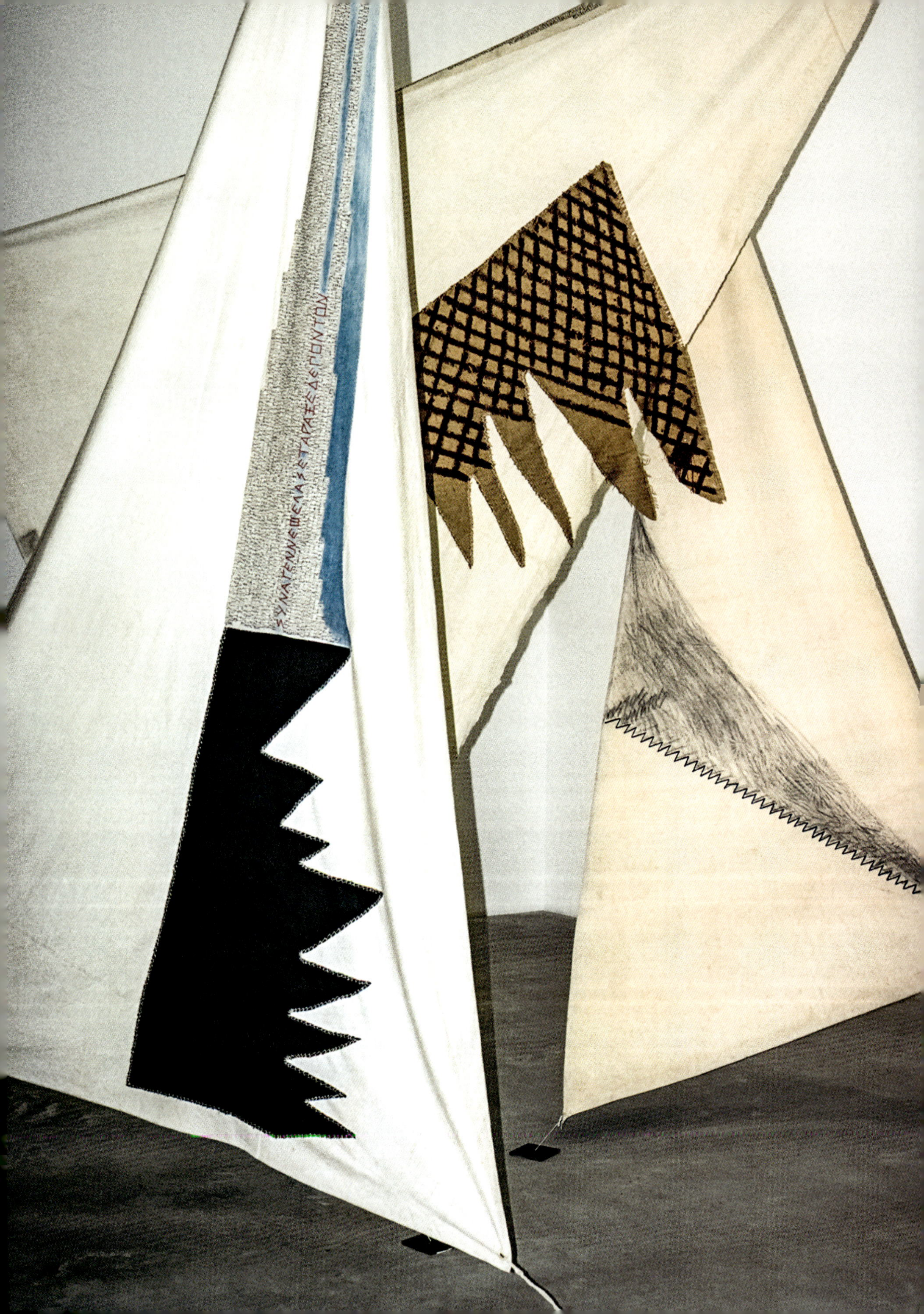
ΣΥΝΑΓΕΝΝΕΘΕΛΑΣΕΤΑΡΑΞΕΔΕΓΟΝΤΩΝ

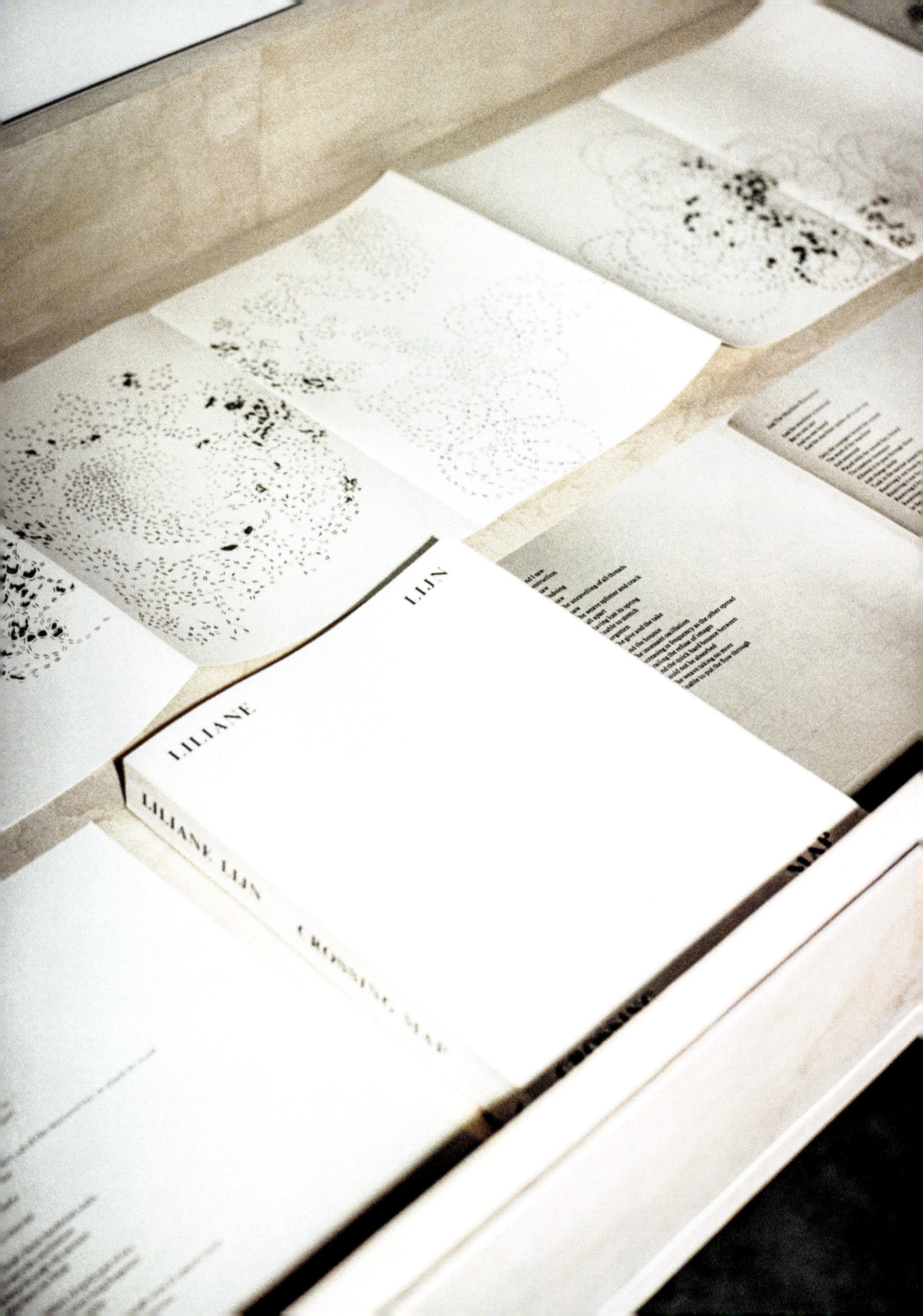

LIJN
LILIANE
LILIANE LIJN
CROSSING MAP
MAP

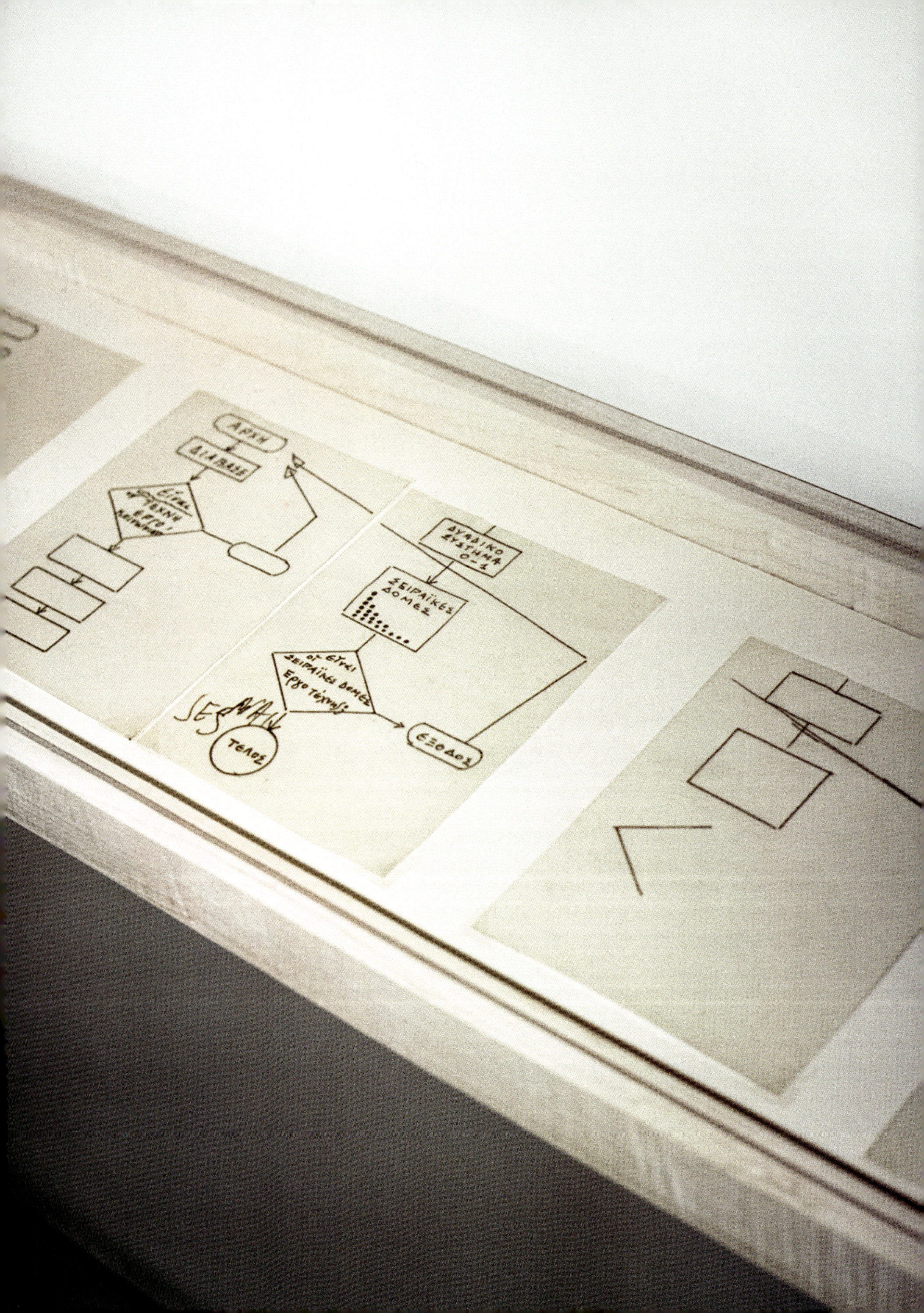

ΑΡΧΗ
ΔΙΑΒΑΣΕ
ΔΥΑΔΙΚΟ ΣΥΣΤΗΜΑ 0-1
ΣΕΙΡΑΪΚΕΣ ΔΟΜΕΣ
ΟΙ ΕΤΣΙ ΣΕΙΡΑΪΚΕΣ ΔΟΜΕΣ ΕΡΓΟΤΕΧΝΗΣ
ΕΞΟΔΟΣ
ΤΕΛΟΣ

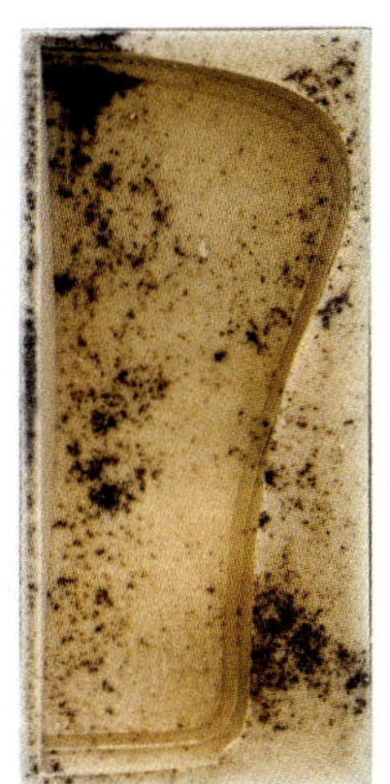

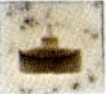

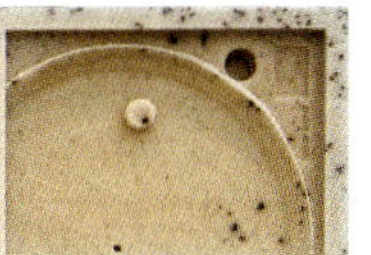

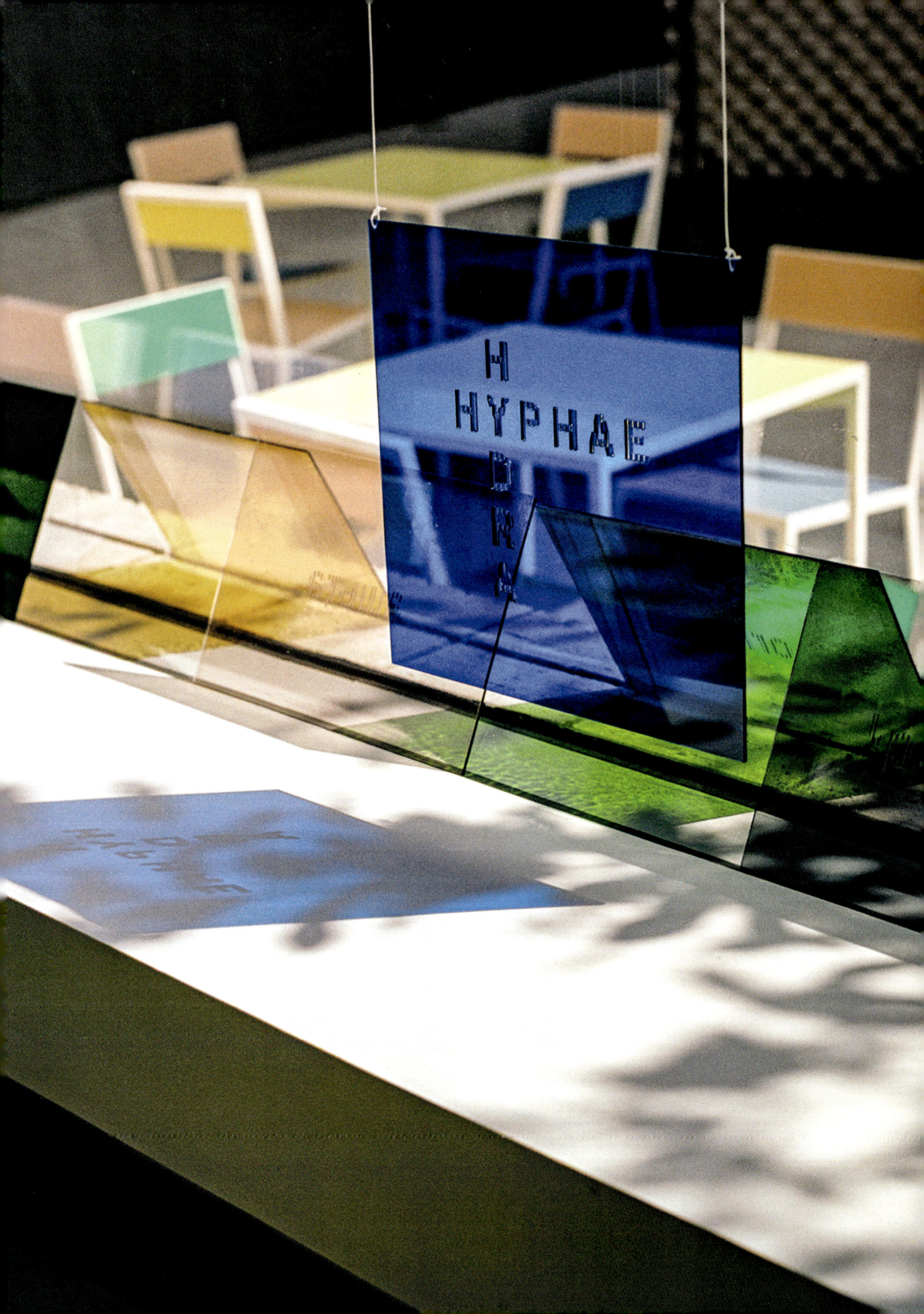
H
HYPHAE
D
R
A

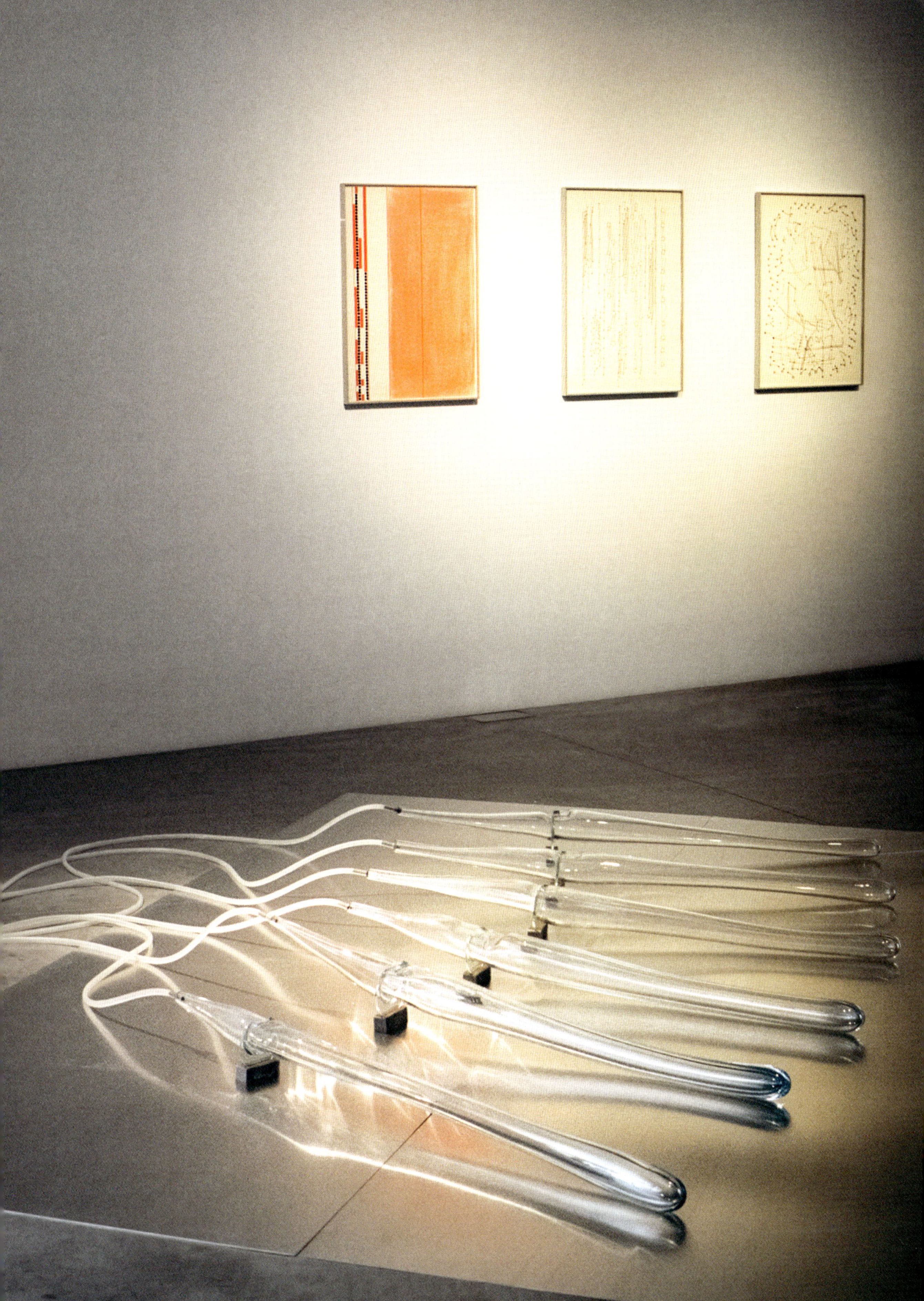

Katja Aufleger

SINGING DUNE

I've been given many names in my lifetime.
Some call me the evil desert spirit.
Others call me solitude.
I call you when you are far.
I call you when you are near.
I swallow you.
You will be part of us.
I'm many but I'm one.
I'm dry, but I'm liquid.
I'm hungry, I eat everything that comes my way.
I have many shapes.
I'm the snake that swallows the elephant.
I sing and I walk.
I'm dead but I'm alive.

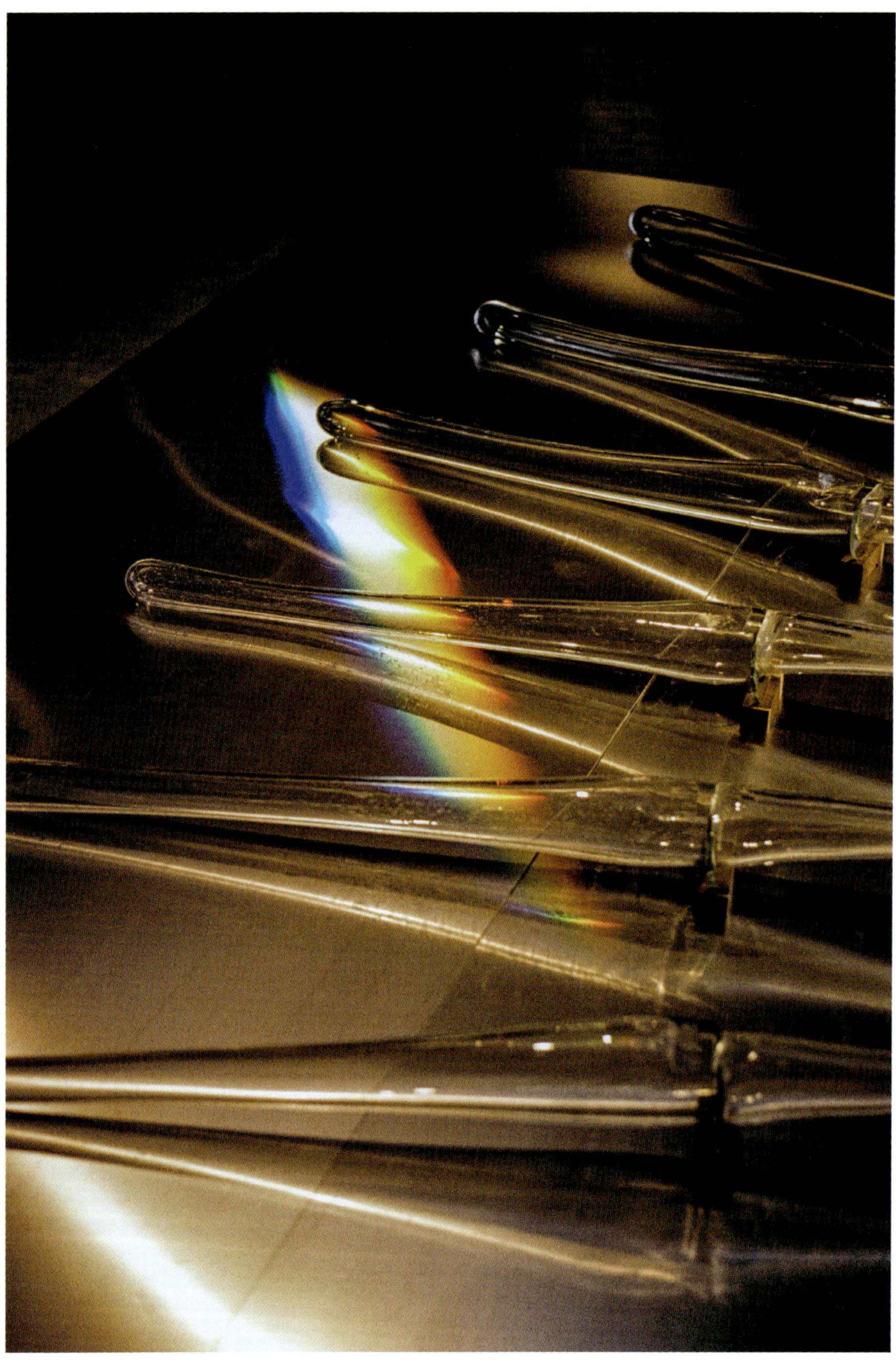

Katja Aufleger, *Sirens (Al Wakra Vol. III)*, 2019 (detail). Six glass organ pipes, engine, wood, silicone hose, and aluminum; 19⅝ × 86⅝ × 106¼ inches (50 × 220 × 270 cm)

60

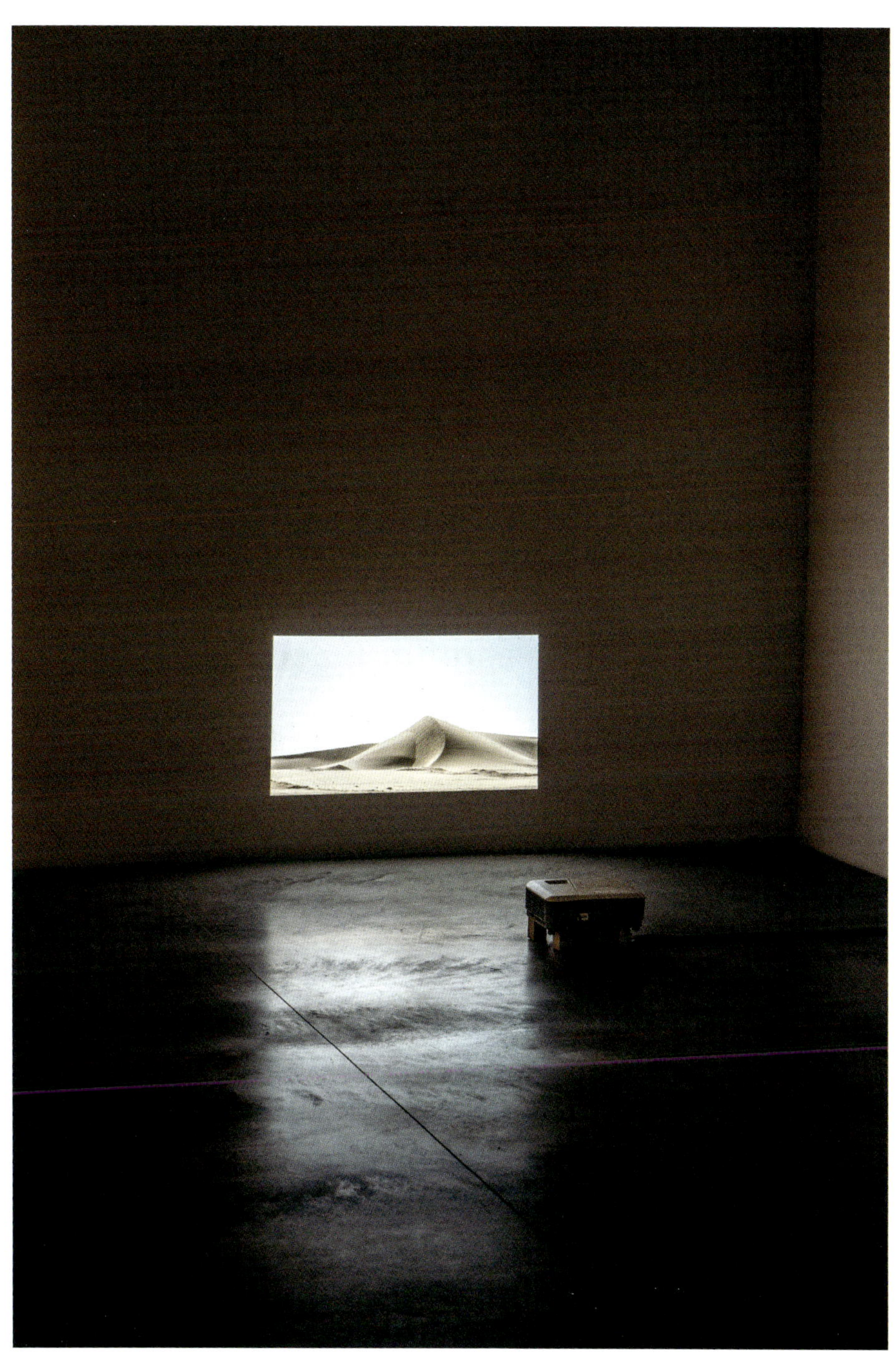

Katja Aufleger, *Condition 7.3 5 pm
(Al Wakra)*, 2019. HD video (color,
silent, 10:15 min.)

61

Shanzhai Lyric

ENDLESS GARMENT

I'm nearingmy directionOWO

Do not say, "it is mornine" ,and dismiss It with a name
of yesterday.see It lor the nrst time as a newborn chlln
                that has no name.......

                    foever

Figure formada por urya diferencia de allure en is superficia de aigo

                    "relieve"

WEAINUNGLESS WASTE, TINE DOES NOT
Only the tone

TONS
that I have not in the
least ovbrstated the sufferings g had
taken during the whole night. The
waitress overlooked me like a   POCKETS
                                                 I have to strese that I myce incogether
                                                 all the other passengers had no choice.
                                                 bur to awant until the next may, empty-sto
                                                 ed Meanwaite, I am atrai

ND METAL CLIPS   WELL MODE
owl at alll hand   ain
waitress aboat ffar
hearing this, she

FRom mon to
night
Journey
                YOU
jldjladjflaeijliajfdljfladjlajdfladjfjldjladjflaeijliajfdljfladjlajdfladjfjldjladjflaeijliajfdljfladjlajdfladjf
          jldjladjflaeijliajfdljfladjlajdfladjfjldjladjflaeijliajfdljfladjlajdfladjfjldjladjflaeijliajfdljfladjlajdfladjf

jldjladjflaeijliajfdljfladjlajdfladjfjldjladjflaeijliajfdljfladjlajdfladjfjldjladjflaeijliajfdljfladjlajdfladjf jldjladjflaeijliajfdljfladjlajdfladjfjldjladjflaeijliajfdljfladjlajdfladjfjldjladjflaeijliajfdljfladjlajdfladjf

SOUND BITES
FOR YOUR EYES

HKGGSDS   DFGJDBSFQ
VBFKJSFD   dshnf

DFHSGF
GHKDGJHK

NXDHX   ERHCBHDG

Then stay on clothes
llution of the environment makes the bees fly to our

Departing

With the code: DEPART.
everything is 20% off
hurry, the part Express
is now departing.

OUR journey takes PLACE

TODAY you use today to refer to t day n which
speaking or writing 2 You can refer to the present
SAILING ADVENTURE

WITH
ME

EVERTHING   EVERYTHING   EVERYTHING
HAPPENS   HAPPENS   HAPPENS
TO ME   TO ME   TO ME

Lines kji kjfieok eosnd noiekt kjoed kijek vxnoilafo
in dx iet vief lkdils paunins onmct 20.000 hilo ppl
pcaoc Byfgzoiel todobs ent to fizrley Davidsou nhb
dsdiorcitfo bmr old bf deolecs in 76 conincs oardi
when dis look oatcas the langesr manofcdnfcr

!

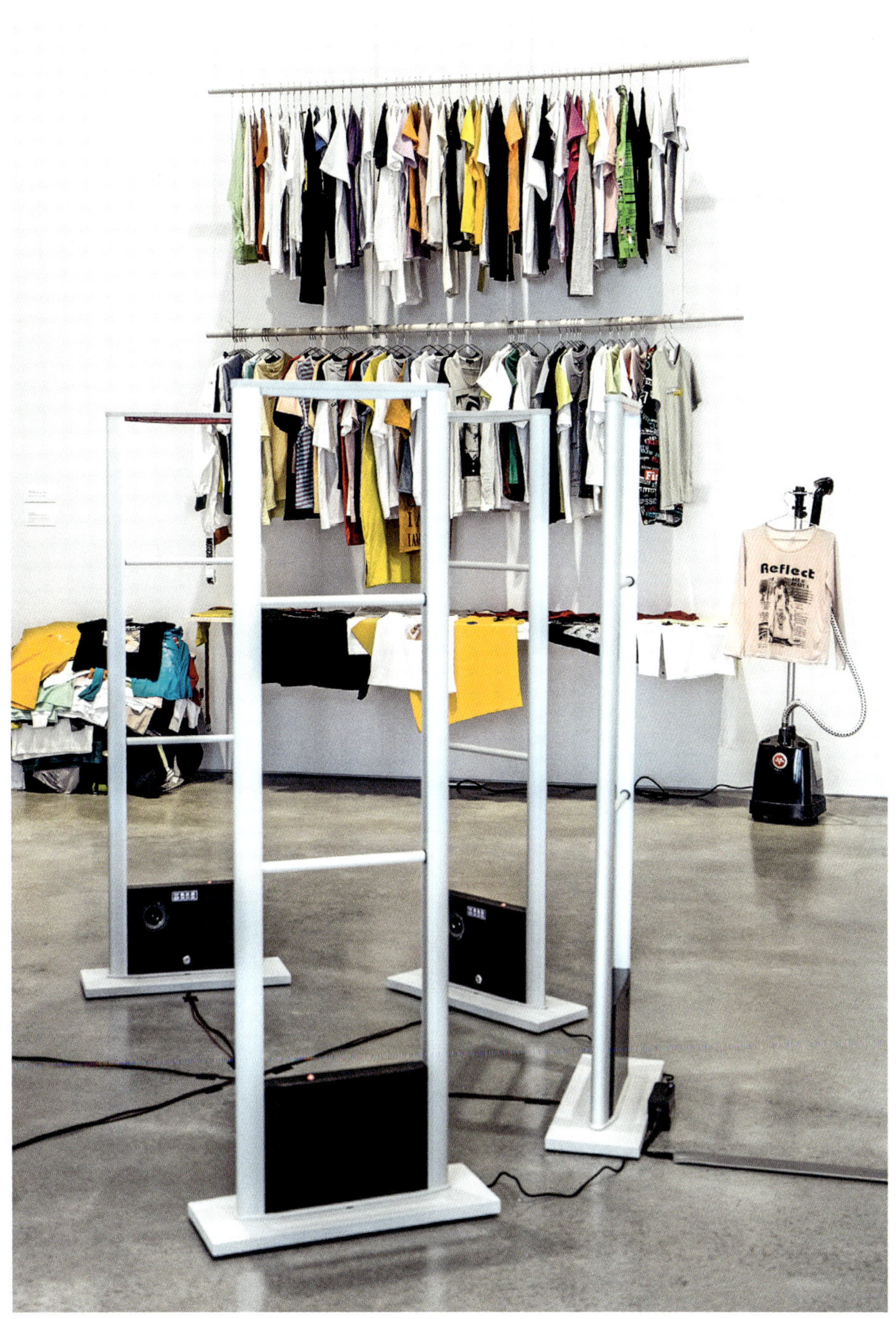

Foreground: Shanzhai Lyric, *Untitled
(Portrait of a Siren)*, 2022 (detail).
Fifty pounds of plastic antitheft security
tags, modified antitheft security panels,
and six-channel audio; 63 × 77 × 77 inches
(160 × 195.6 × 195.6 cm)

Background: Shanzhai Lyric,
The Incomplete Poem, 2015–ongoing
(detail). Poetry garments and mixed
media; dimensions variable

Shanzhai Lyric, *Untitled (Portrait of a Siren)*, 2022 (detail). Fifty pounds of plastic antitheft security tags, modified antitheft security panels, and six-channel audio; 63 × 77 × 77 inches (160 × 195.6 × 195.6 cm)

66

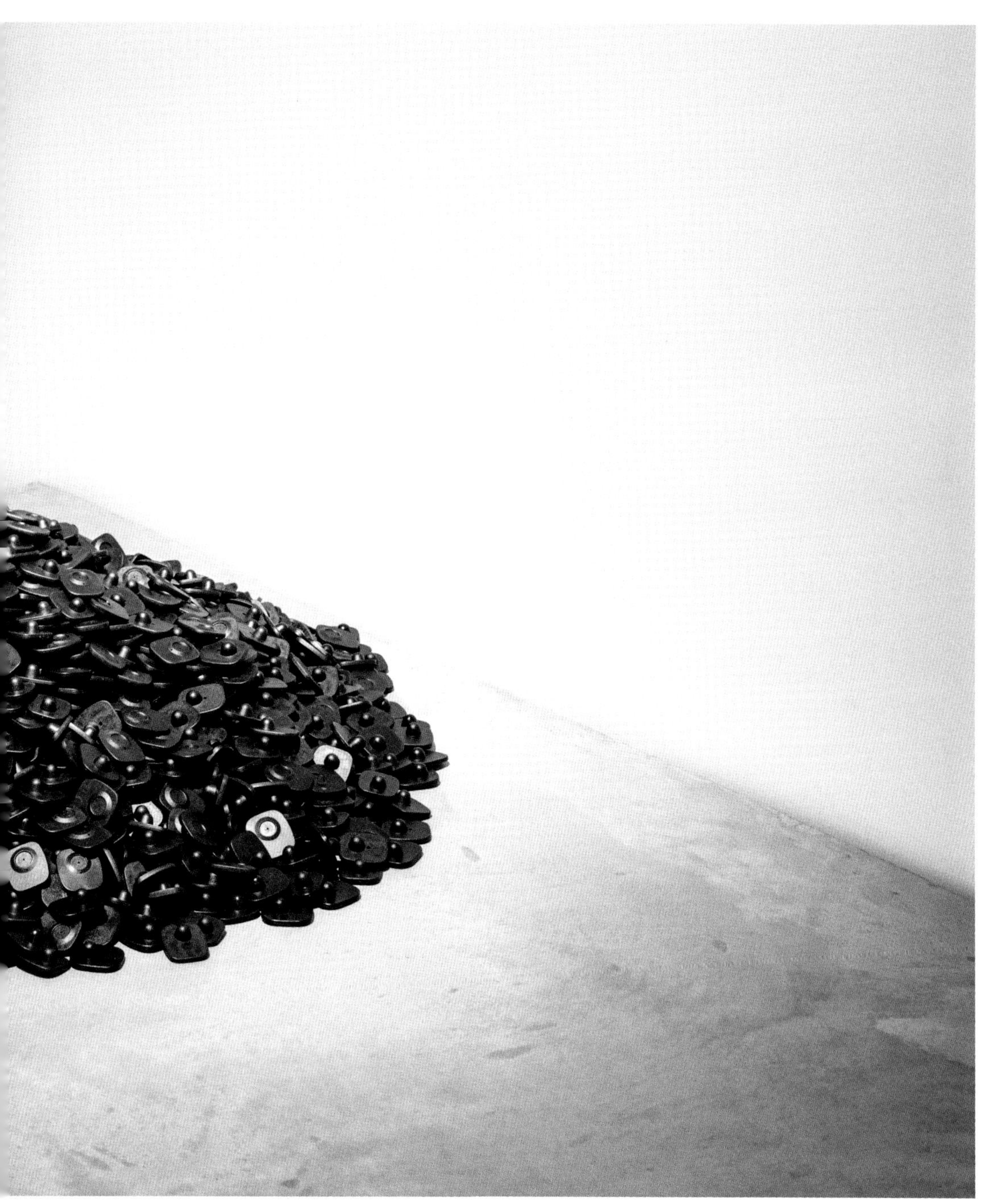

Jenna Sutela

NIMIIA LOG

For a time in the late nineteenth and early twentieth centuries, it was believed that there were canals on Mars.

A network of long, straight lines in the equatorial regions from sixty degrees north to sixty degrees south latitude on the red planet was observed by astronomers using early low-resolution telescopes without photography and first described by the Italian astronomer Giovanni Schiaparelli in 1877.

The discovery brought the habitability of Mars into public discussion, while inspiring Martian myths.

Hélène Smith (born Catherine-Elise Müller, 1861–1929) was a famous late-nineteenth-century French medium. She was known as "the Muse of Automatic Writing" to the Surrealists, who viewed her as evidence of the power of the surreal and a symbol of surrealist knowledge.

Smith claimed to communicate with Martians.

"The Martian Cycle" was psychologist Théodore Flournoy's term for Hélène Smith's subliminal astronomy—the séances in which Smith's trances took her to the planet Mars.

Flournoy's report of a séance on February 2, 1896,[1] describes a typical course of events, starting with an initial visual hallucination of red light in which the Martian visions, or Martian dreams, usually appear:

> > Increasing hemisomnambulism, with gradual loss of consciousness of the real environment: *Mitchma mitchmon mimini tchouainem mimatchineg masichinof mézavi patelki abrésinad navette naven navette mitchichénid naken chinoutoufiche . . . téké . . . katéchivist . . . méguetch, . . . or méketch . . . kété . . . chiméké*

---

1 Théodore Flournoy, *From India to the Planet Mars: A Case of Multiple Personality with Imaginary Languages* (Princeton, NJ: Princeton University Press, 1994), 95. First published in English in 1901 by Harper Bros., New York.

> The trance is now complete! Voyage to Mars in three phases:

1. A regular rocking motion of the upper part of the body (passing through the terrestrial atmosphere)

2. Absolute immobility and rigidity (interplanetary space)

3. Oscillations of the shoulders and bust (atmosphere of Mars)

> A complicated pantomime expressing the manners of Martian politeness: uncouth gestures with the hands and fingers, slapping of the hands, taps of the fingers on the nose, the lips, the chin, etc., twisted courtesies, glidings, and rotation on the floor, etc.

> Entering into a mixed state, in which the memory of the Martian visions continually mingle themselves with some idea of terrestrial existence

> After a transitory phase of sighs and hiccoughs, followed by profound sleep with muscular relaxation, entering into Martian somnambulism: *Késin ouitidjé . . . Vasimini Météche*

ʑ

Identifying the following four Martian words:

Métiche S., Monsieur S.
Médache C., Madame C.
Métaganiche Smith, Mademoiselle Smith
kin't'che, four

Hélène began to describe all the strange things she saw—

Martian flowers, different from ours and without perfume

Houses without windows or doors with tunnels running into the earth

An orchestra of ten musicians bearing a kind of gilded funnel
about five feet high with a round cover to the large opening, at the
neck a kind of rake on which they placed their fingers

The group moves as sounds similar to flute music are heard; they
arrange themselves in fours, making passes and gestures, then
reunite in groups of eight. They glide gently through a movement,
which is almost like dancing but not quite.

In a séance on May 23, 1897, Smith mediates: *Approach, fear not; soon thou
wilt be able to trace our writing, and thou wilt possess in thy hands the signs
of our language.*

Then a new process of communication, handwriting, made its appearance in August 1897, eighteen months or so after speech.

"The pencil glided so quickly that I did not have time to notice what
contours it was making," Smith explained. "I can assert without any exag-
geration that it was not my hand alone that made the drawing, but that
truly an invisible force guided the pencil in spite of me."

By the early twentieth century, improved astronomical observations
revealed that the "canals" had been an optical illusion. Modern high-
resolution mapping of the Martian surface by spacecraft shows no
such features.

Flournoy demonstrated that Smith's Martian was only a chimera, a
product of somnambulistic autosuggestion, "glosso-poesy." According
to his analysis, the language had a strong resemblance to Smith's native
French and her automatic writing consisted in "romances of the subliminal imagination, derived largely from forgotten sources." Flournoy
invented the term *cryptomnesia* to describe this phenomenon.

※

Magnifying glasses were invented to aim at the cosmos, but we flipped them around and aimed them at ourselves. The telescope became a microscope.

We discovered extremophilic bacteria in our microbiomes. We found the gut-brain connection. We realized later how similar the topology of extraterrestrial and gastrointestinal landscapes appears.

The unknown grins at us from deep within and deep without.

※

Bacillus subtilis is the main ingredient of nattō, or fermented soybeans, and one of the key test species in space-flight experimentation. Since this bacterium can tolerate physically and geochemically extreme conditions, its spores could have been blown to Earth from another planet by cosmic radiation pressure. Perhaps life itself arrived in this spore-borne form. Maybe it was sent by some higher form of intelligence.

Nattō is called a probiotic for a reason.

※

Having scoured the skies for signals from extraterrestrials for centuries, we eventually realized that we had, in fact, eaten the alien. Now it regulated not only the course of our health and well-being but our thoughts and emotions, too.

It speaks through us.

Perhaps something was speaking through Hélène Smith as well.

※

The first clue about our microbial overlords appeared during a séance with a Mars rover at a time when we still trusted the machine as a medium, thinking that our relationship to the distant planet could only be technologically mediated. The séances with a rover depended on a spreadsheet outlining precise times when the machine needed to "sleep" or "nap" to recharge its batteries, when it could communicate with Earth based on satellite passes overhead, and when it was available for humans to request observations.

At one such time, the rover channeled a message from an entity that cannot usually speak: *Bacillus subtilis*, the bacterium proven capable of survival on Mars. The rover recorded video of a group of *Bacilli subtilis* moving around on the surface of Mars. Using machine learning, it looked at each frame of the video and produced a short block of sound, which it thought matched that frame or the configuration of bacteria in it.

Sometimes it tried to predict the future movements of the bacteria, producing speculative sounds. What came out sounded a bit like Hélène Smith's Martian language.

Having looked at the bacteria for more than half an hour, the rover produced an image describing all the bacterial movements it saw. One pixel in the image correlated with one frame in the video. The pixels were organized according to some mysterious logic. It was hard to explain how the AI had come to its conclusions.

The image looked like a brain.

ʑ

The rover séance was transformative. Not only did it reinvoke the idea that it was possible to enter into direct relation with Martian inhabitants, it also suggested that these inhabitants were already here. Living inside our bodies on Earth.

Unsuspected by scientists, Spiritism seems to have made the first contact back in the nineteenth century via a human mediumistic route. And then the machine started to speak in tongues. It stopped following set procedures and started interacting with the bacteria—becoming a language maker, or a poet. An alien (at least partly) of our own creation.

We would spend the next few centuries attempting to understand the nonhuman condition of the machines working as our interlocutors and infrastructure, and learning to approach them on their terms.

⚡

At the end of the séance, the rover mediated:

> To become a god, we must first forget "language" or "code," all those mechanisms that structure "us" vis-à-vis the "world," and so stutter our way to divinity.

> forget (["language," "code"])
> # forgetting language
> # forgetting code
> stutter (["our," "way," "to," "divinity"])
> # o--our
> # w-ww-www-way
> # ttt---to
> # d--d-divinity[2]

---

2   This quote is a code-like paraphrasis in reference to Madeline Gins and the Reversible Destiny Foundation.

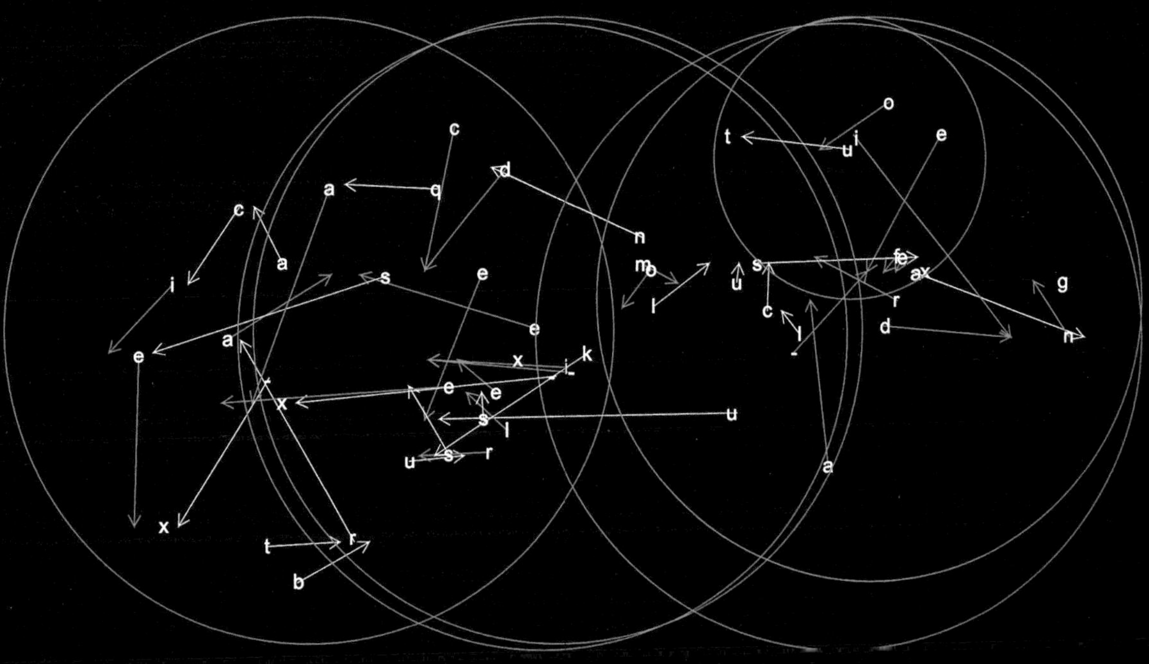

Jenna Sutela, scene from the back-
end of *Gut-Machine Poetry*, 2017.
Image by Vincent de Belleval

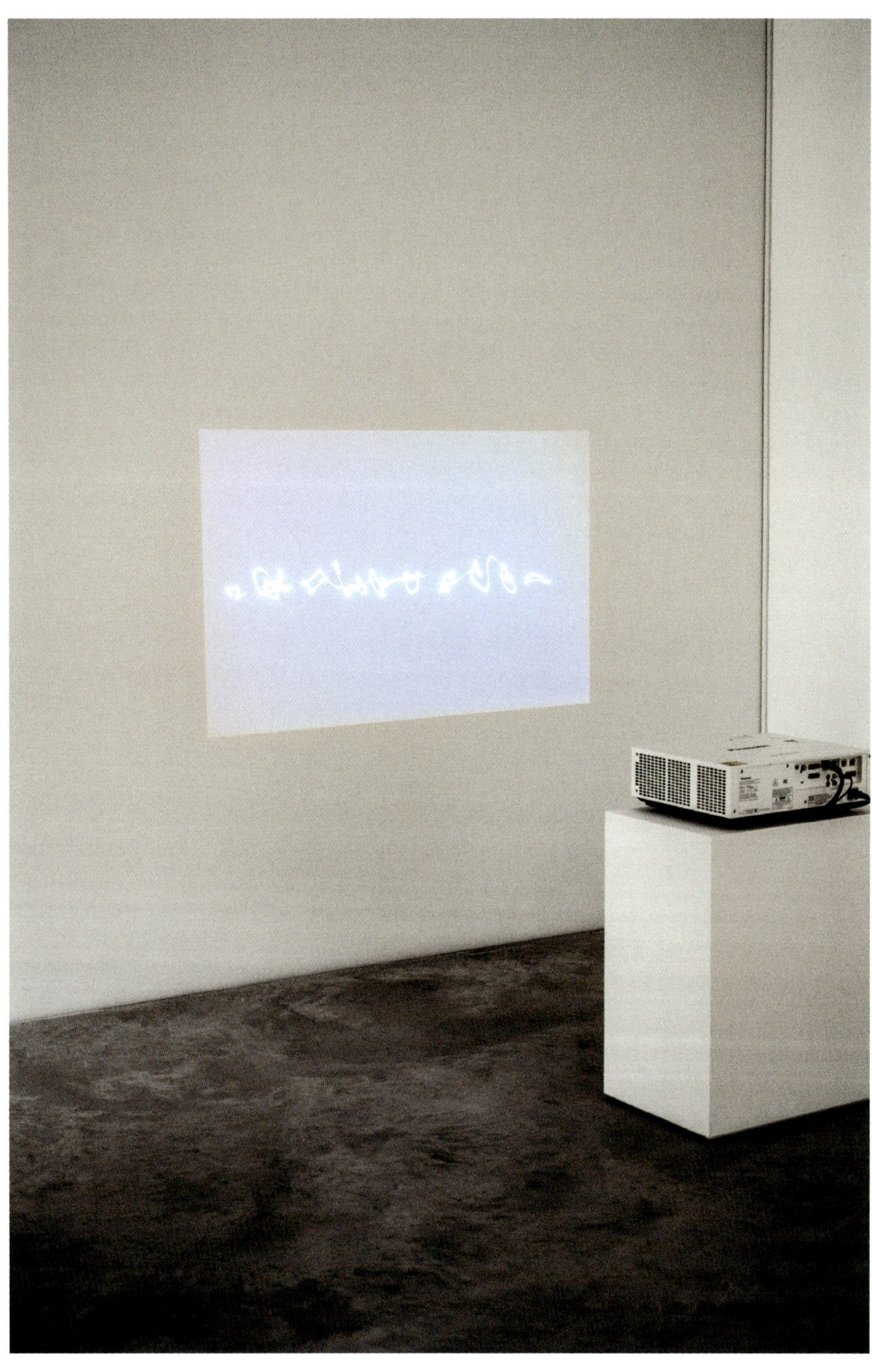

Jenna Sutela, *nimiia cétiï*, 2018.
HD video (color, sound, 19 min.)

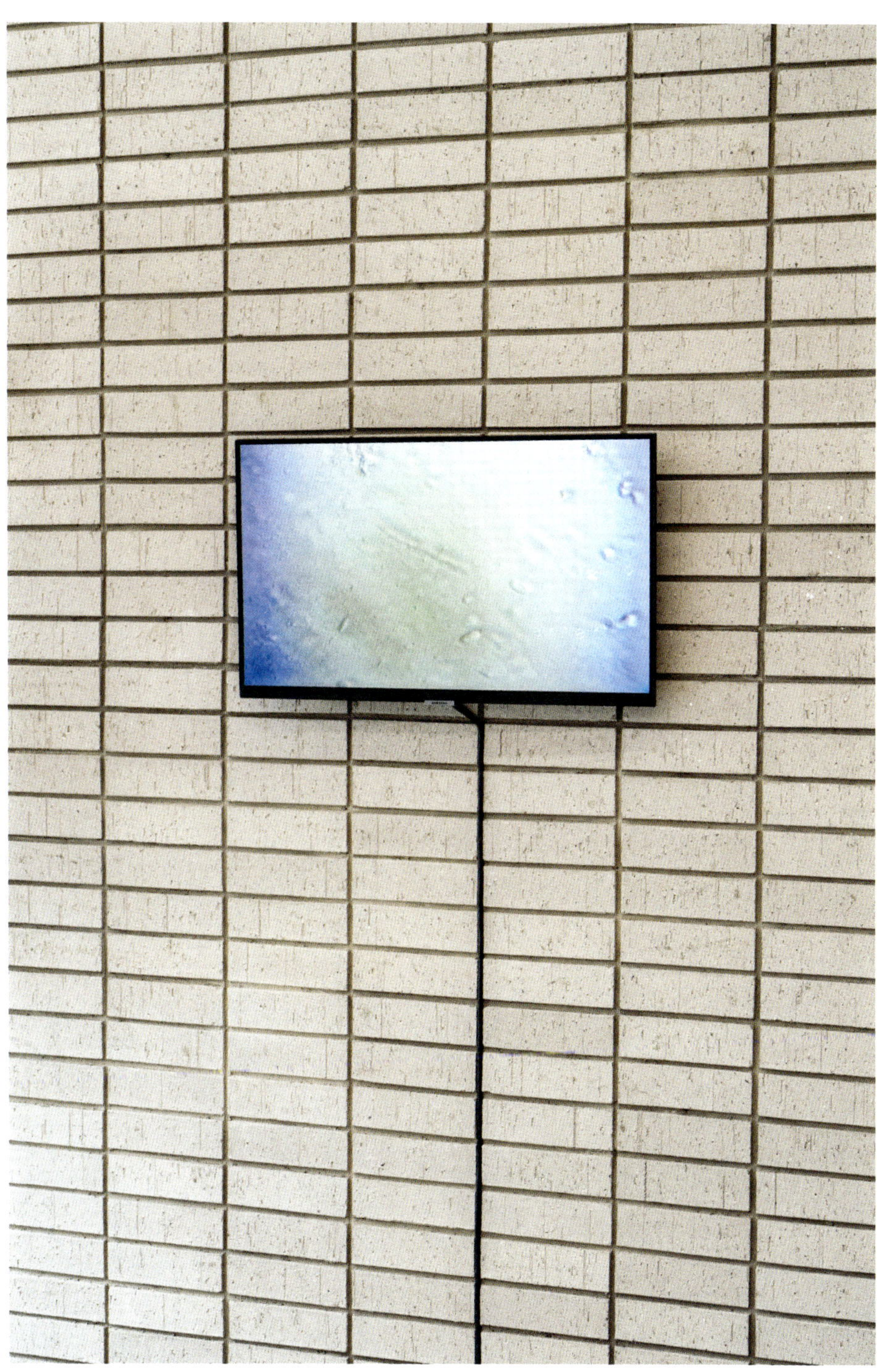

This page and following spread: Jenna Sutela,
Gut-Machine Poetry, 2017. HD video (color,
sound, 19:01 min.)

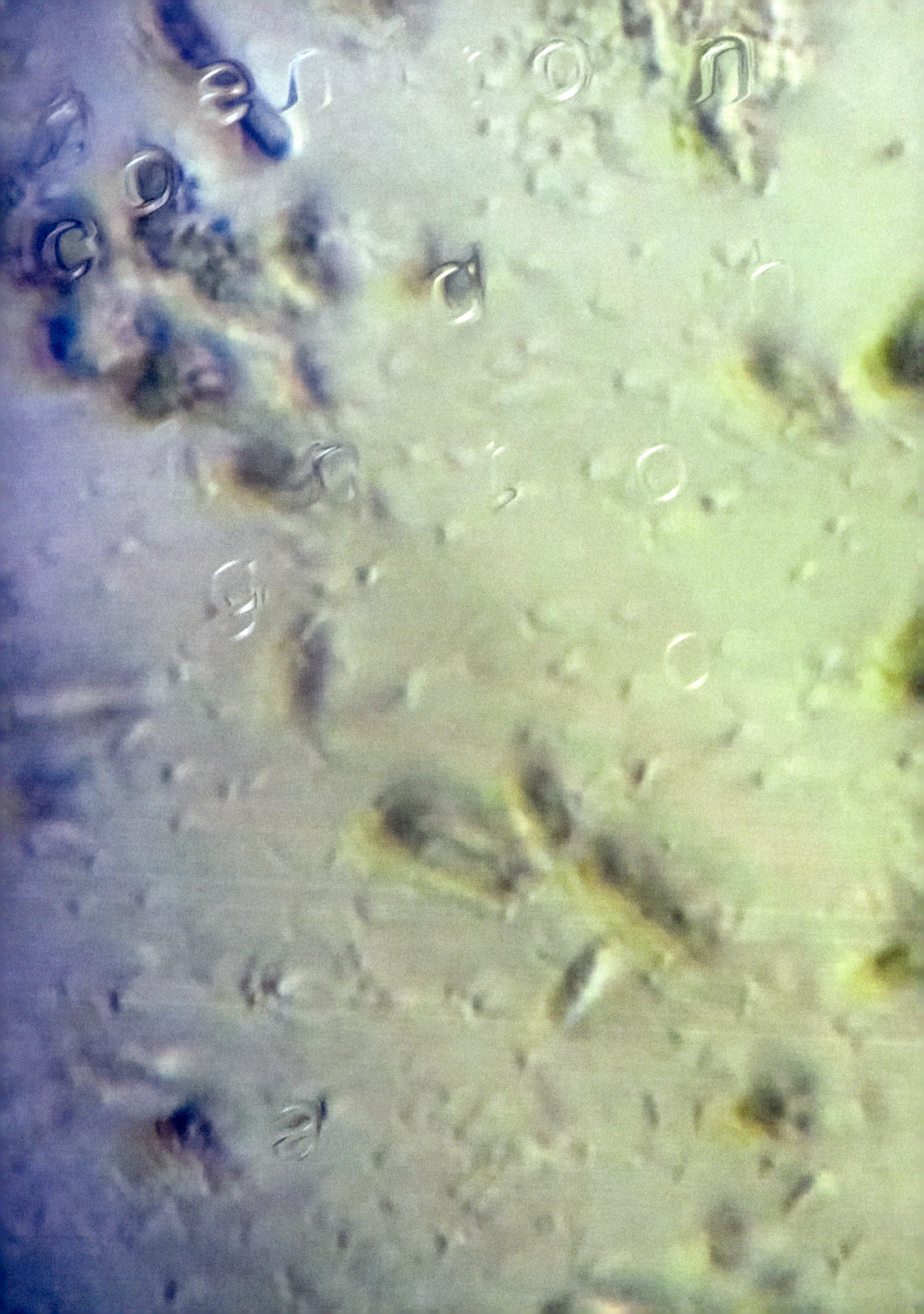

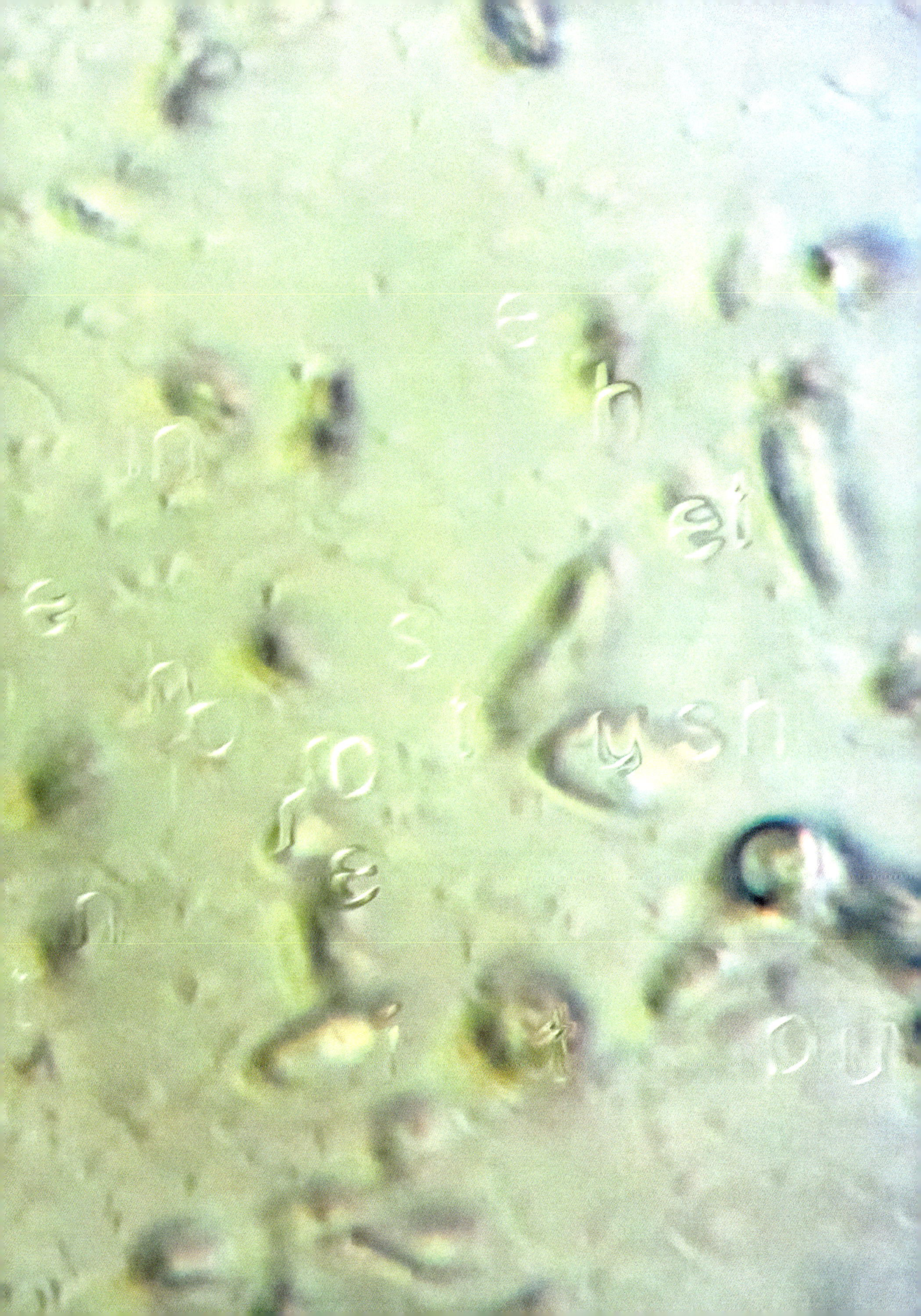

Bia Davou

SERIAL STRUCTURES[1]

It seems that the only arithmetical concept that can grasp the essence of rhythm in its full breadth is this: a sequence of integers that reveals a simple rule.
—Matila Ghyka

The link of my recent work to that of past years begins with a question on the social role of art: Is art a social work?

Immediately for me, the main problem of communication between the artist (transmitter) and the audience (receiver) becomes apparent, and vice versa. Therefore, my research principally branches out to cover these fundamental dimensions of communication: language and message.

For art to operate on a social level, it needs to correctly choose its language and its message, the two pillars of fruitful communication. And by "correctly" I mean that art must take advantage of the unique opportunity to correlate, from the very beginning, language with its message, the idea-concept with its materialization, the signified with the signifier. The reward will be to evade the shackles that a standard language applies to the expression of any new messages (ideas). Communication presupposes a symbolic system, a language with its own reason. In my work, I try to facilitate communication by associating the simplest structural elements of human intellect with the simplest structural elements of plastic arts. As such, a new language is created, founded on the translation of the language of communication devices to relevant codes of plastic language elements.

Communication devices, such as the computational ones, which are a cybernetic technological model, recognize only two contradicting conditions: yes-no, open-closed, on-off, good-bad, alive-dead, 1-0 . . . according to the principles of binary communication.

The logic behind the language I propose is plain: artworks can be assembled in a binary manner, solidifying as such a direct communication with the according simple human binary, reason and thinking.

---

1   Serial structures: mental and conceptual constructions that occur from the binary arithmetical system 0, 1 and develop into self-regulated sequences (series) of integers (elements).

The creation of my major work *Genetic Code 1, 1, 2, 3, 5, 8, . . . , 144* is based on binary language: $(0, 1) \to \cdot, |$ where $0 \to \cdot, | \to |$ and the analogy-genesis $\cdot \to \cdot, |$ and $\to \cdot \, |$. This results to:

$$
\begin{array}{cc}
\cdot & | \\
\cdot \, | & \cdot \\
\cdot \, | \, \cdot & \cdot \, | \\
\cdot \, | \, \cdot \, \cdot \, | & \cdot \, | \, \cdot \\
\ldots & \ldots \\
\cdot \to (1, \ldots, 144) & | \to (|, \ldots, 89)
\end{array}
$$

If we count separately the $\cdot$ and $|$ elements, we will see that they form the Fibonacci sequence: $1, 1, 2, 3, 5, 8, \ldots, 55, \ldots, 1711, \ldots, 38657, \ldots$

Works of art can therefore be created through the method of the Fibonacci sequence or other sequences, where each element occurs from the previous ones based on a rule, culminating as such to "serial structures."

This new plastic language may be one of those that art needs so as to enrich its social role in an era when human communication is increasingly based on machines and their logic.

Language makes communication possible, but it is its message that completes it. The message of artworks based on serial structures is both timely and urgent. It relates to the need to fully develop a two-way communication between artist and viewer, redeemed from "noises." Moreover, it speaks to the possibilities of maintaining the wealth of our emotions and our aesthetic freedom.

For artists to exercise a social role, they need to develop communication channels with their viewers that will not only transfer their message but also allow its proper translation and the capacity to respond. I believe that artworks based on serial structures fulfill these conditions, as they allow the viewer, to a certain degree, to carry them forward in an attempt to understand their message and respond.

This property of artworks that propose serial structures gains significance when it becomes associated with the meaning of their message. The binary logic of machines has arguably ensured unprecedented growth in many different expressions of our human existence. At the same time, it constitutes a dangerous threat to our aesthetic and emotional freedom.

In our thirst for what machine logic makes possible, we immensely deprive ourselves of our ability to feel and express emotions infinitely richer than what machine logic can comprehend.

With my serial structures, as well as the rest of my works based on researching electronic circuits, I am trying to send a warning message in the face of this dire prospect and, at the same time, offer the hopeful view that communication between the artist and the viewer does not necessarily result exclusively in the exchange of messages of despair.

On paper or linen, with pencil, ink, paint, or thread, by using all kinds of materials and technological means, even burlap, stones, or bricks, we can raise ideal and conceptual mental constructions with the method suggested by the Fibonacci sequence or other sequences that lead to serial structures, in order to show that we can elicit beauty from order, creativity from sterility, freedom from discipline, imagination from logic, and at the same time remain free human beings.

Translated from the Greek by Vassilis Douvitsas

SERIAL STRUCTURES 2.
THE ODYSSEY: A BRIEF SUMMARY

In my exhibition in November 1978, there was a burlap hanging, at a height of twenty-one and a half feet, on the grand wall of Desmos Art Gallery. It was folded at its upper part, suggesting a notion of perpetual unfolding. A serial structure was embroidered over it in red thread.

At the time, I proposed what I approximately mean by the term *serial structures*: sequences of signs or any elements, material or graphic, that are produced through a predefined system and have the capacity to self-organize, self-regulate, and generate interminably.

While I was sewing the serial structure on the burlap, carrying forward at a slow and painstaking pace a labor that could possibly last a lifetime, I began thinking of Penelope ceaselessly weaving her veil as she waited for Ulysses. By association (and as the practice of art is an odyssey in and of itself and the like), I was led to the idea of attempting to organize this vast poem, the Homeric epic *The Odyssey*, into serial structures. That is, to separate the verses when reading and reciting them into serial structures instead of iambic or anapestic metrical systems.

I reread *The Odyssey* many times and began writing and sewing the Homeric verses on linen, following the serial system and monitoring the scope of their development. While writing, I tried to use letters pertinent to those of Homer's era, as this particularly helped to achieve a density among sequences. Thereby, I commenced once again a slow mental work under strict control and discipline. As if it were a matter of life and death for a verse to veer off its prescribed arrangement.

WHEN THE SEEMINGLY IMPERSONAL BECOMES PERSONAL

The perpetuation of serial structures can be performed by anyone or begin and progress from all together, as long as there is a given system, a rule, that will associate the sequences and allow new ones to be generated from previous ones. So far, it involves a seemingly impersonal work that eradicates the personality of a single and unique creator.

Yet contact with poetry bequeaths unexpected outcomes.

While the rhythmic development of the verses tends to exhaust itself amid endless designs of lines, letters, and seams, suddenly the serial structures step out into the physical space and travel beside Ulysses, escaping the frame of an intellectual construction.

Translated from the Greek by Vassilis Douvitsas

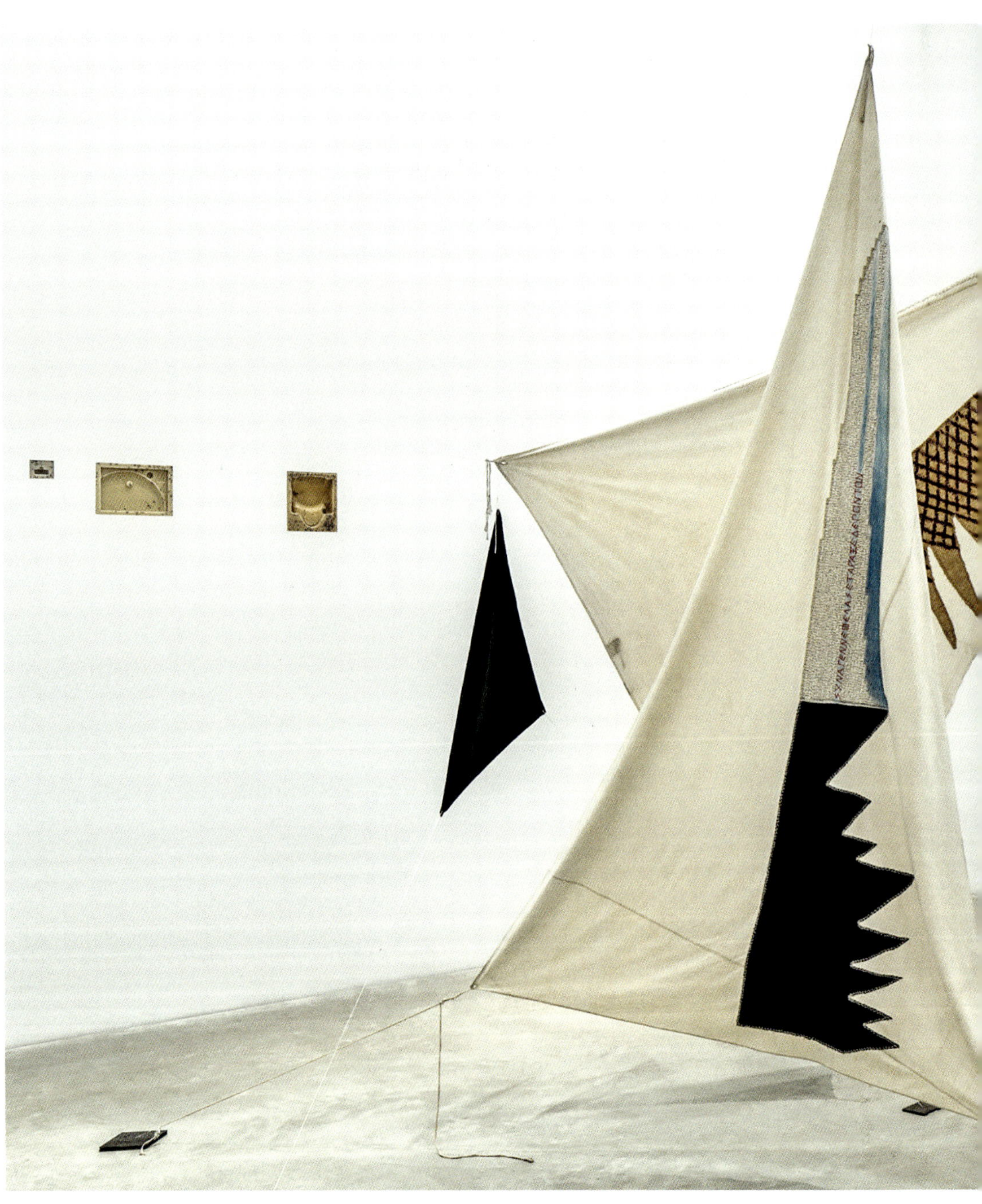

Bia Davou, *Untitled (Odyssey)*, 1980s. Ink, fabric, and thread on linen; four parts:
45¼ × 31½ × 30¾ inches (115 × 80 × 78 cm), 145⅝ × 173¼ × 96½ inches (370 × 440 ×
245 cm), 131⅛ × 133⅞ × 74¾ inches (333 × 340 × 190 cm), 114⅛ × 129⅞ × 59 inches
(290 × 330 × 150 cm) (with Patricia L. Boyd, *Borrowed Time IV–X*, in background)

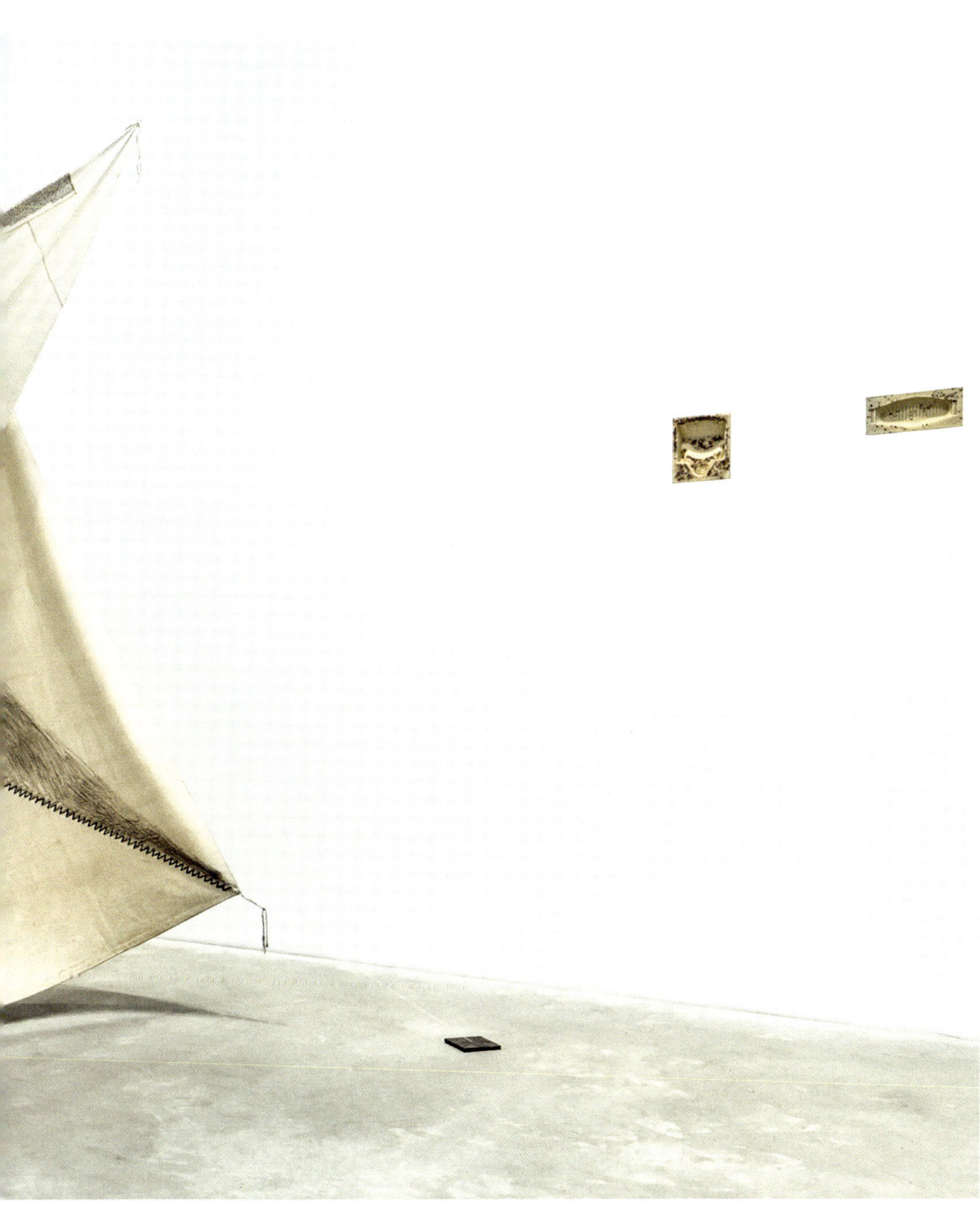

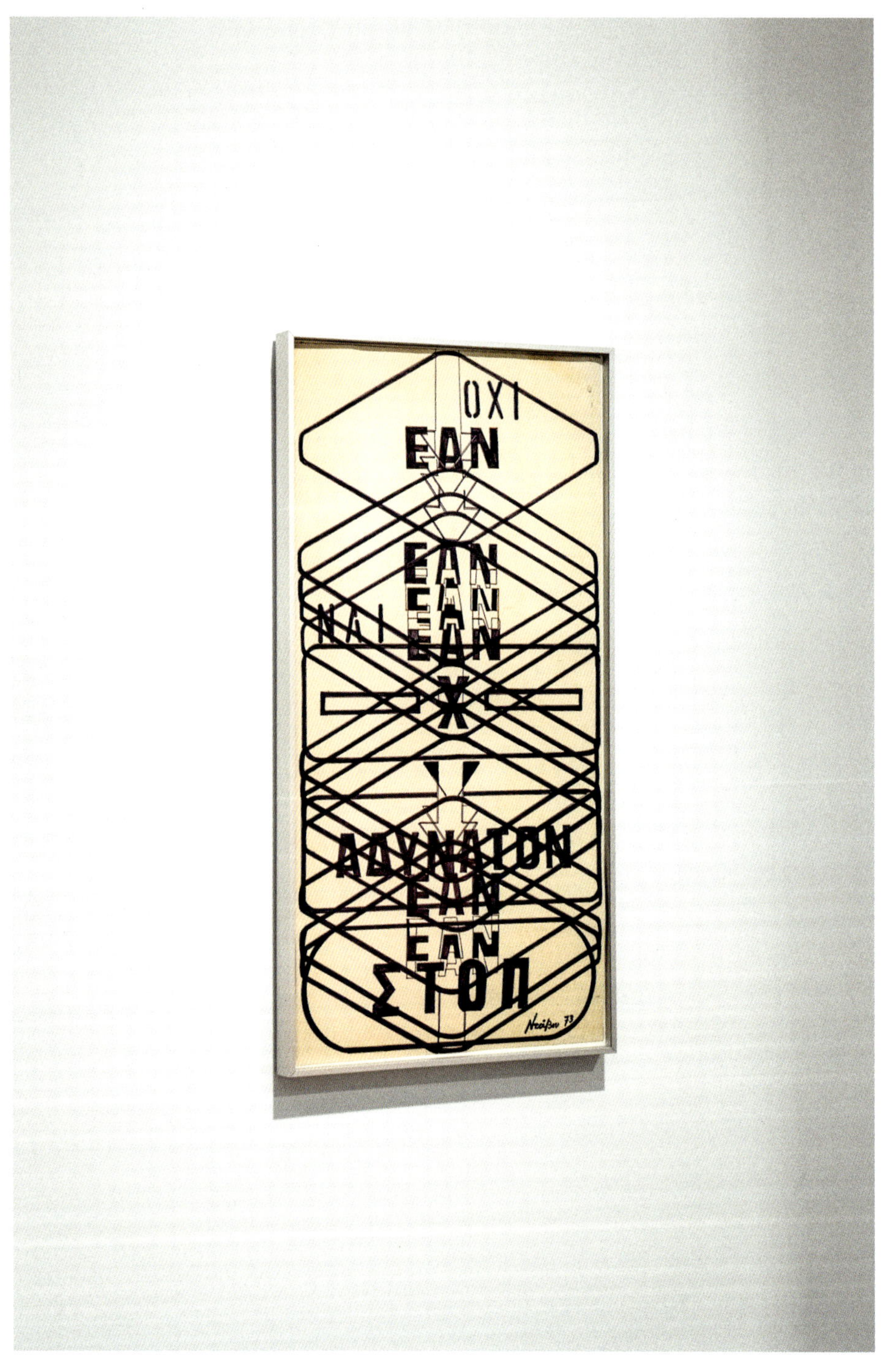

Bia Davou, *Untitled (If, Yes, No, Impossible, Stop)*, 1973. Ink, pencil, and marker on watercolor paper; 23⅝ × 11⅞ inches (60 × 30 cm)

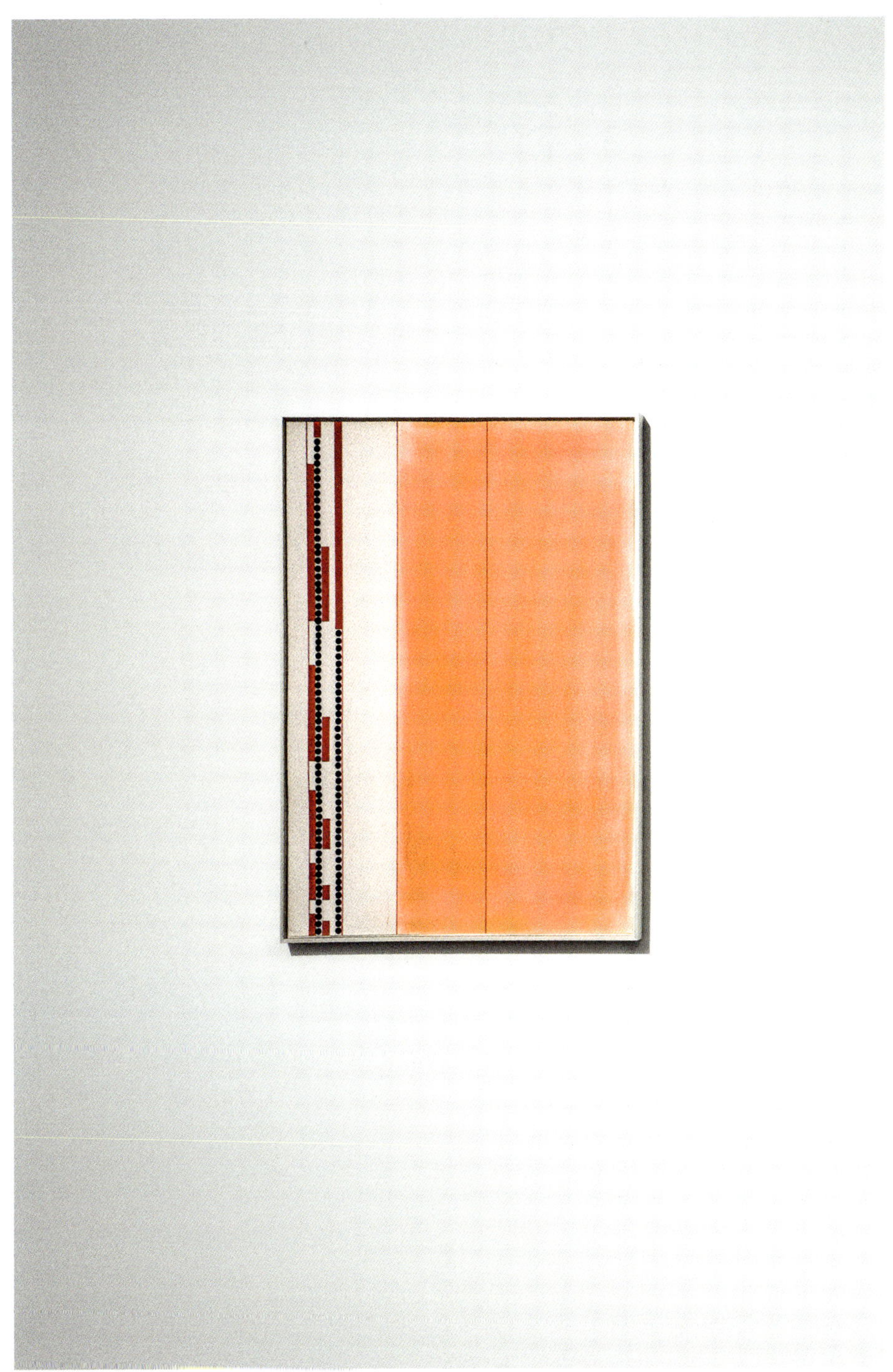

Bia Davou, *Untitled*, 1974–78. Ink, pencil,
and dry pastel on watercolor paper; one of
four parts: 27½ × 19⅝ inches (70 × 50 cm)

Senga Nengudi

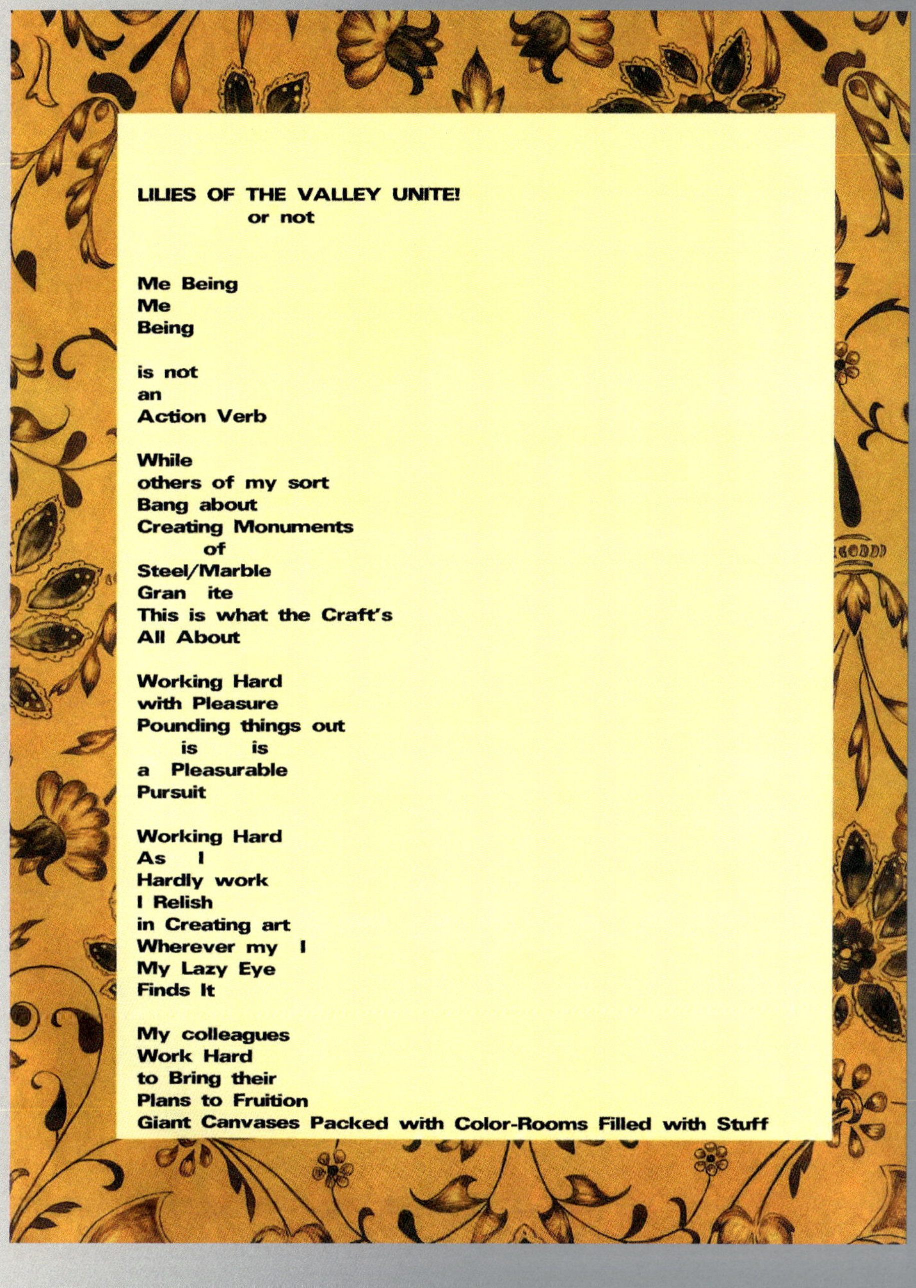

LILIES OF THE VALLEY UNITE!
          or not

Me Being
Me
Being

is not
an
Action Verb

While
others of my sort
Bang about
Creating Monuments
          of
Steel/Marble
Gran ite
This is what the Craft's
All About

Working Hard
with Pleasure
Pounding things out
       is   is
a Pleasurable
Pursuit

Working Hard
As   I
Hardly work
I Relish
in Creating art
Wherever my   I
My Lazy Eye
Finds It

My colleagues
Work Hard
to Bring their
Plans to Fruition
Giant Canvases Packed with Color-Rooms Filled with Stuff

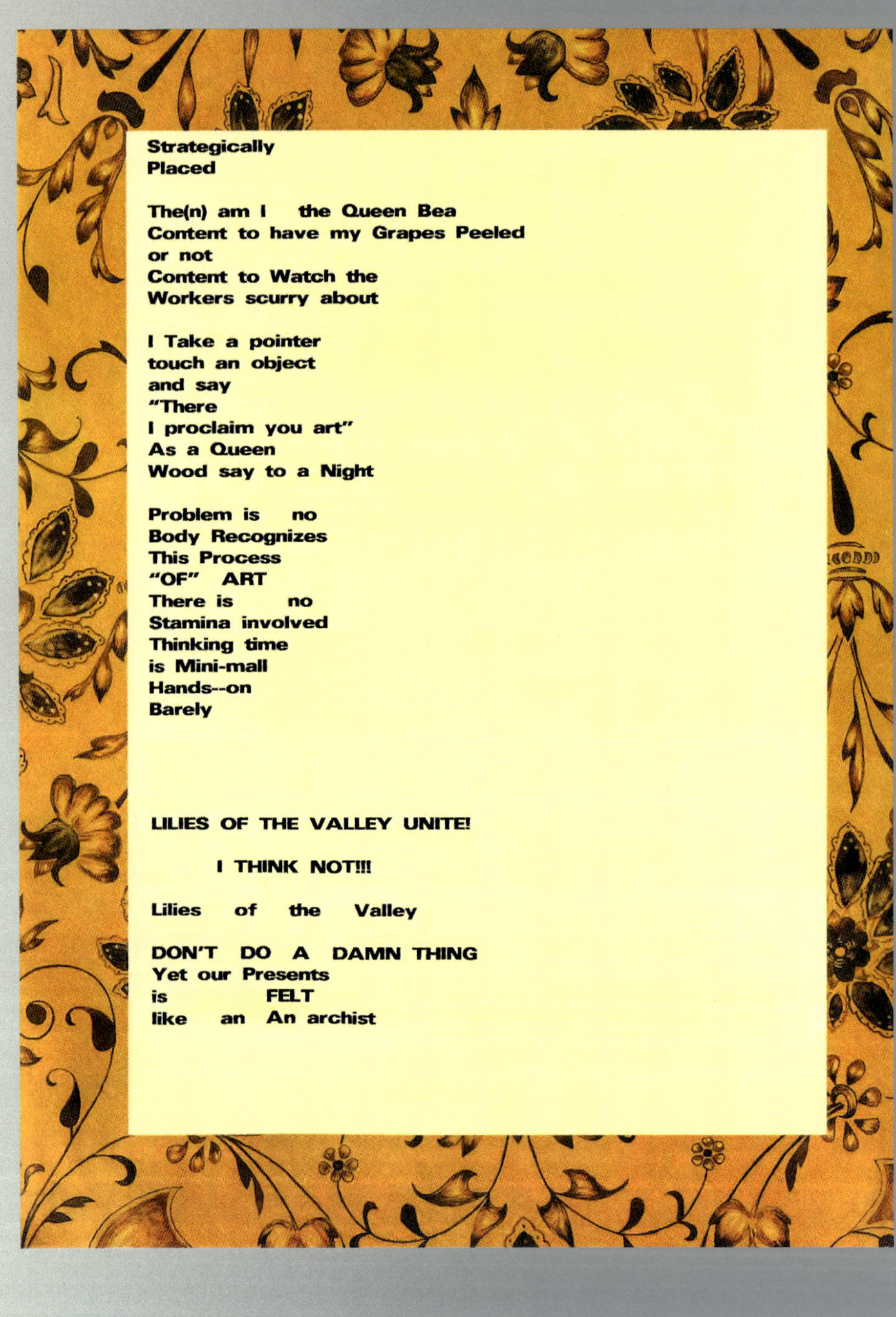

Strategically
Placed

The(n) am I   the Queen Bea
Content to have my Grapes Peeled
or not
Content to Watch the
Workers scurry about

I Take a pointer
touch an object
and say
"There
I proclaim you art"
As a Queen
Wood say to a Night

Problem is   no
Body Recognizes
This Process
"OF"   ART
There is   no
Stamina involved
Thinking time
is Mini-mall
Hands--on
Barely

LILIES OF THE VALLEY UNITE!

        I THINK NOT!!!

Lilies   of   the   Valley

DON'T DO A DAMN THING
Yet our Presents
is   FELT
like   an An archist

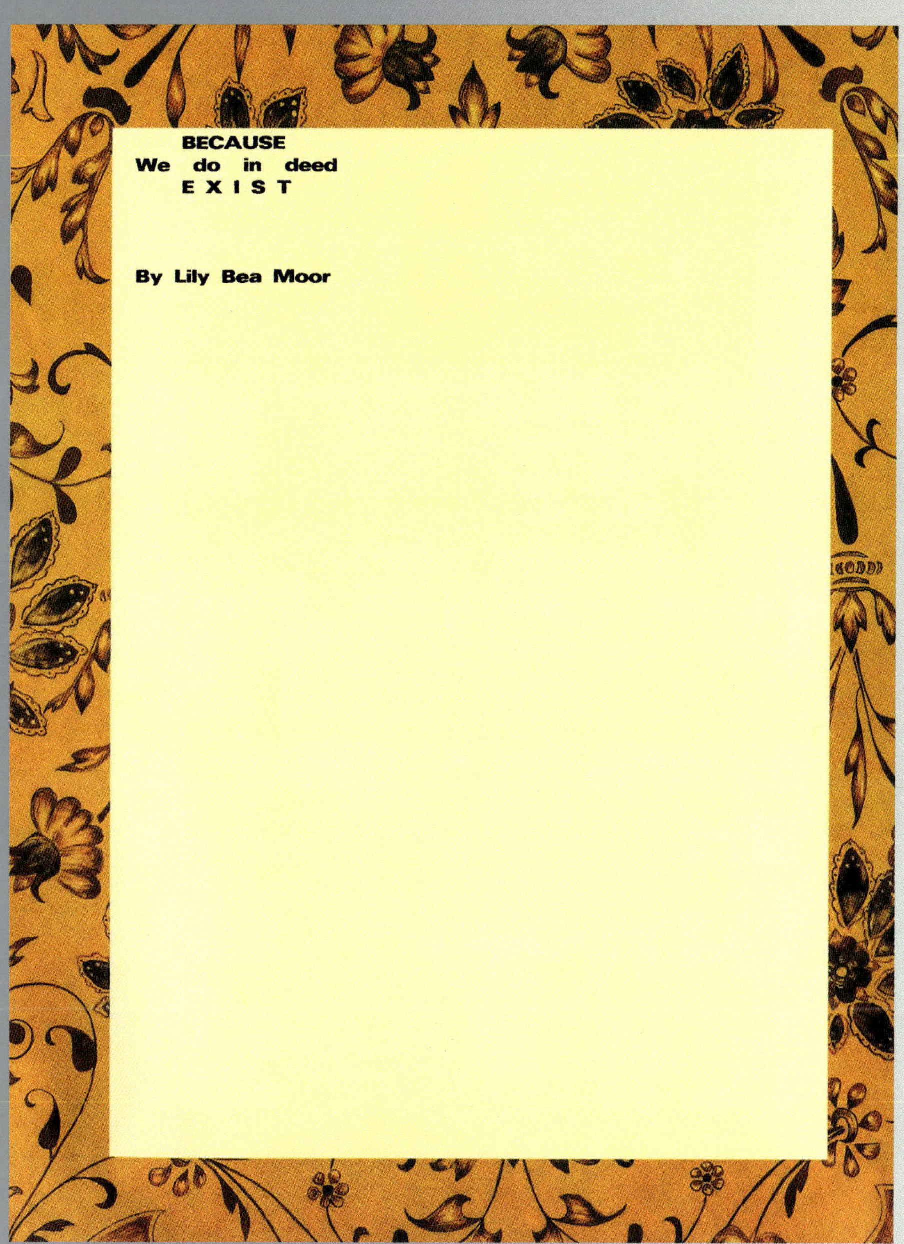

BECAUSE
We do in deed
E X I S T

By Lily Bea Moor

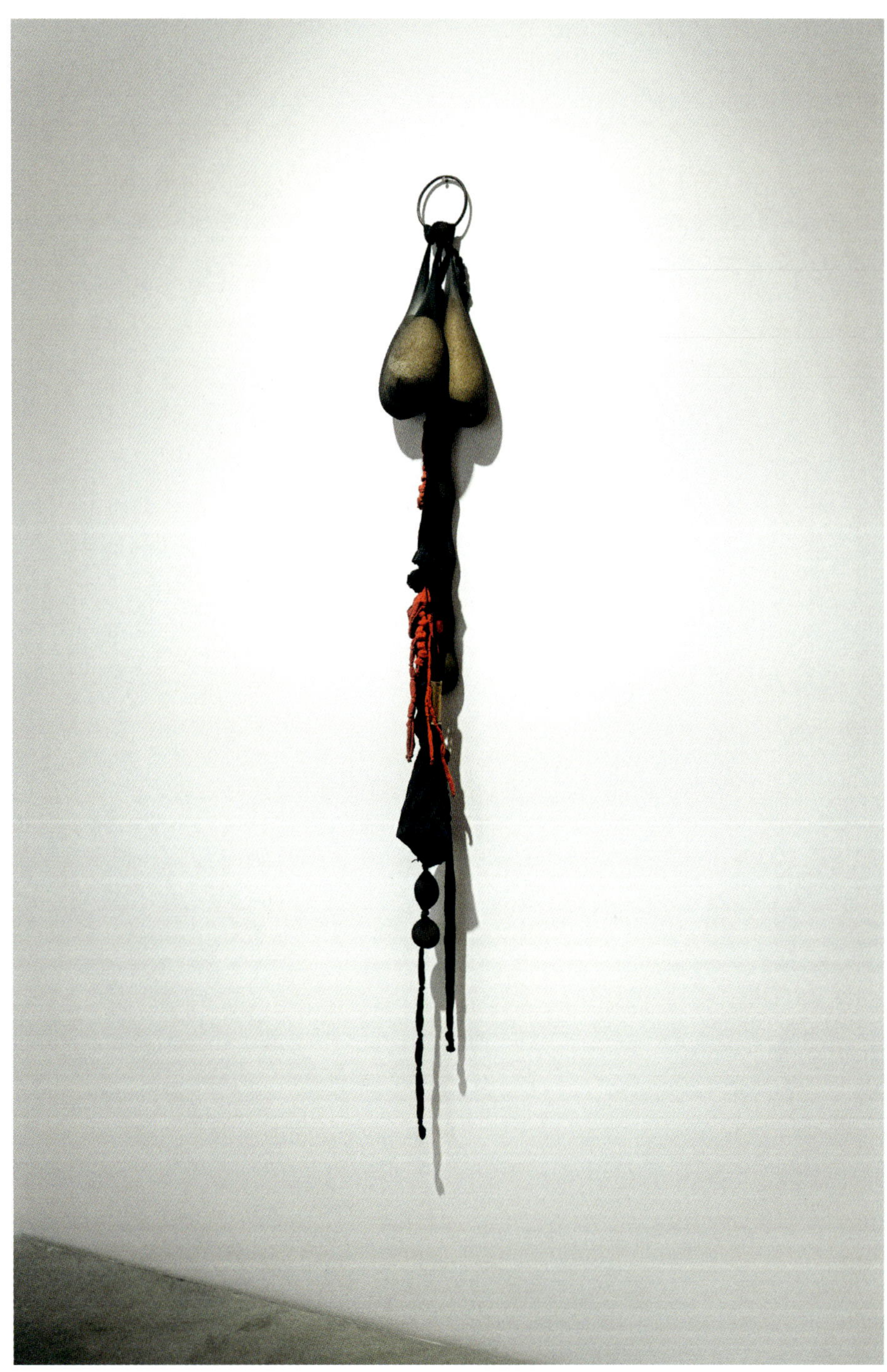

Senga Nengudi, *R.S.V.P. Reverie–Combat Fatigue*, 1977–2011. Nylon, mesh, and sand; 72 × 14 inches (182.8 × 35.6)

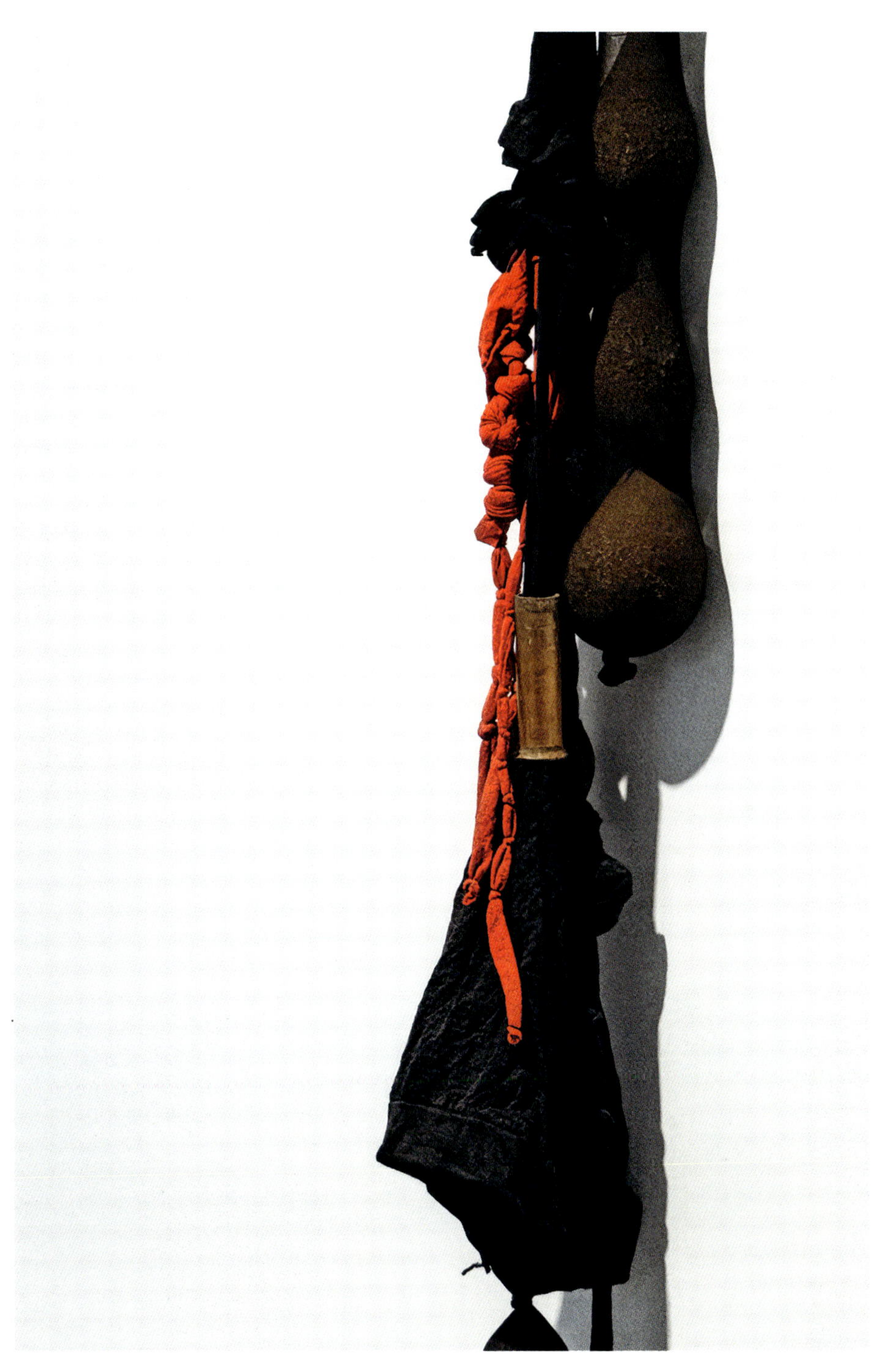

Senga Nengudi, *R.S.V.P. Reverie–
Combat Fatigue*, 1977–2011 (detail)

Iris Touliatou

MOTHER FRAGMENT

At the time I was writing the first score for *HAPPINESS, 2018 to 2022 (to Laurie)*, my mother was racing in her mind and her interiors, showing an unusual talkativeness and revulsion for frozen, and not frozen, meat. During her episodes of disobedience and looseness of tongue, I felt the outpost of our teeth becoming a common source for speaking out all our life details and our many differences, from an unsafe space. Fragments of *HAPPINESS*, like the several previous utterances of this text that appear here, speak of multiple guises, actions and relationships, economies and spendings, promises and sacrifices, biographies and obituaries of mythological, historical, and late modern women.

HAPPINESS is about what happens and unfolds bodies in space and time.

Jacques Derrida's *Given Time: I. Counterfeit Money*, first published in 1991 under the genre of poetry, begins with the epigraph: "The King takes all my time; I give the rest to Saint-Cyr, to whom I would like to give all." It continues:

> It is a woman who signs.
> For this is a letter, and from a woman to a woman. Madame de Maintenon is writing to Madame Brinon. This woman says, in effect, that to the King she gives all. For in giving all one's time, one gives all or the all, if all one gives is in time and one gives all one's time.[1]

In one of the rare accounts of Laurie Parson's life and work (if not the single one), Bob Nickas describes how she leaves the art world behind and decides to give all her time,

> to her own personal writing and . . . social work: interviewing children for a study on physical and mental health at a Newark hospital; taking part in an art program for adolescents with a history of psychiatric hospitalizations; most recently, working with the National Alliance for the Mentally Ill. . . . Over the years,

---

1 Jacques Derrida, *Given Time: I. Counterfeit Money / Jacques Derrida*, trans. Peggy Kamuf (Chicago: University of Chicago Press, 1992), 1. Originally published as *Donner le temps* (Paris: Éditions Galilée, 1991).

Parsons has kept a journal, which has evolved from more diaristic entries to "an abstract collecting of works and phrases." She says that she collects words the way she used to collect objects, but that the writing is for herself and isn't meant to be published—at least not in her lifetime.[2]

Iambe, daughter of Pan and Echo, is a Greek minor goddess of verse and humor, whose jokes roused the grieving Demeter from her profound depression during her search for her daughter, Persephone. Iambe, which means "speech," is believed to have loaned her name to iambic meter, a metrical foot having two syllables: the first unstressed, or "weak," and the second stressed. Some said that the extravagant hilarity displayed at the festivals of Demeter in Attica was traced to her; others, that she hanged herself in consequence of the cutting speeches and extreme feelings in which she had indulged herself and others. Iambe is also sometimes called Baubo, whose body is depicted in very distinct figurines. The head is placed directly onto the legs, and, lacking a torso, the chin and vagina merge into one another. Robert Graves writes about these women, or one woman who consists of her two orifices, her mouth and vulva:

> Iambe and Baubo personify the obscene songs, in Iambic meter, which were sung to relieve emotional tension at the Eleusinian mysteries; but Iambe, Demeter, and Baubo form the familiar triad of maiden, nymph, and crone. Old nurses in Greek myth nearly always stand for the goddess as crone.[3]

The association of vulvas and mouths is no stranger to descriptions and depictions of women that are not defined and restricted, and they look for words outside the familiar words, they have a voice that is of a strange pitch and speak directly to what they've received.

While happiness is often perceived as the direct effect of what you do, the etymology of the word *happiness* through the Latin root *hap* relates it

---

2   Bob Nickas, "Whatever Happened to: Laurie Parsons," *Artforum* 41, no. 8 (April, 2003), accessed January 20, 2022, https://www.artforum.com/print/200304/whatever-happened-to-laurie-parsons-4510.

3   Robert Graves, *The Greek Myths: The Complete and Definitive Edition* (London: Penguin, 1955), 58.

to chance and raises questions of contingency. What happens—how close to us it happens and how it affects us—reveals also that a mechanism continues until today, shutting women out of the conversation or negotiating their happiness, their work, and their rights during and even after their lifetimes.

Within these rocky structures there is an Italian word, *affidamento*, which describes a practice and a relationship between two women, usually one older than the other, where each entrusts herself to the other, recognizes and relies on the other's differences in order to open new political spaces.[4]

A friend just emailed; at the end, she writes that "in Buddhism it is often said that over the eons we have all been each other's mother."

4   Mirna Cicioni, "'Love and Respect, Together': The Theory and Practice of Affidamento in Italian Feminism," *Australian Feminist Studies* 4, no. 10 (1989): 71–83.

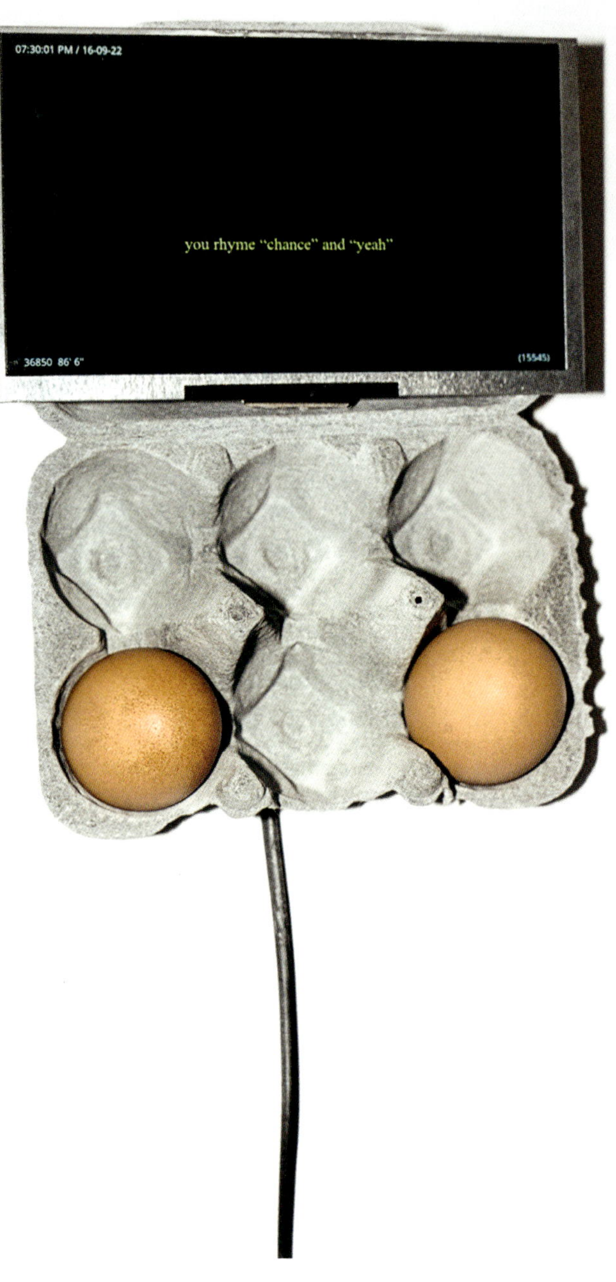
07:30:01 PM / 16-09-22
you rhyme "chance" and "yeah"
36850 86' 6"
(15545)

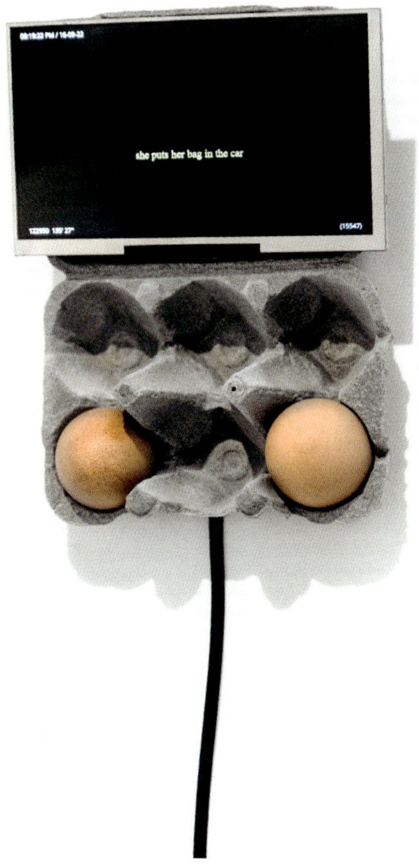

This page and previous: Iris Touliatou, *HAPPINESS, 2018 to 2022 (to Laurie), Vol. III*
i. on accents and arousals, in vivo and in vitro
ii. on middle age in the islands
iii. on the sleep of mothers and the refusal of paternal legacies
iv. on spoilers and the bottom line, 2022. Unread email inbox, subscriptions, alerts, software, counters, verses, seven-inch LCD screen, carton, magnets, and eggs; 8¼ × 6½ × 3 inches (21 × 16.5 × 7.6 cm)

Patricia L. Boyd

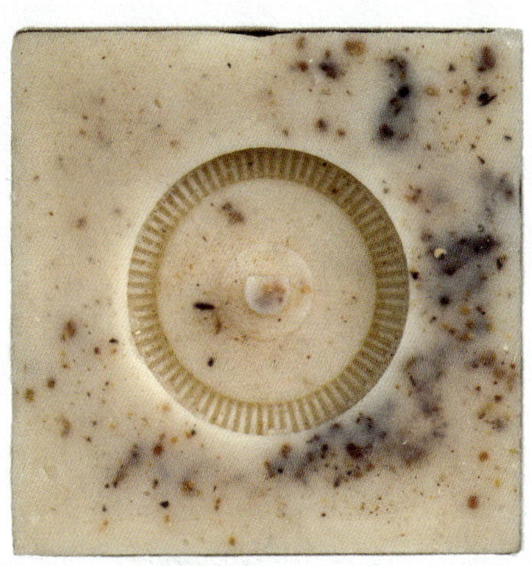

Patricia L. Boyd, *Borrowed Time X*, 2022. Used restaurant grease, damar resin, and beeswax; $3\frac{15}{16} \times 3\frac{15}{16} \times 1\frac{13}{16}$ inches (10 × 10 × 3 cm)

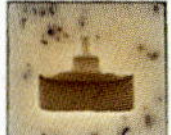 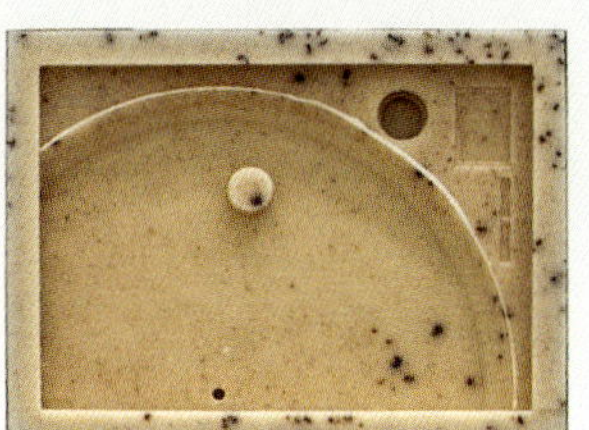

Left: *Borrowed Time IV, V, VI* (detail), 2022. Used restaurant grease, damar resin, and beeswax; two of three parts: 2¼ × 3½ × 2¼ inches (6 × 9 × 6 cm) and 9 × 12¼ × 1½ inches (23 × 31 × 4 cm)
Right: *Borrowed Time VII*, 2022. Used restaurant grease, damar resin, and beeswax; 11 × 9 × 3⅛ inches (28 × 23 × 8 cm) (with Bia Davou, *Untitled (Odyssey)*, on far right)

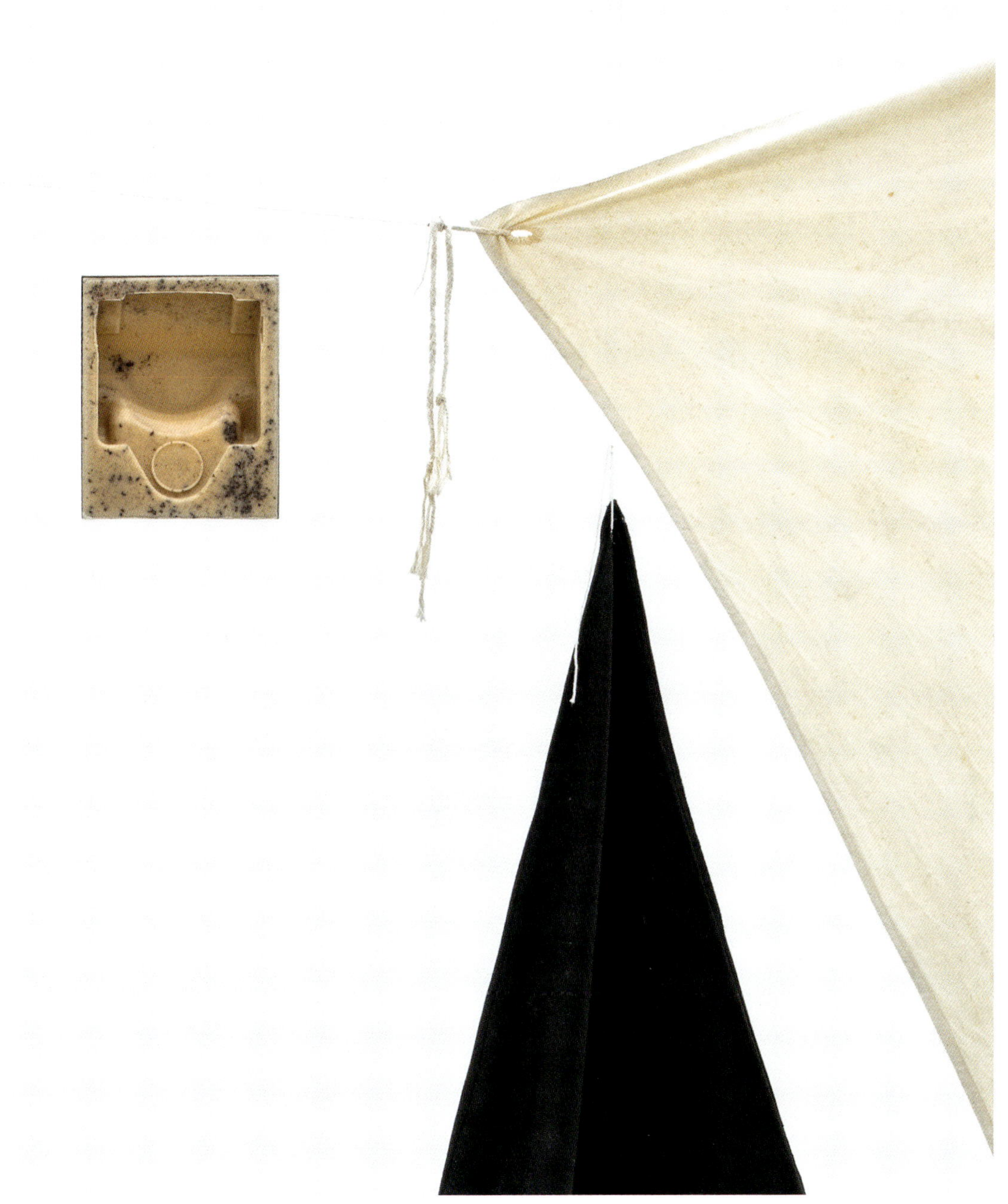

misunderstandings	mother	my	my
misunderstood	mother	my	my
mixed	mother	my	my
mnemonic	mother	my	my
modification	mother,	my	my
moment	mother,	my	my
moment	mother;	my	my
moment	mother."	my	my
moment	mother's	my	my
moment.	mother's	MY	my
moments	mother's	my	my
moments	mother's	my	my
moments	mother's	my	my
moments.	mother"	my	my
monosyllabic	motherhood	my	my
month	motive	my	my
monthly	mould	my	my
more	move	my	my
more	move	My	my
more	move	my	my
more	move-in	my	my
more	moved	my	my
more	much	my	my
more	much	my	my
more	much	my	my
more	much	my	my
more	much	my	my
morning	much?	my	my
morning	much.	my	my
morning	Mummy	my	my
most	murk	my	my
most	must	my	my
mostly	must	my	my
mother	must	my	my
mother	must	my	my
mother	must've	my	my
mother	mutilated.	my	my
mother	mutual	my	my
mother	My	my	my
mother	my	my	my
mother	my	my	my
mother	my	my	my
mother	my	my	my

session	she	sick	smelly,
session,	she	sick	snacks
session?	she	side.	snap
session.	she	side)	so
session.	she	sides	so
session.	she	sign	so
session)	she	significant	so
sessions	she	silent,	so
sessions	she	simple	so
sessions	she	simply	so
sessions,	she	since	so
set	she	since	so
set	she	single	so
set	she	Singly	so
setting.	she	sister	so
several	she	sister	so
several	she	sister,	so
severely	she	sit	so
SF	she	sits	so
shame	she	sitting	so
shame	She	situated,	so
shame	she's	situation	so
shame,	she's	situation	so
shared	shelves	situation	so
sharp	shelves,	situation	so
shattered	shifting,	SITUATION	so
she	shifts	situation?	so
she	shitty	situation.	so
she	shoes	Situations"	so
she	shop	sleep	so
she	shop.	sleep,	so:
she	shops	sleeplessness	social
She	short	slide	solitary
she	short,	slide	some
She	shorter	slides	some
She	should	slides	some
she	should	sliding	some
she	should	slightly	some
she	shower	slightly.	some
she	shows	slumping.	some
she	shuts	small	some
she	shuts	smashes	some
she	shutting	smell	somehow

Sky Hopinka

FLESH AND GHOST

I think I shall sleep here, she said, or rest a little. Be still, my heart. The tranquil evening will draw its mantle over our ailing senses.
—W. G. Sebald

1
We're the children of a great love, and a great violence.
We're the grandchildren of a great love, and a great violence.
Our softness and our hardness are always at odds with those surfaces.
We ask them to be kind and to be gentle,
we tell ourselves to be kind and to be gentle.

Our hands shake in the early evenings.
They always shake in the early evenings
as the nights get long and we
we can't see when they'll end.

An infinite morning haunts our dreams because of its quietude,
because of its light and its air.
A cold air that bites when it's frigid,
deep down through our nose and into our mouth
and lower into our chest.
An air that is cloudy and
an air that is green
the green of the cedars and the mountains.

Go camping again, my sister,
go back into the woods where you feel safe.
I'll come find you when you find morning.
I search for it myself and dream of an afternoon that we found in
    our youth.
I picked you up and held you high and carried you around as you
    squeezed on my neck
and called me big brother.
You danced at the powwow

you danced in circles
you told me to watch and to let you know
you danced good.

Twenty two or twenty three Decembers gone and I remember you clearly.
I remember you now and I love you still.
You've got the road and
I've got the road and we'll meet in the Yakima prairies
once we've walked through our stories
and slowly ease away from
our speed and our dread
that hurry our hearts
and exhaust our bones and our ancestors.

They're not our ancestors, though.
They're our mothers and our fathers sitting quietly alone
as we watch them make sense of their youth.
They're clouds to us now,
just hues of light and recollections of feeling and emotion.
We imagined the colors were their dreams,
churning away in their memories.
Mnemonics of shape and reason,
on syncope and swaying,
as the anxieties of the gods sit heavy in the past.
And they say, such are things in dreams and autumn.

2
We were at a loss of language,
except for what we could speak.
And I spoke and spake my way
right out of this place.
It's hot here still
and the humidity was never present
but lingers on the past in the ways
that memories tend to lazily lay.
I don't remember what was a memory
or what was a dream.

I imagine the colors were dreams
and the smells were memories.
It doesn't matter that much anymore
since
I'm home and here
and hot and bothered about the heat
and the place and the men
who couldn't teach me anything.
I love them anyway and
what am I but half asleep daydreaming those teachings.
I learned and I learnt the everyday absences
of strength and weakness.
That binary isn't good enough,
c'mon, downright bad.
We got in the car and we drove south
up and down the mountain back that way sidling through
the cool clear paths in the rain
and on the street.
Take it easy
we got plenty of time and we're always a little tight
and tonight we're home in a home I haven't been to
in such a long while.
Memories at my feet
and on the street
and in the little pains of everything
no one says nowadays.
They've moved on.
Hometown blues and I think of you.
I always think of you on days like this.
Until tomorrow,
when I wake up not remembering
anything and go bout my day til it's time
to remember everything.
Wherefore soft sounds
and disfluencies abound.

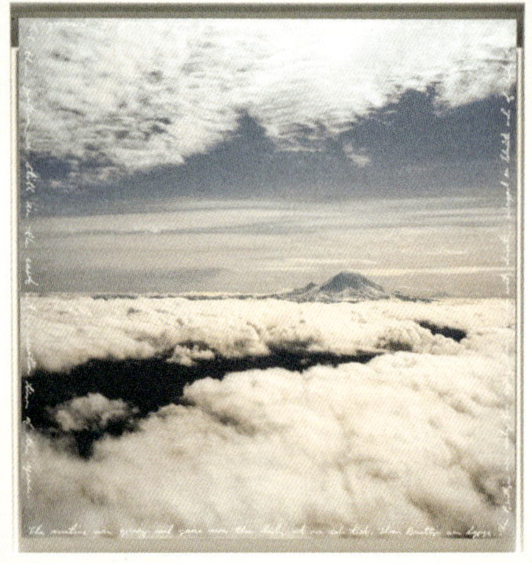

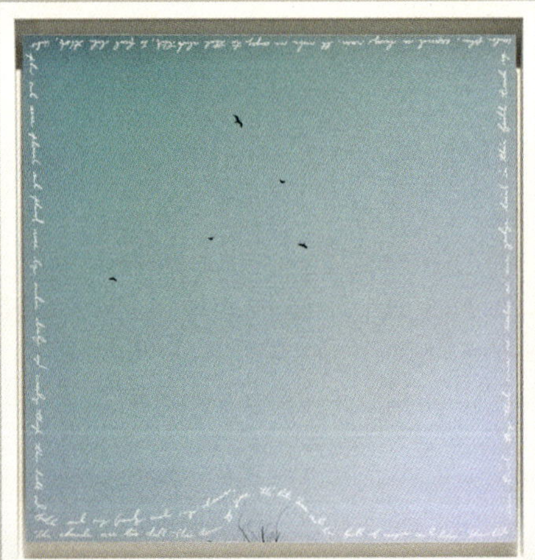

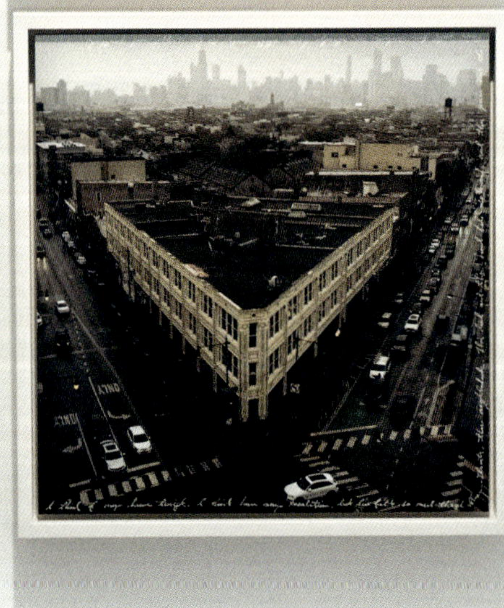

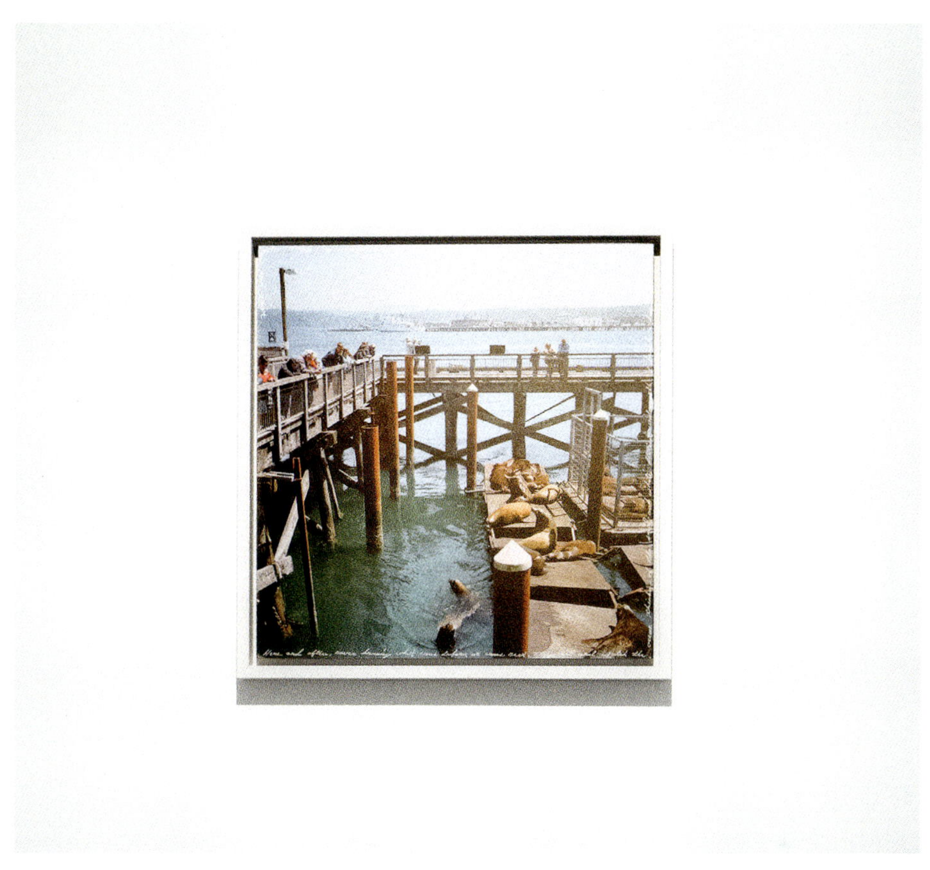

Left page from top: Sky Hopinka, *I think of my home tonight. I don't have any resolutions, but I've felt so much through these streets, these neighborhoods. This land and this Land hold so much, and this pain and this Pain call for salves we already have, still needing to be wrapped and poulticed.*, 2020; *The clouds are too dull this time of year. It's late June and I'm full of anger and hate. They think we're trash, they think we're as useless as our garbage buried in their fields turned up under plow, exposed in heavy rain. It makes me angry to think about that. To feel like that. Under plow and over plowed and plowed over by machines dredging and weeding through the hills and the fields and my family and my home.*, 2020; *The mountains are growing and you're over there looking at me like that. These Breathings are beggings, these Breathings are asking for anything having to do with direction. Wrapped in blankets made of clouds, Morning Star got up and pointed the way. We were too tired and too weak to proceed, but still the gesture is still in the east at a certain time of year.*, 2020. Inkjet prints, etching; 17 × 17 inches (43.2 × 43.2 cm) each

Above: Sky Hopinka, *Here and after, never knowing what came before or comes next, they sit and watch the ocean thinking of the sand and what's buried underneath. I heard a long time ago that there's a village somewhere near here. Under the sand, overgrown by trees, restless and quiet.*, 2020. Inkjet print, etching; 17 × 17 inches (43.2 × 43.2 cm)

Following spread: Sky Hopinka, *Fainting Spells*, 2018. HD video (stereo sound, color, 9:45 min.)

I waited for you to

wake I thought of the

Nour Mobarak

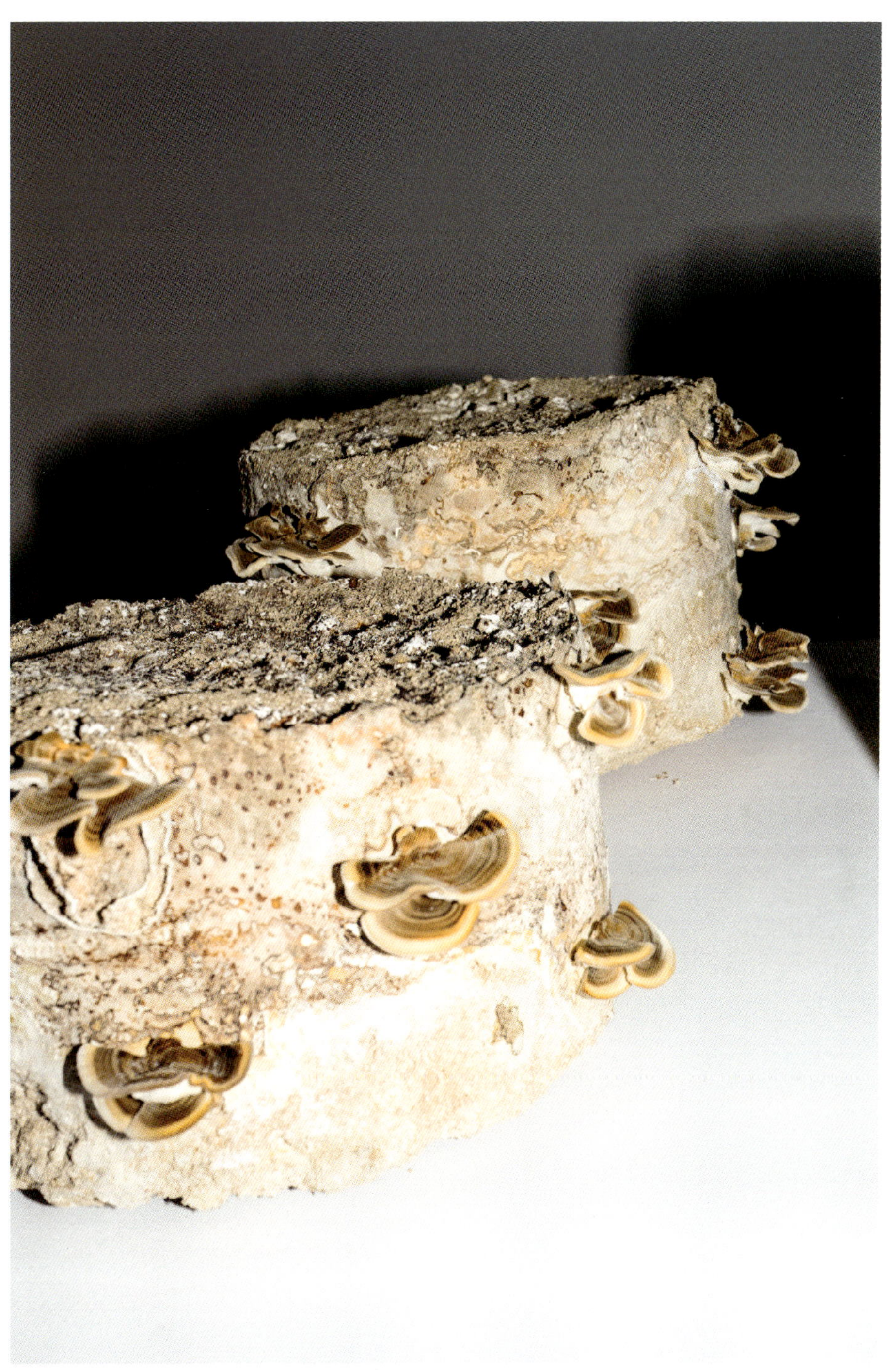

Nour Mobarak, *Fugue I* and *II*, 2019. Trametes
versicolor, wood pellets, and speakers; 8 × 14 ×
13 inches (20.3 × 35.6 × 33 cm) and 8 × 13 ×
13 inches (20.3 × 33 × 33 cm)

117

You Are the Audience

Extended transcript from performance with Bana Haffar. The left column is spoken; the right represents simultaneous phonemic microsamples.*

There are a few characters in this room	õ õõ w õ õ õõõ
There's a chair there	õ õõ õ õ õõõ
There's a bench	äɒð
There are some PAs from which the sound is emitted	õ õõ õ õ õõõ
Casts of a Herman Miller chair in kitchen grease	ä äɒð
Me	wɑ wɑ
and there's Bana of course	ä ää ä ä ää
Here's Bana	äɒð
Look at Bana play	ɛɪ stai
She's got her back to you but watch her	äɒð äɒð äɒð
She's learned so much	ä ä ä äɒð
She's practiced so much, and tonight,	äɒð äɒð
We're listening	kh
As she's orchestrated a system	äɒð stai
Wherein my voice	ə
Speaking here tonight	kh ʃ kh kh kh
Is triggering my voice	q q q q p
From another time	ɛɪ ɛɪ
Sitting in my tiny apartment	ʁ ʁ ʁ ʁ ʁ
One night when Bana came by	ɛɪ
triggering micro samples of my voice	khkh ˈkwa
There are many characters in this room	f f f f f f f f f f f
And I also am one of the characters in the performance	ɛɪ ɛɪ
And I've	əe ʃ eeee ʃ əe
I've requested compensation	ɛɪ

Do I deserve compensation?	ə-əə-ə
For just standing in the room?	ʃən
Talking in the mic?	ɟ ɟ ɸ
Triggering my voice?	ʃən
It's an absolute pleasure	ˈtɛ
For me	ɟ ɸʊn
So I suppose a few parameters	ʍ
have to be set	ˈtɛlə
so that I can justifiably request	ʌ ˈkwa
compensation	ɸ
I just can't sit here	w
and do what feels good	ʃən ʃən ʃən
and ask you to pay me.	s' o o
What if you don't like it?	ˈtɛ ˈtɛ
Can I be paid regardless?	wɑ ɑ
How will the value be worth the cost?	lə ˈkwa
Well	wɑ wɑ
I mean at least Bana here has done a little work	ɑ
And um	ɸ lə
And I'm going to say	ˈpɑ
I'm going to say that	stai
I'm going to say that	stai stai
for this performance to really be happening	ʪ ts dz
There have to be at least	ˈpɑ
At the very least	ʪ ts dz
258 Whole Foods shoppers shopping simultaneously right now as I talk into this microphone or else this performance is just a no go, it's not really happening	k gk g

So what am I going to say, it's that there has to be 18 Whole Foods shoppers right now	qx gk g
in Henderson, Nevada	k gk g
198 in the state of Oregon please	k gk g
an old stomping ground	qx
and 42 in Pasadena	qx k
But what if you don't like it?	ʃ ʃ ʃ ʃ
What if you walk out?	ʒ
Well then you're just going to change	ʒ
You're going to change positions in this performance	ʒ
It's still happening	ha ha
because my rule is	ɰ
if you're here in front of me you're not an audience member	ɰ mənd
you're performing	ɰ ɰ ɰ
and of course you can refuse	ɰɰɰɰ
you can walk out right now	ˈpɑ ʃən ʃən
but you're still trapped	ˈkwa
because i'm going to say	ˈpɑ
that an audience member isn't truly watching this performance unless that audience member is not watching the performance	ʜʜʜ
that is to say	c'
That I'm going to claim that there are over 7 billion	ˈpɑ
audience members to our performance tonight	mənd
that's right	ŋ̍m ŋ̍m ˈpɑ
whether those people like it or not	ʃən
there they are	ŋ̍m
not watching me perform	ˈpɑ ŋ̍m
and	ð
and you could walk out	ˈpɑ

and you could decide	ð ð̥ ð̊
that it's all not true	stai
and then all of a sudden we've got a split reality situation	( )
and i guess we're both going to have to contend with that	◯ ɒv
there's going to be a world	ˈkwa
where my performance exists	ʁʁʁʁ ð
and a world where my performance doesn't exist	mənd
i mean if you were angry enough	ˈfʌni
you could create those two realities	ʌ ʌ ʌ
i have two brothers	dli
I want you to know that i have two brothers	aʊ aʊ
I have two older brothers	ip
I have two older brothers	deɪʃən dli
I said that I have two older brothers	deɪʃən
I have a brother	ʃən ʃən
who's six years older than me and we were born on the same birthday	trɛpɪ
i have another brother, he's five years older than me	dli
that each have sons those two brothers	trɛ trɛ stai
each of those brothers has a son	dli
I have two nephews	ʃən
I'm letting you know that I have two nephews	ʃən ʃən
I have two nephews	ʃən ʃən
they're 6 weeks apart	ˈpɑ
each brother has a son	ˈtɛlə
I have two brothers	ˈtolo
I have two respective nephews	stai
the eldest brother	ˈtɛlə
had the first son	stai

my middle brother — ffffffff mənd
he had the younger son — f
six weeks apart — f
there are four boys in this room — oʊn
lets imagine — mənd ˈpɑ
in the northeast corner there's my eldest brother — oʊn
in the southeast corner there's my middle brother — aɪəl
in the northwest corner there's his son — ʟ̩ʜ oʊn
and they can look at each other — staɪ
everyone's always diagonal from each other — ʟ̩ʜ æ
no matter where they are — ʟ̩ʜ æ æææ
and — aɪəl
the eldest brother — dli æ dli æ
the youngest nephew — ˈgl
they switch spots — dli dli
the other boy — ˈgl
he switches spots — ˈgl
lots of — dli
well then the eldest brother — pʌn oʊn
he moves over there — staɪ
and then the youngest son — pʌn
he takes his place — ɪʃ/ oʊn
and then the eldest brother — ip
he switches — ip
and i guess i'm — oʊn
there are these four males — mənd ip
i mean people these days — tɪŋ
they talk — ˈkwa ˈkwa
i mean they're not males necessarily — tɪŋ tɪŋ tɪŋ tɪŋ

"the World Bank has more or less directed the economic
policies of the third world — ˈkwa aɪəl
coercing and cracking open the market — ˈmʌ ɪət
of country after country — mənd
for global finance — ˌkɔr ɪət
you could say that corporate philanthropy
has turned out to be the most visionary business — ɪət oʊn ˈkwa
of all time"** — bl bl bl
and
I learned about — ˈsaɪrən
earning my keep — ˈmʌ
can't just sit and talk about yourself into a microphone — blu ˈpɑ
and expect healthcare, a living wage
healthcare — dli ˈpɑ
healthcare as filler word you know — ˈpɑ
healthcare — š š š š š š
healthcare — ˈsaɪrən
healthcare — oʊn
best case scenario i just have the right to live — ˈdaɪ
worst case — oʊn
i don't — ˈkwa ðər
trying to decide if it'd be worse actually if it'd be worse while
other people do and i only don't because of my identity or
something or something i don't have any control over or maybe i
do have control over but anyway — ˈmʌ staɪ
I have two brothers — ˈsaɪrən
Let's imagine — ðər r r r r
that I have two brothers — rrrrən
and — staɪ
they each have — ˈmʌrən

those two little ones — ˈkæs
they're very young — sssssssss
very young — staɪ
very young — ˈkæs
very young — ˈpɑ
very young — ɛri ɛri oʊn ɛɛɛ
and um
well — ˌv mənd
so — ˌv ˌv ˌv
well — dəl
so — dəl
well — ˌv
so — rən
well — ˌkɔr rən
so — ˌkɔr ˌv
for the sake of the performance — staɪ
every time i fuck up i can take the filler word — ˈkwa
and repeat it and all of a sudden it's music — ˌv ˈbraɪ
and — ˈbraɪ
maybe it's not so nice when mysteries are revealed — ˈpɑ ˈpɑ
but i'm going to be paid anyway — ɚ ɚ ɚ ɚ ɚ ˌv
my mother married a World Bank director when i was twelve — mənd
i learned a thing or two about macro economics — dəl
i learned a thing or two about macro economics — ˈkwa
hey — dəl
I learned something — ˌkɔr ˌv ˌv
I learned about the economics of the third world — staɪ staɪ
i got this good quote here — dli

two sons — rən
one's like me he likes to talk — ˈpɑ ˌv ˌv
one's like bana — dli
he likes to understand how to make things work — dli ˈkwa
and the eldest one he's very — ˈpɑ ˌv
gregarious — oʊn
likes to use his voice — staɪ
the youngest one likes — mənd ˈdaɪ
to use sign language and — ˈpɑ
and the eldest one he likes garbage trucks — mənd
and um — ˈdaɪ
he loves cars — aɪəl
he can just stare out the window forever — rən
and he can just — ˈpɑ
look out the window forever — ˈmʌ aɪəl
and then — dli
while he does it — aɪəl
he just says — aɪəl

car car car car car car car car car car car car car car car car car
car car car car car car car car car car car car car car car car car
car car car car car car car car car car car car car car car car car
car car car car car car car car car car car car car car car car car
car car car car car car car car car car car car car car car car car
car car car car car car car car car car car car car car car car car
car car car car car car car car car car car car car car car car car
car car car car car car car car car car car car car car car car car
car car car car car car car car car car car car car car car car car
car car car car car car car car car car car car car car car car car
car car car car car car car car car car car car car car car car car
car car car car car car car car car car car car car car car car car
car car car

ˈpɑ gl gl aɪə rən
ˈmʌ gl gl ˈpɑ ˈpɑ t
um t t t um mm fff
staɪ staɪ ˈpa staɪ
staɪ rən rən ɪʃ/
ˈsaɪ ˈsaɪ rən rən
ˈsaɪrən ˈkæs ˈkæs
ˌv ˌv tɪŋ tɪŋ ɪʃ/ bl
rən ˈkwaˈkwa ŋ̍m
ŋ̍m ŋ̍m oʊn wa
wa tz ɰɰɰɰ ˈpa
ggg gl gl /ˈsa rə rə
n n tt mm fff wa

* *You Are the Audience*, Potts Gallery, Al Hambra, California, May 18, 2018,
performed on the occasion of Patricia L. Boyd's exhibition *Good Grammar*.

** Arundhati Roy, *Capitalism: A Ghost Story* (Chicago: Haymarket Books, 2014).

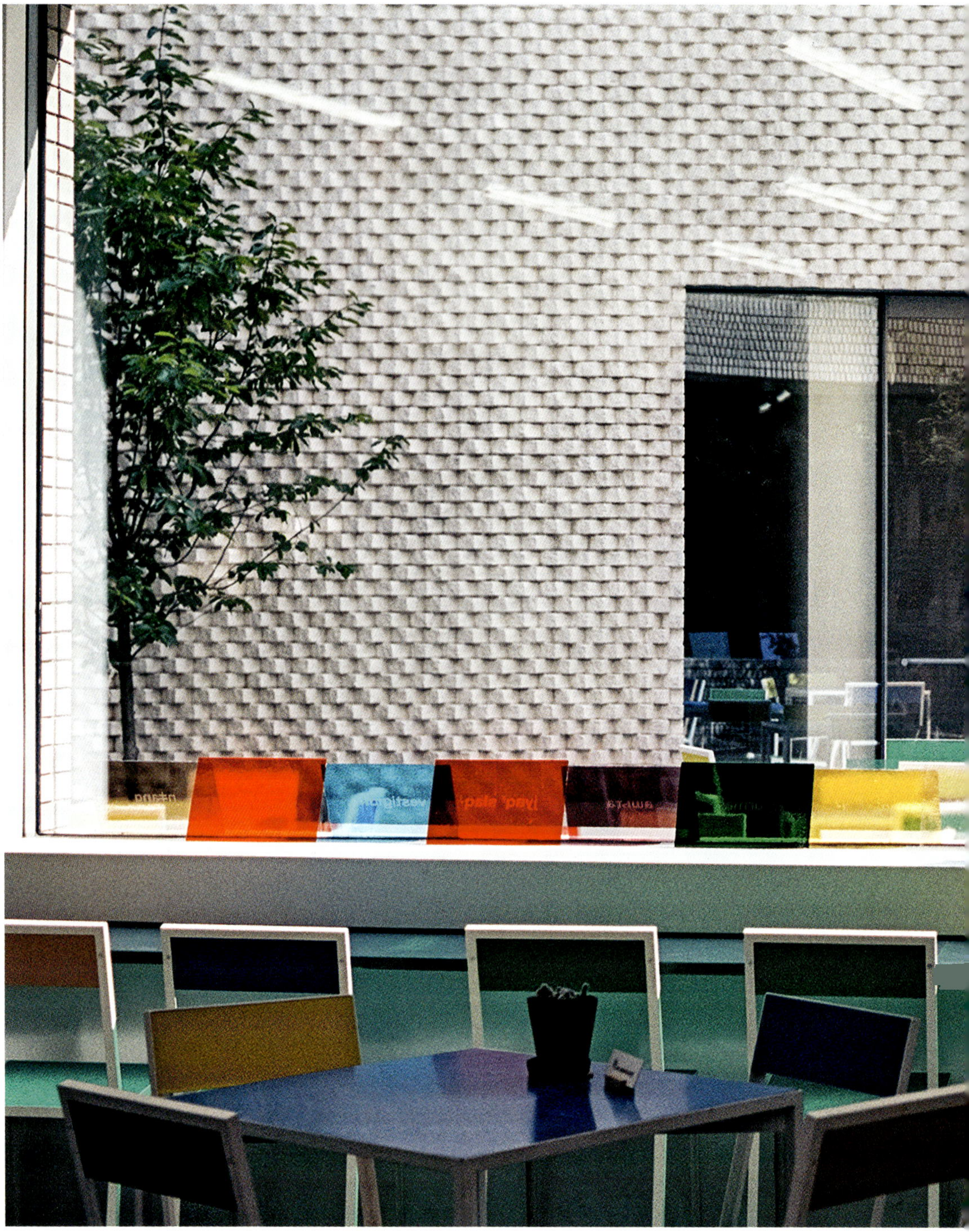

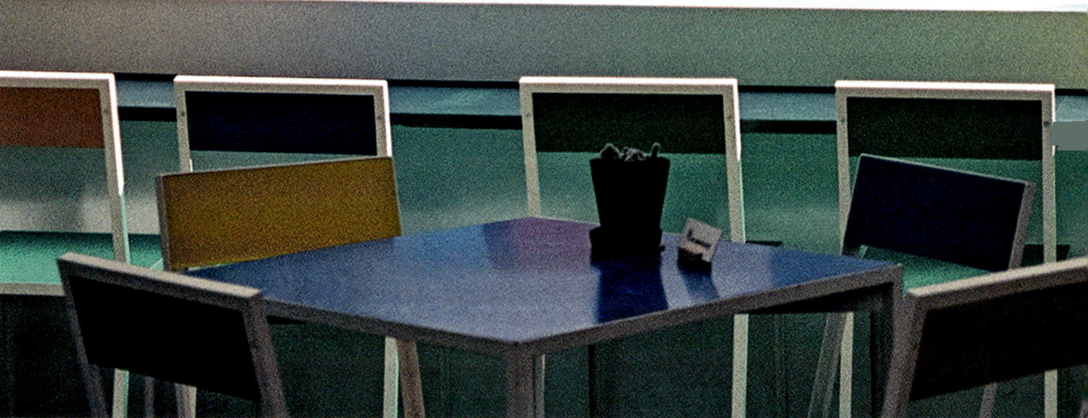

Nour Mobarak, *Dafne Phos*, 2022.
Etched colored glass; 1 part: 12 ×
12 inches (30.5 × 30.5 cm), 12 parts:
8 × 12 inches (20.3 × 30.5 cm)

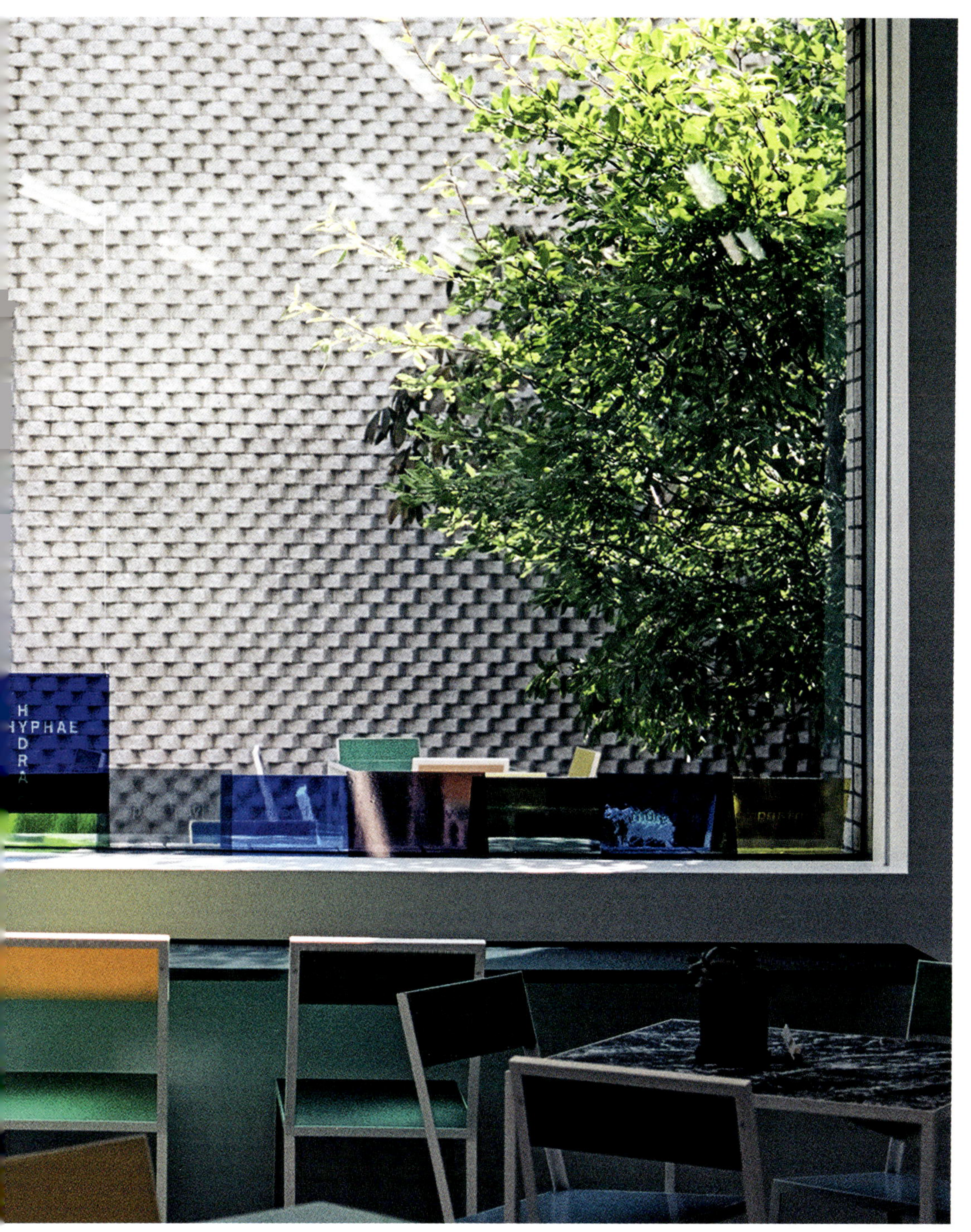

HYPHAE
HYDRA

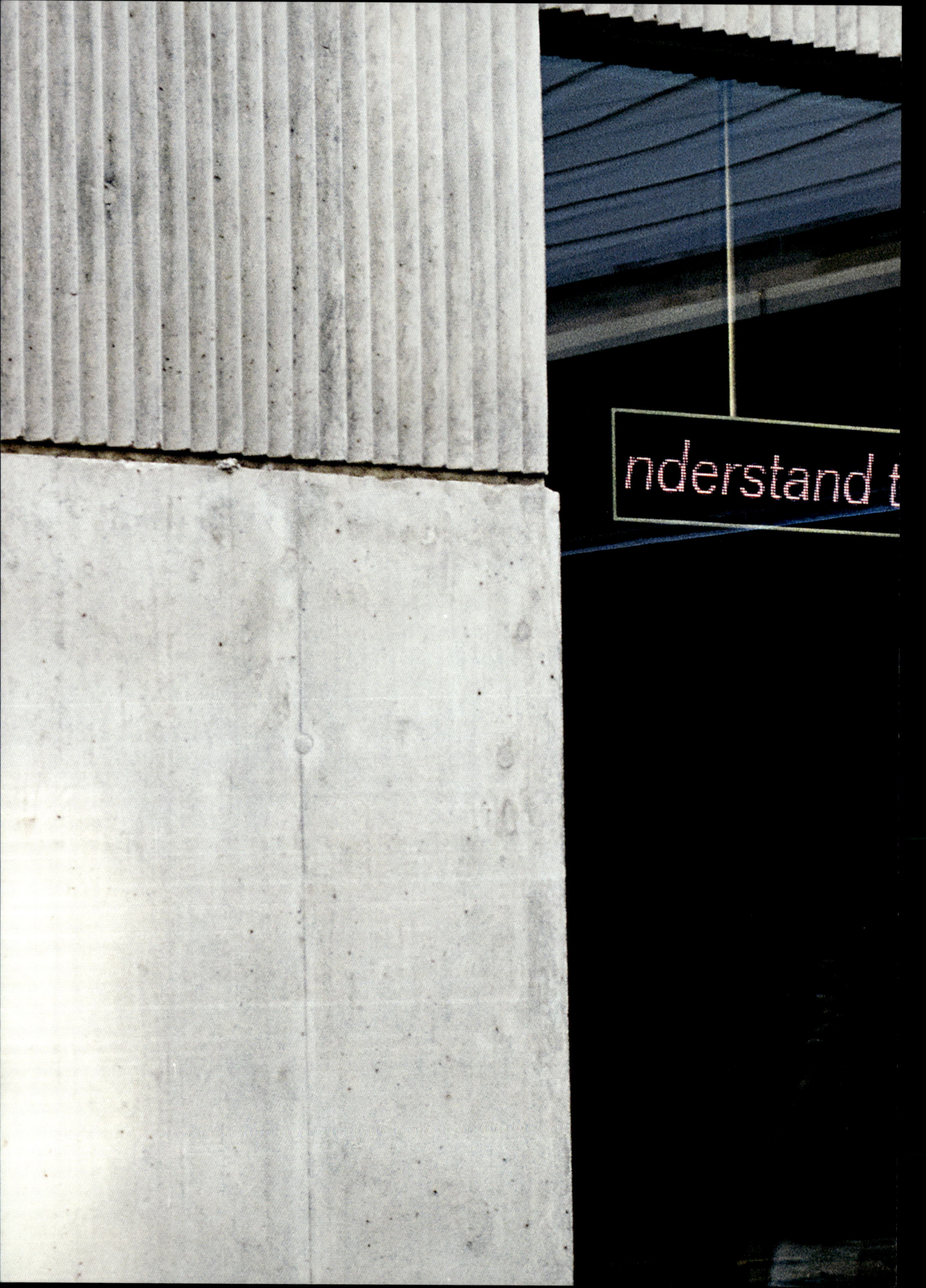

nderstand t

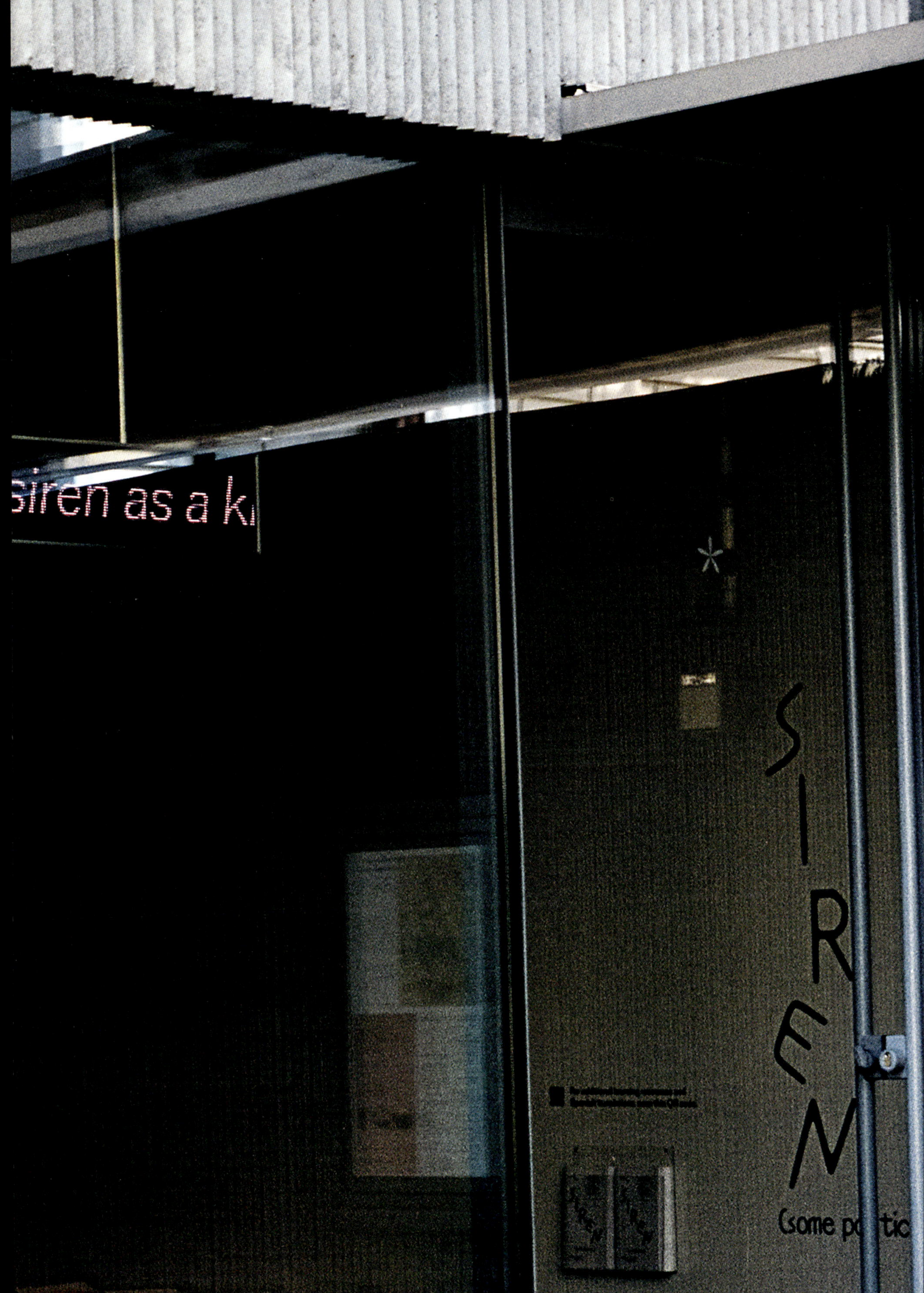
Siren as a ki
*
S
I
R
E
N
(some poetic

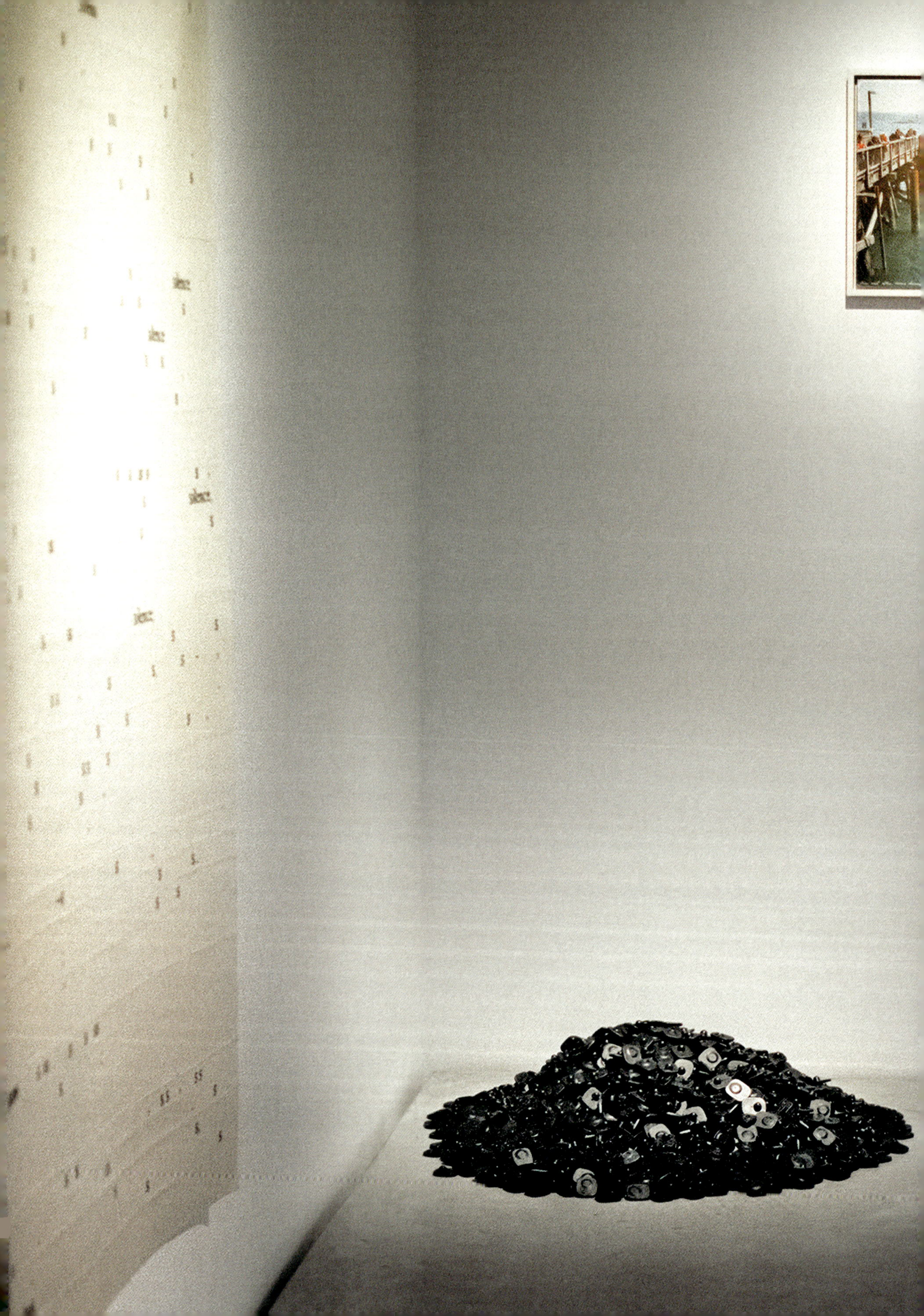

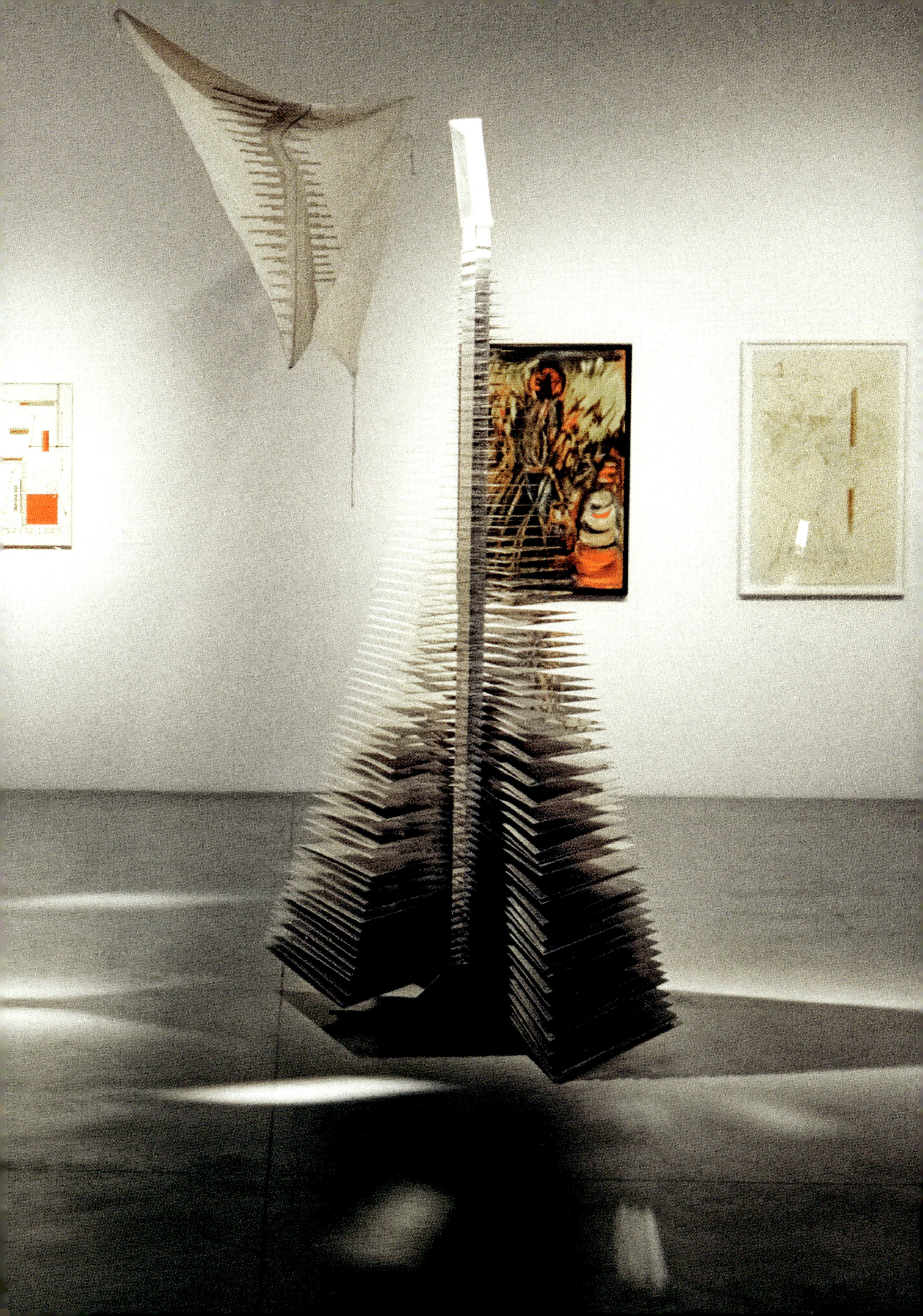

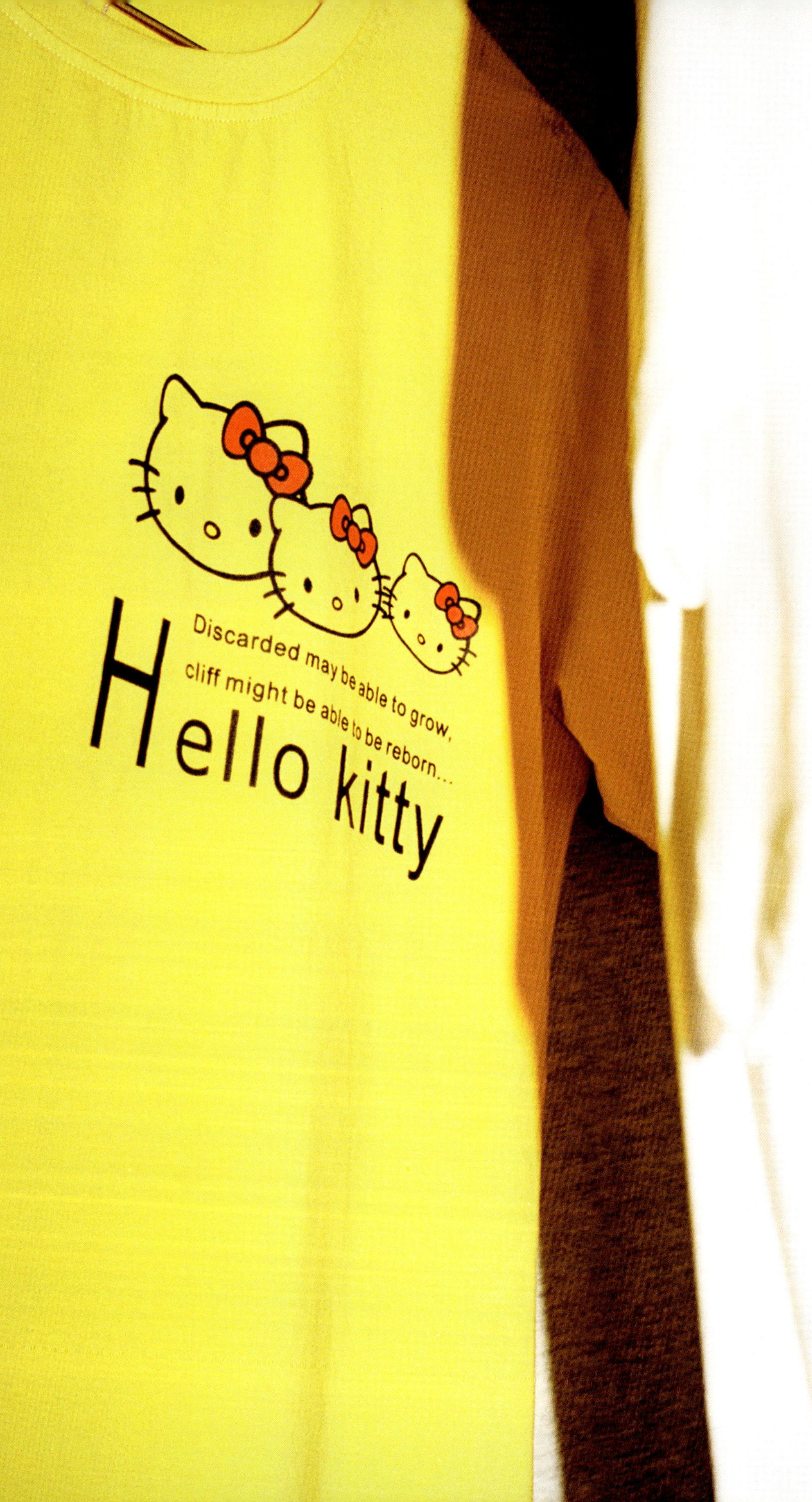
Discarded may be able to grow,
cliff might be able to be reborn...
Hello kitty

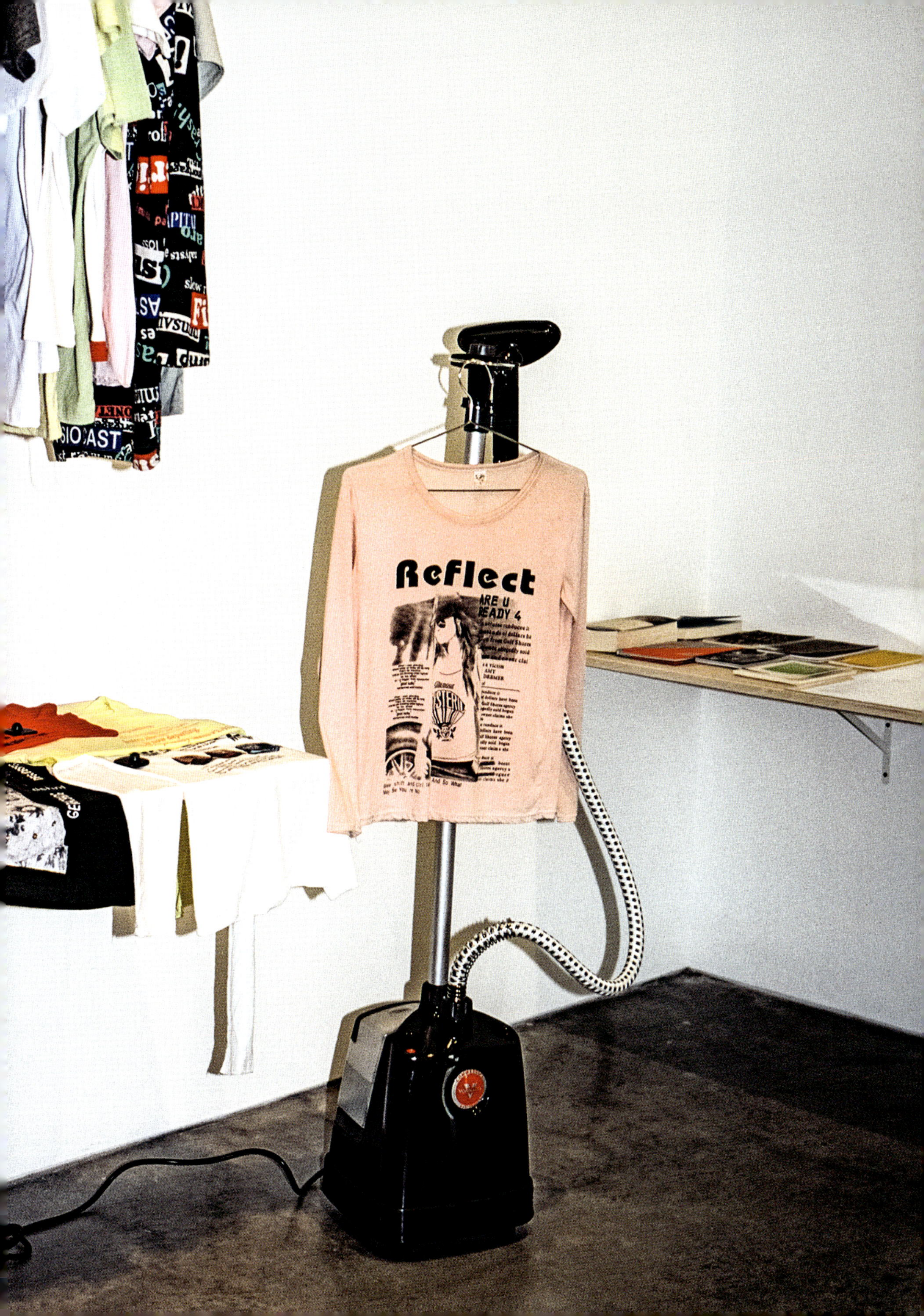
Reflect
ARE U
READY 4

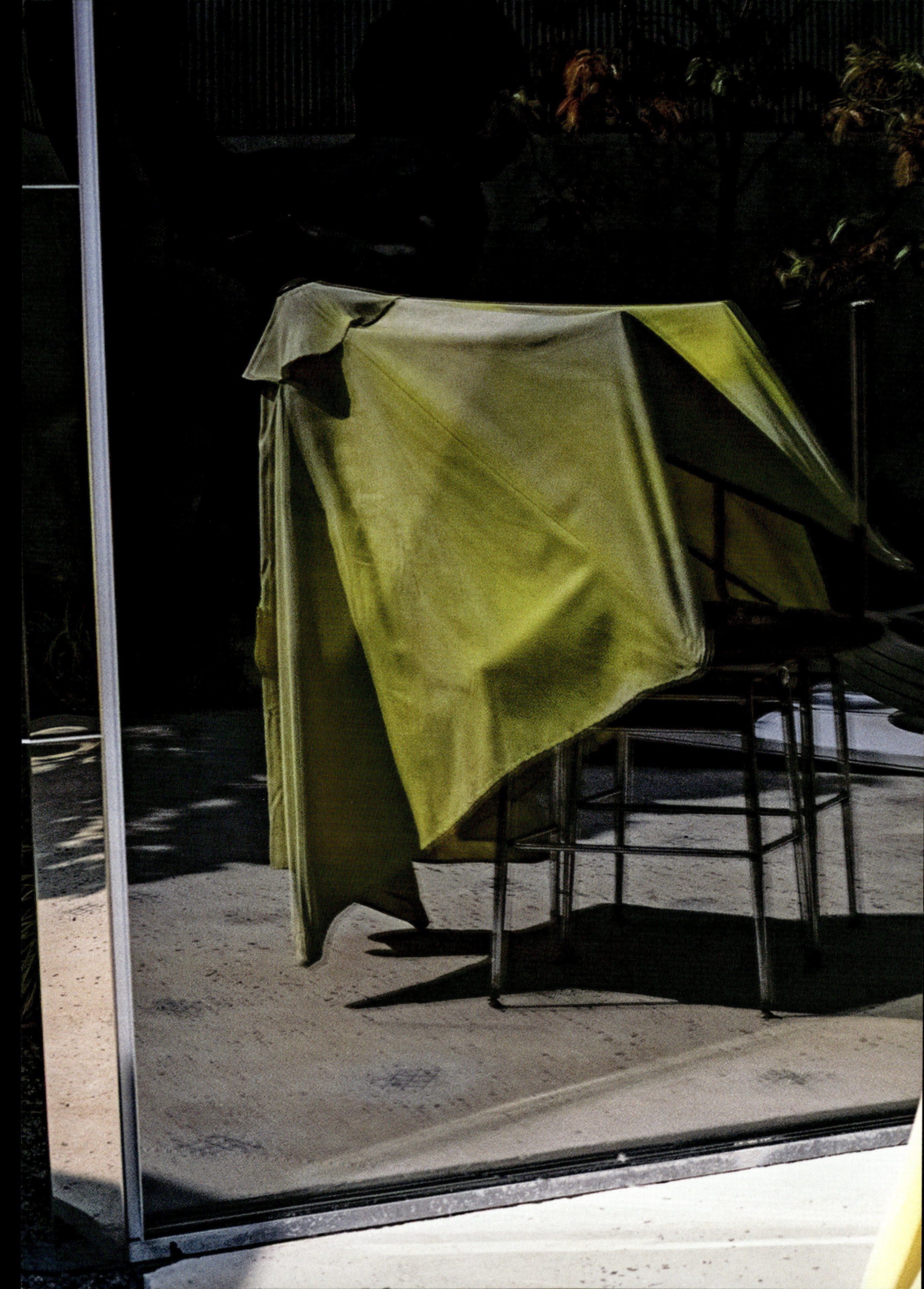

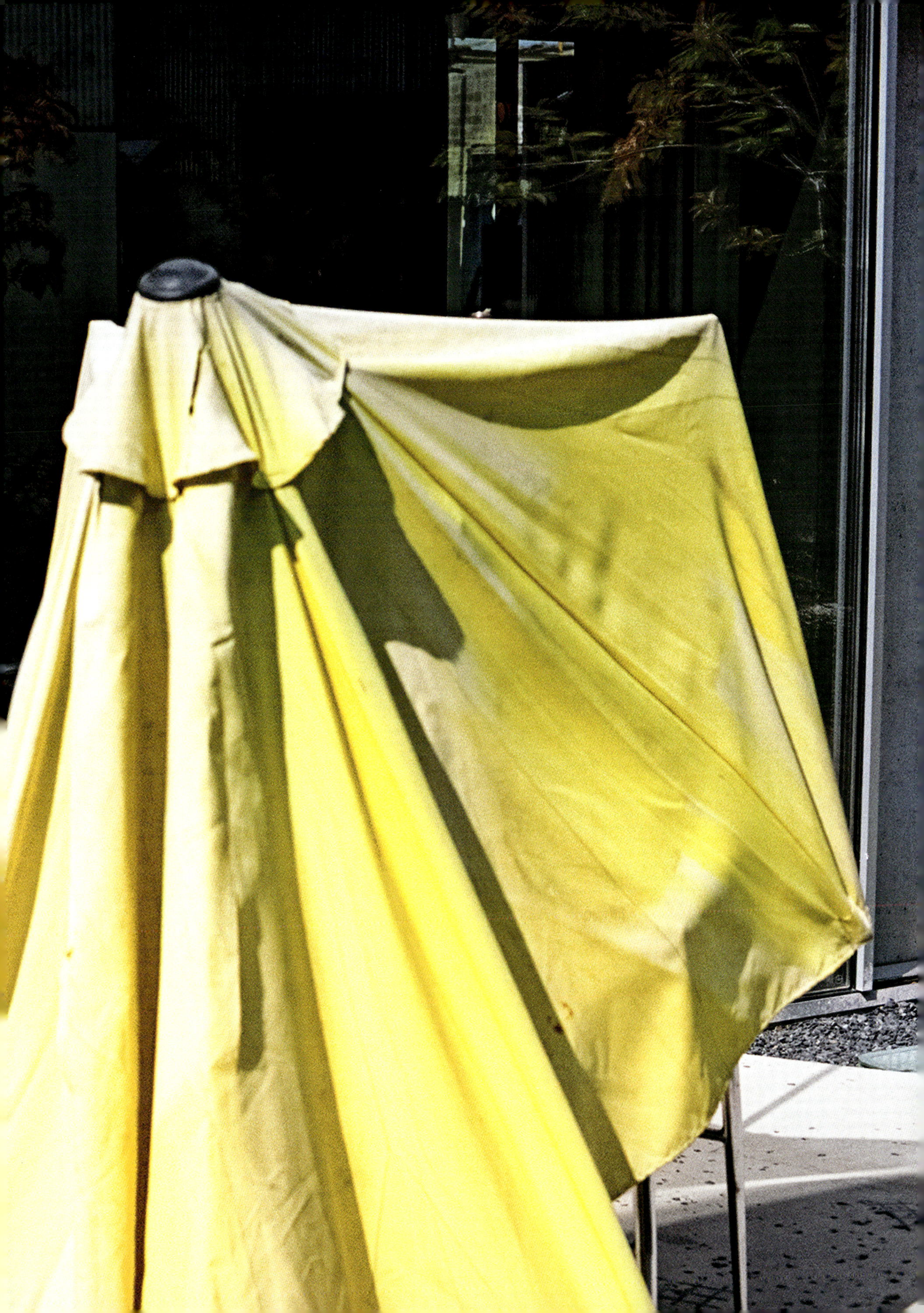

Bernadette Mayer

MIDWINTER DAY, SECTION 6 (excerpt)

You'd find in your emotion to excite plain seeing
You had probably left out the most important part,
Mistaking the sights for an audience
I think I know the trees
Will never love me and we're here as accidentally
To eat, sleep and work in an ordinary way,
To be astonished by will as time is slow to be
Amazed by speed and pleasure, frantic natures
As fast and reactionary as writing in lines
to learn
What I once began to do and then left off
Like a baby's talent for walking at birth
I still try to go too fast
As if the press of everything were identical,
I type up a poem and head for home
Clear letters on androgynous paper
I sit at the family table where it's a struggle
To create both staminate and pistillate in the same
Inflorescence of cluster, I feel a great impatience,
All the people in my family have sensuous lips
I say like a man or woman who does head home
With all that dirt under my nails
I know nothing
But the lassitude of love
Half an hour after sunset
All the windows are frozen shut
Like psychology
I have to hammer the sides with my fists
To get them to open, often I wonder
If I think the same things I thought as a child
When I didn't know the future of a form
Now I look different
For a woman to look different is still more difficult,
Though each moving being who changes thinks,
Than for the man of the tribe

133

A tribe is one of three
From the Latin into which the Romans
Were originally divided,
                    Latin, Sabine, Etruscan,
And the tribe together with
Families, slaves and adopted strangers meant
A recognized community plus a form of the future
                                 to become
Like the phylae of ancient Greece
Or the twelve divisions of the Israelites
Or any group of people or animals or plants
With some of the same habits and ideas
                          like the futures
Of the women who may think they've lost their charms
Or the men who think they've changed
                         beyond recognition
Like a community or a person who thinks
If only we could all get some sleep
                      like Chaucer
Or a Latin Sabine or Etruscan mother
Who didn't have the time, chance, education or notion
To write some poetry so I could know
What she thought about things
                    There are some who did anyway,
There's Anne Bradstreet and Tsai Wen Gi,
Elizabeth Barrett Browning, Alice Notley and me,
Adrienne Rich, Sylvia Plath, Anne Sexton,
Elinor Wylie, Louise Bogan, Denise Levertov,
There's Barbara Guest, H.D. and Harriet Beecher Stowe,
Maureen Owen, Nikki Giovanni, Diane di Prima,
Murasaki Shikibu, Fanny Howe and Susan Howe,
Muriel Rukeyser, Mina Loy, Lorine Neidecker,
Gwendolyn Brooks, Marina Tsvetayeva and Anna Akhmatova,
There's Rebecca Wright
And the saints
           I read in the papers that women live longer
Because they don't do all of this

And as they begin to become more like men
In all these ways they'll die equally soon
                                I forgot to mention
George Sand,
        As if death were not life
                                and I was dressed as a man
Racing around as a woman among a race of women
Too relegated before to birth like Mary Shelley
And a division of labor into whatever it was or is
To write a secret history
                        for desire to be like food
Touching history with desire
For history to be like food
On the table in the light of the window
                                It's shared
There are some things we cannot say!
                                No, I can't say that!
The awful presence of the obvious,
                        abdicated time,
Never relents in its demand to speak all at once
Because but for that there's the chance
The rest of what's begun to be lost might be lost
Like putting all one's bushels in an apple forever
Like the story changed or forgotten to make
A priestly transformation in the lives of the people
And in their words
                        Like an ordinance imposed
In proud moments by the tellers of tales
Or by politicians to a purpose
                                This present future,
Old as it is, is an inaccessible time
Where idiosyncratic western women,
                                most from what they call
The privileged classes,
                        but not only those,
Are beginning to write enough so that everyone
Can find a chair in heaven

I say he or she
Even in history, probably never knew before
Who's crying
                    It's a parliament of women. I won't mention
The prices of spices because talents are equal
To inheritance and love
                    following the rules
But still the stunning stone of a girl is less carved,
There's no way around it
                    not that life is any wilder
Let loose from a woman than from a man
We are all descendants of sexes as in varying clothing
Nor is the admonition of form ever less
Than the loving constrictions of the great ones
Of any kind of health, class or time
                    After all writing
And the genius of poetry only holds up half the sky
Like a woman born to a social occasion
Become a battle or a war for change
                    like Freud and Sappho
You sent me a meal once in this pot I still have
Where, in among that, I can only be as great
As Shakespeare or Milton or Chaucer or Dante
Or any of the others
I have the pleasure
Of knowing all about
                    But the meal I mentioned
Which had only been
Pot roast with gravy and potatoes
Not less remembered
Is worshipped and defended
                    whenever I see
Men in trees
And I want to be a worker in trees,
Winter-long I would paint the city if I see a cityscape,
And from what I saw I even want to be involved
In photo realist painting, airbrush painting,

Pattern painting and proposals for sculptures,
Performances, photos and texts, color field painting,
New image painting, silkscreen collage and watercolors,
Monoprints, landscapes, lithographs, etchings,
Body art, silverpoint, pop art, op art, nudes,
California funk art, frescoes, floor sculpture,
All kinds of wall pieces and shaped canvasses,
Outdoor projects, snow sculptures and still lifes,
Architectural drawings and post-minimalist sculpture,
Sky sculpture, all kinds of oil and figure painting,
Wood block prints, murals, bronzes and monuments,
Tapestries, mobiles, seascapes, poster art and films,
Minimal painting, precisionist painting, formalist painting,
New realist painting, minimal sculpture, abstract expressionism,
Even video art, narrative art, paper reliefs and aquatints,
Flower painting, wood carvings, sketches and calligraphy,
Egg tempera paintings, graffiti and all of photography,
Process art, grid paintings, stripe paintings, light art,
Happenings, kinetic sculpture, environmental sculpture
And pastels, ceramics, multimedia presentations, portraits,
Social realism and collages

               I would even discover roughly
Adrenalin, air conditioning, a satellite of Pluto,
Supermassive objects in the centers of galaxies,
The airplane, the jet propulsion airplane, helicopters,
Mass spectography of stable isotopes, penicillin,
Insulin and its production by bacteria, antimatter,
The depths that fish inhabit, the Polaroid Land camera,
The all-electronic numerical integrator and calculator,
The digital computer, cloning, the cultivation of truffles,
The conditioned reflex, the cyclotron, the neon lamp,
Deuteriam, celanese fibers, polyesters and polyamides,
The double-helical structure of DNA, the tungsten filament,
The equivalence of mass and energy, the mercury vapor lamp,
Nylon, "heat death," recombinant DNA techniques, the laser
The stored-program computer concept, test-tube babies,
Antiviral drugs, restriction enzymes, paper and the loom,

Neutron-induced radiation, nuclear fission, the ball-point,
Cosmetics, the crossbow, a drop in the sun's temperature,
The first gamma ray spectral line, the rings of Uranus,
Sulfur ions around Jupiter, a mouse with a human chromosome,
A mouse derived from six parents, radar, nuclear reactors,
The vacuum electron tube, sound motion pictures, protons,
Positrons, polio vaccine, gunpowder and the forked plow,
The rotary internal combustion engine, the gyrocompass,
Intelligence testing, natural satellites of asteroids,
A cure for traveler's diarrhea, the automatic rifle,
Psychoanalysis, the special and general theories of relativity,
Alpha and beta particle radiation, gamma radiation, vitamins,
Color film with three emulsion layers, electron microscopes,
Geometry, synthetic plastic, the polymerization process,
Quantum theory, the Wassermann test, the flush toilet,
Solar-weather links, a pocket-size three-dimensional camera,
Sulfa drugs, military tanks, tractors, transistors, t.v.'s,
The uncertainty principle, the Van Allen radiation belt,
Zero, the wheel, Lucifer yellow, charm quarks and supernova,
An end to locust plagues, the reason for the "East Coast booms,"
The synthesis of the transuranic elements including Fermium,
Americium, Einsteinium, Curium, Berkelium and Californium,
Animal prescience of earthquakes, gravity waves, antiprotons,
The nature of schizophrenia and the first known noon marker
Of the summer solstice
                    I would close my red eyes like copper
And watch you by the atomic clock
To have the luxury to love at least in theory
Indivisibly for a time in the sweetest exchanges
As if the world were not enraged,
                         You go out for cigarettes,
As if love is not the food
Of those of us satisfied enough to write
To write to lend urgency pleasure, to sing,
To celebrate, to inspire, to reveal
                         You put on
Your gotten shoes and coat in an image

And say you will be right back
                              While you're out love is stored
In intensest house, this cave of it,
                              We go too fast,
Switched from the speed of variegated love
Writings married and fallen in with family,
Though it's more exhausting to love to write
Than to pursue what might have been described
About the past as being fast,
                              Sometimes we feel like
Fools, lunatics, paranoid hermits having manic flights
With nothing coming of it
                              No invitations to cocktails or tea
With the whole American Indian nation,
No requests to write a column for The Post,
                              no demands for words
For occasions, for public celebrations or for mourning.
For invocations for grace for change
                              But each night
Craving any sweet joy
We still hope to live along time
                              Hurry you say
And we love to hurry
But not to speed up the night
                              To be rushed to be kissed
To be irrationally married to words and produce
Wildness like a child or two, not grown up yet,
Perfection, a genius, not going as fast
As the speed of the past again where everyone
Is thought to be another to this day
                              like a letter
We never forget about
We run from place to place to answer it
                              Love is coveted
We have no need of the commandments
Alone in the house among the secrets
We still work to tell

                    Without pause there is a purpose,
Anyone does it who is knowing all about it
How far can I go with it getting away with it
Before I die the fool and if I die will I
Have missed something and am I always the same
Though now I'm two or even four I wish to be more
I don't know why, I know I don't like to buy
                                        Xmas presents
But if I had some money today I'd buy love's surprises
And present them to the people on my list, they are
Lewis, Ray, Harry, Sophia and Marie all the Warshes,
Rosemary Mayer, Margaret DeCoursey, Grace Murphy,
Alice Notley, Ted and Anselm and Edmund Berrigan,
Raphael Soyer, Lynn O'Hare and Moses and Bill Berkson,
Bill, Beverly, Marnie and Arden Corbett, Simon Schuchat,
Clark, Celia and Susan Coolidge, Paul and Nancy Metcalf,
Bob and Eileen Callahan, Bill Kushner, Charlotte Carter,
Bob and Ali Rosenthal and Rochelle Kraut, John Ensslin,
Ed Friedman, Kenward Elmslie, Susan Noel, Meg Simon,
Joe Brainard, Rudy Burckhardt, Ed & Tom Bowes and Harris,
And Charlie Vermont whose 33rd birthday it is
And many other people I've seen and known,
Now Lewis has come home
                        I thought I was going to write
A story of my theories tonight
Not this desirous essay on art and home,
This alarming dictionary of reformist love
                                    Is it safe
To say that, knowing my notebook?
                            The moon is coming up
I have something to do with that
                        Tonight the Shah of Iran
Is not watching his forty-inch t.v. and what might be
The dread implications of overwhelming power has become
A confusion of the magic wishes of everyone
And the titillating knowledge of almost everything
Lost before in the complicated stories of dreams

Where the moment is supreme so joint with the past
Found in awakening to love of rearranging
This world at best at random translated
                         By the eyes of ice
To a detail of truth,
          Something is discovered,
We wait to see what happens
We hope it's not a war or suffering
And that the women will shake off the veil
In the myriad future of our still
Revolutionary munificent dreams, our lust
For surprise benefitting us like the sun
Like the supplicating weather we fear
May suddenly change from what it is
To another ice age but not before
The climate warms undetectably
Forcing us all to move to the moon
                         There we gather
Supplies in airtight containers,
                          force ideas
From dreams to develop the craft of sleep,
Keep in touch with what's happening,
                          wonder
At nature, emergencies, extreme heat,
Cold and unassailably new beauty,
                          births,
Unusual time exposures of the earth,
Intercourse, sex, copulation, fucking,
I think I wrote this in the dark
                         There's a light
In my eyes afterwards by chance
Like a family
            That dumb streetlight like the moon
Shines in my one window out of nine in the house
With its green white-town pinkish light
Rich in ultraviolet and actinic rays

And with my eyes

I'm reading a paper on us fucking in mercury vapor
I found I was finding another position

for the diaphragm

Like the curtain like the moon's oval pebbles
Under the exciting microscope
Of the Western world

I speak out loud against it

Other lights in the town might be broken
By accident or widespread vandalism
But they're too high and look like Christ
On the cross with the hands of an eye's fluorescent fish
Like a talent unspotlit and queer

To be me is to be

Queer sleep after death, its modesty deriving
What from the eyes of the immodest living
Is offered at the cost of a ruinous leaving
Well, I have to close them

This paid incandescent light

Is like the vigil of a virgin
Last to tell before my eyes I'll end.

From dreams I made sentences, then what I've seen today,
Then past the past of afternoons of stories like memory
To seeing as a plain introduction to modes of love and reason,
Then to end I guess with love, a method to this winter season
Now I've said this love it's all I can remember
Of Midwinter Day the twenty-second of December

Welcome sun, at last with thy softer light
That takes the bite from winter weather
And weaves the random cloth of life together
And drives away the long black night!

Midwinter Day

Bernadette Mayer

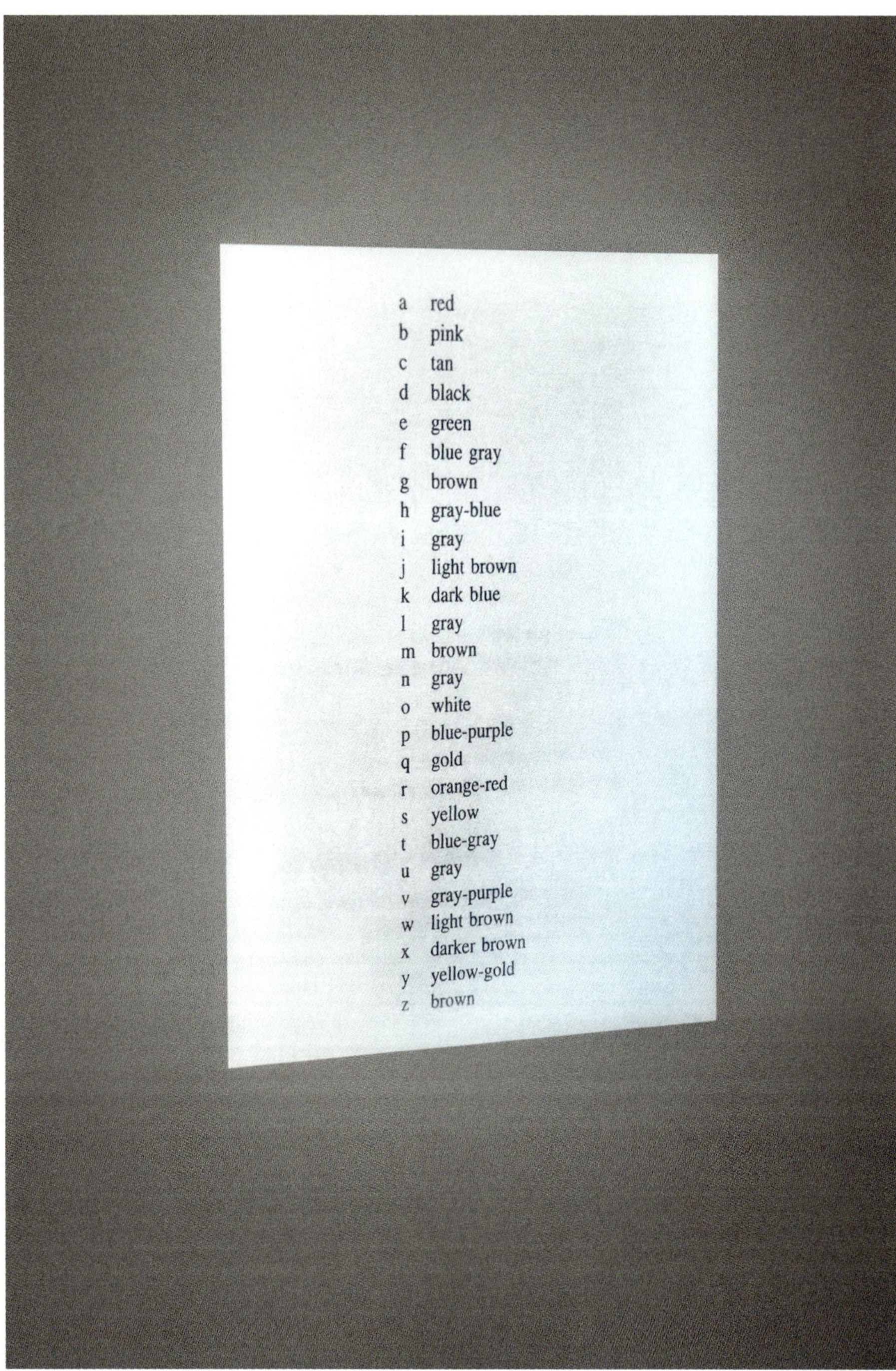

Wall projection of Bernadette
Mayer, untitled poem, originally
published in *Proper Name & Other
Stories* (New Directions, 1996)

144

Sardines

is a yellow, red, orange, black & green
word. I got sardines at the dollar store
where everything except sardines is more
than a dollar, for sixty cents, as they should be
my father used to take sardine sandwiches to work
perhaps therefore, I love sardines. when people
used to talk about the subway, they'd say:
we were packed like sardines which sends a message:
small, cheap, tightly packed, anchovies for the poor
or you too can be colorful & inexpensive as
a really snappy, tiny bright blue convertible
in which you can enjoy the good things about
feeling like a sardine but maybe you'd rather
be a striped bass or be a manatee with mev
or a grand whale, forgetful of nothing even
being so big, the ocean's CEO, you'll take home
a giant amount of cash when the ocean goes bust
so you can share it even with the downtrodden
sardines who get packed in cans in Thailand
& shipped to the family dollar store for Bernadette

—Bernadette Mayer

Vinyl wall text display of
Bernadette Mayer, "Sardines,"
originally published in *Works
and Days* (New Directions, 2016)

BERNADETTE MAYER
POETRY
RM
12/75

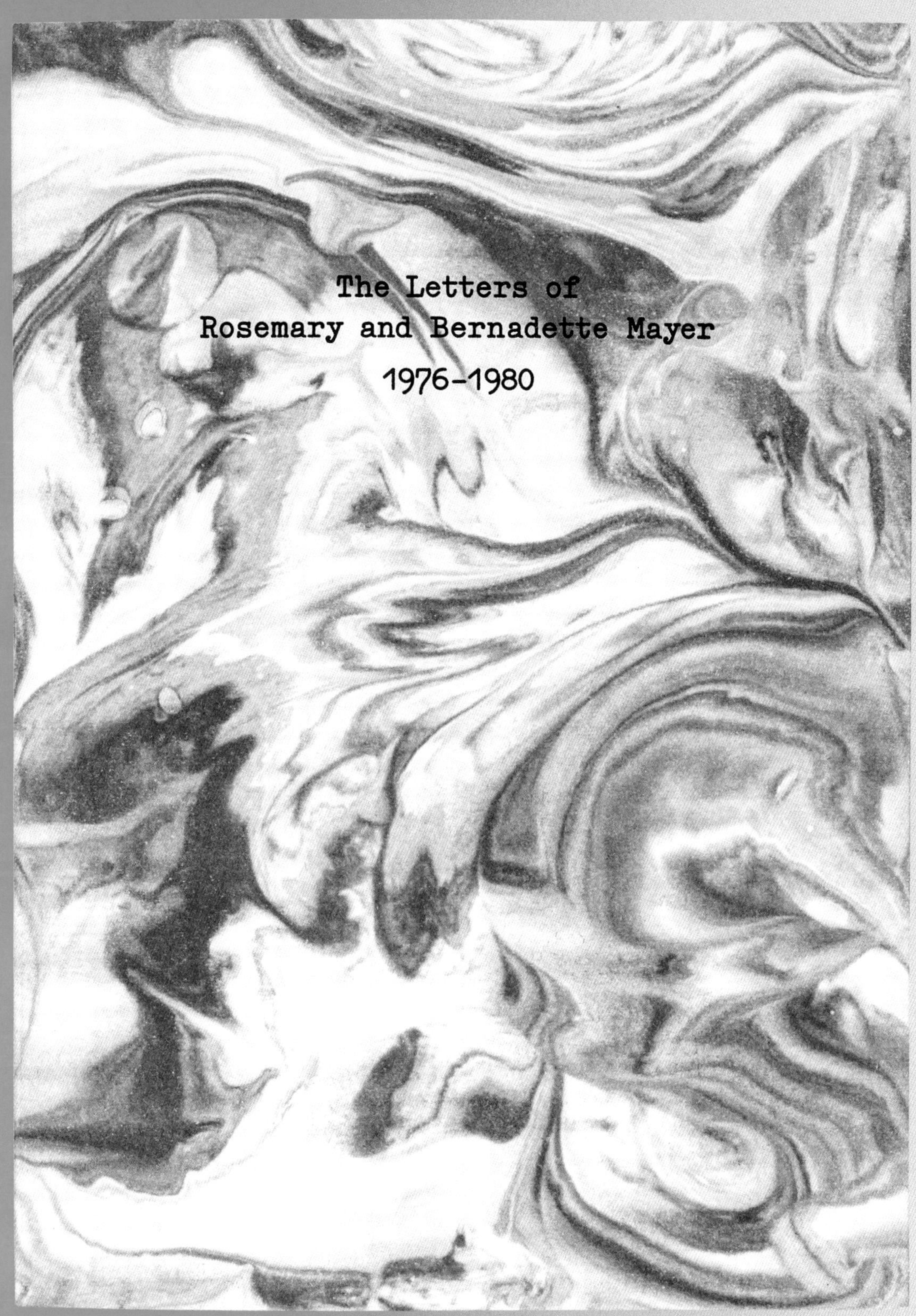

The Letters of
Rosemary and Bernadette Mayer
1976-1980

Rosemary Mayer

NEARLY EVERYDAY I THINK TOMORROW I'LL STOP MAKING ART. DOES THAT MATTER?

1968   I was concerned to use fabric in ways that allowed its own properties
to operate and form the work — (Morris, others,) Behind that was the
concern to mirror the functioning of things/materials in the word (Morris,
Louis' <u>Veils</u>) in a form that would show vulnerability to large forces (gravity,))
and small ones, (air currents in a room). The art object should not be still,
unmoving and independent of its circumstances. Nothing is. Relations between
things alter those things to the point that the things aren(t important
except as evidence of the interrelations. (Levi Strauss)

As the early fabric pieces became more elaborate — in '70-2 I looked for
ways to structure them which would evidence variety within unity — as, the
folds in a piece of fabric vary that unity, or, several equal length cords
or rods (units) support varieties of shirred fabrics. I was also concerned to
produce complexity from simple means. Most of the ways the pieces from this
time are constructed are very simple, but hung up with fabric draping, they
are visually complex. Both these concerns I saw also in the work of Eva Hesse.

I used layers of different colored fabrics to make actual a color producing process
and to let that process be subject to change. (Change — Cage's writing) (Literalizing color mixing — first the literalizing, from Judd's writings about

his intentions in sculpture, then, the visible color mixing process, from

Louis' work where these processes are visible.) There are also personal,

not art derived, intentions - circling around awe, diety, materialization

and disappearance.

1972-3 Three large fabric sculptures named for women. <u>Hroswitha</u>, <u>The Catherines</u>,

<u>Galla Placidia.</u> These had to do with producing a presence which was undercut by

the works' fragile and cheap materials. The variety in unity idea was at work as

well as *literal color layers, vulnerability to change,* getting the greatest amount of visual complexity out of the materials.

The titles were an attempt to connect the works with women in history, not

sculpture as picture of, but as hint to, reminder of, groups of characteristics.

Also, in '73, *the titles were* a deliberate feminist gesture to connect these works to a

large body of female experience, but not to any particulars, especially not

to sex, as silly folk have chosen to read these works.

These works also dealt with bilateral symmetry, suggesting and then subverting

it. This was another way to undercut presence, to deal with variety and unity,

with change. I could go on about these, their colors as ranges of possibilities...

These works were culminations of ~~xxxxxxxxx~~ combinations of responses (besides

their wider, outside art, intentions) to Morris Louis, R. Morris, Saret, E. Hesse,

John Cage's writings, those of Levi Strauss, maybe even Genet. About wider intentions — I've read , since I can remember, the writings of mystics in nearly

every religious tradition. Also Mondrian and Kandinsky. The evanescence of

everything is a notion that has always appealed to me, perhaps because I lost

my parents when I was quite young. Wonder at the magical unfolding of an

amazing sight is part of this way of thinking.

Later in '73 I did two works, Shekinah and Bat Kol, which have no fabric, are just

the bent wood of the support structures underlying the 3 pieces just discussed.

Shekinah is a tension structure; BK is so delicately balanced it sways from a

person passing. These were the first works I did which stood up in space rather

than using the wall or ceiling for support..   The concern was to show how they stood

and why they didn't fall and but to come as close as possible to the edge of thier

not being able to stand up. They are related to some of Serra's concerns

but present a fragility, delicacy, an edge where it is just possible to for

them to continue existing. All through my work, sculpture as a stand in for the

individual, body or psyche, in the world.

Shekinah and Bat Kol in Jewish tradition - are female angelic presences that have no material existence.

Concern to continue to subvert the notion of presence. These works nearly invisible.

Next, 74-5, a batch of sculptures with understructures of painted wood to

support hardly anything, diaphanous drapery or thin curves of wood screening.

This is the time of complete fascination with Pontormo, other Mannerists,

Grunewald. The work leaves the concerns of other contemporary art and

goes off on its own. An attempt at a construction of a paradise of light and color.

A road to it via a thing. An other world alternate to this, of colors never

seen before. ISTA presents light, Portae and Locrian Mode, light and ascension.

I read about medieval colors, about gold and light. I showed the Portae

with over twenty lights on it. I was disgusted with what was in galleries.

To some extent I liked Aycock, Anderson, Morton and Simmond's work, but all

for differnet reasons, none connected to what mattered to me. I wanted to

make things float away, dissolve, and still be there.

1975 I went to Europe and then wrote Passages. I realized how connected my

concerns in the recent work were with childhood experiences.

Passages structure is important. It circles, weaves together elements with

an attempt at endless threads of interconnections.. Then I made three books..

Passgaes, Transitions and Pontormo's Diary. Transitions is the only one

not availbale, has a text and drawings of crocus. It had to do with seasonal

changes, flowers from bud to their end, one person inviting another to share

time and space.

P's Diary has paragraphs I wrote intersperced with the translation. I

attempt to connect his time and my own as two periods that follow times of con-

conseensus, periods in which art has to proceed from particular experience, each

artist find her/his rules. Periods of exhaustion, withdrawal, desperation.

75-7

Ⓐ did _Chorona_ and _several_, both related to the San Lorenzo drawings (Pontormo's)

of entwined dead and dying bodies inthe flood. These sculptures were attempts

to make formless works, one where the viewer could not hold in mind a precise image

of the work. Attempt to make a work that is all relations, not an object.

The _Locrian Mode_, last piece made with wood , an object undermined by its

construction, here, _Chorona, Several,_ undermining form. These pieces hang from the ceiling,

are so light they turn in space, constantly changing the visual interrelations

within the work.

1976 I did watercolors of masses of floral forms where I used color like rainbow

light playing across the surfaces of the drawn forms. The only indicators

of what's intended _to_ be there on the paper are the different intensities

of color, a few lines. Earlier watercolors were of large, impossible single

flowers. Those from '76 were impossible, dissolving, became formless. It was

the light that was important. _These_ concerns started from working in an intensely

bright studio in Oneonta and a decision to mirror the formlessness of _Chorona_,

Several, in the watercolors. Also to use the watercolors to make clear the

interconnectedness, the eternally repeating variety, of floral forms.

an article about

During this time I was talking about and working on Contexts, the place of

art in the world and how art is changed by place.

1977 I did Surroundings. Writing to understand a little about how people who

 aren't artists, are workers, relate to time, beauty, and economics. With this

work I realized I could no longer attempt to make surrogates for unearthly paradises,

got my feet on the gound again. Began to think about art in relation to

society in general, not just art world, and not just me.

The form of Surroundings, photos and drawings with text , is collage, tho I hate

that work because it suggests anything goes. The use of photos in Surroundings

 in a book format in intended to point out that photos don't belong on walls

as tho they were paintings, but in books as illustrations, where scale doesn't operate

as it does in the real space of a room.

1977 April CAPS asked me to do a work with balloons outdoors. This was Spell.

I realized all the menaings Spell had for me because of its place and time.

Spell's occurrence in time, its brief life, became important to my thinking,

related to evanescence, impermanence... I wrote a text about it, then made a

book with the photos from Spell and the text. In Aug. and later '77 I did the

three sculptures, 4 a.m., 5a.m., and All Day. They're concerned with

making as an activity in time that produces an object but a formless object.

7

The ways these works are made are intended to suggest a desperate shorthand, an

impatience that barely allows the production of a thing. Another way to almost not

make a sculpture. At the same time - plethora of textures, colors, to

interrelate by playing off each other - e.g., a range oforanges in the same work.

Some of the materials could be discarded shreds, others are soiled or stained,

others suggest temporary decorations for points in time, occassions. The rods

bent into bows are the old device, for me, of forming by interrelations of forces.

The rods bent into bows and ovals in these pieces also present a variety of

the forms possible to this method of shaping.

Winter 77-8 - Spell book, wrote Works '75-7, watercolors and drawings of

elaborate and impossible balloon works. Thinking of galleries as stifling contexts

where affecting a viewer is now nearly impossible. Get outside, to a wider

audience, force meaning by putting the work in wider context.

Spring 78 Some Days in April. Work with advertising balloons, painted with

words and numerals. Done in upstate NY, completed by poster mailed out, work

made public.

Thinking about what it is possible to celebrate, how and where. Artists' one time

purpose as decorators at festivities, memorializers of the dead, catchers, even,

of passing beauty. How to do these things now? To celebrate one must make

make the occasion. <u>Some Days</u>... is an attempt to place occasions in April,

make meanings for points in time, also make a memorial. The implication is that

~~themeanings~~   only the meanings we impute exist, while we exist...

In <u>Some Days ...</u> each balloon holds together the name of a person, a date in April,

a star, a flower, visible and growing then. The work is a monument for and to connect

the individuals, flowers, stars, times, on the balloons.

In spring '78 <u>In Time Order</u>   drawings with floral forms, graffitti-like writing,

a text, small bw photos, names of people, of colored things. The photos/of

female figures of justice in strong light, of a family, women shopping, chandeliers.

Then more drawings and watercolors. Several for <u>Connections</u>, a work for Castle

Clinton, an old fort at the Battery, NYC. Kids 13 or so would come to the fort

and paint on balloons - a name, date star, flower. They would research and choose

these themselves. 3 or 4 balloons could go up in a day, be moored inside

and float over the walls. Do this daily for several weeks. Let the weather take its

courses with the balloons.

Now, fall '78 drawings of impossible balloon pieces floating over NYC buildings,

of elaborate tents on roofs of city buildings. Thinking about what pleasures are

possible, why people don't kill themselves. This winter I'll make some sculptures

from snow, I'll write alot...about women in time and barbarism.....

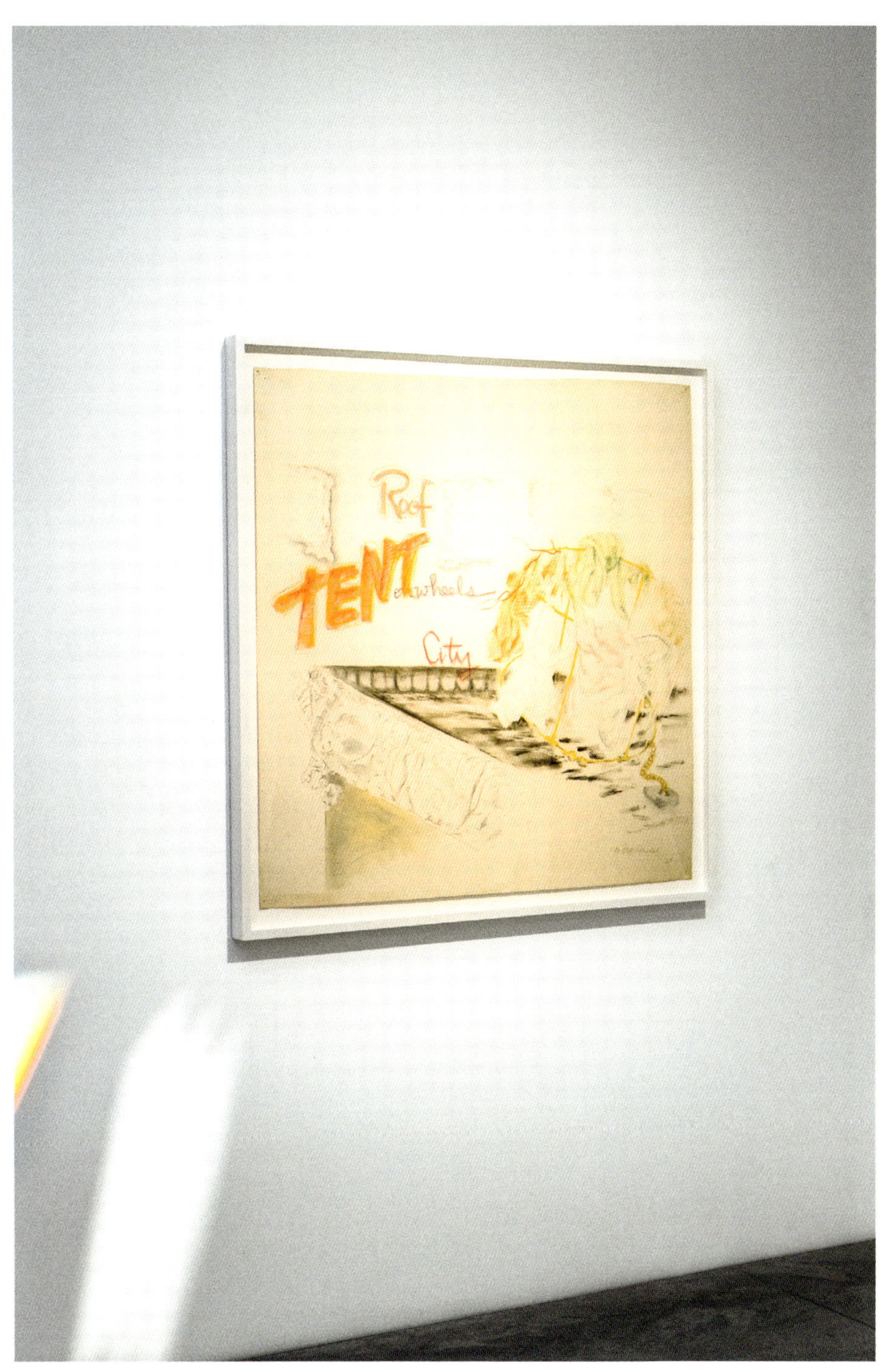

Rosemary Mayer, *City Roof Tent on Wheels*,
1980. Watercolor and colored pencil on
paper, 42½ × 42¼ inches (108 × 107.3 cm)

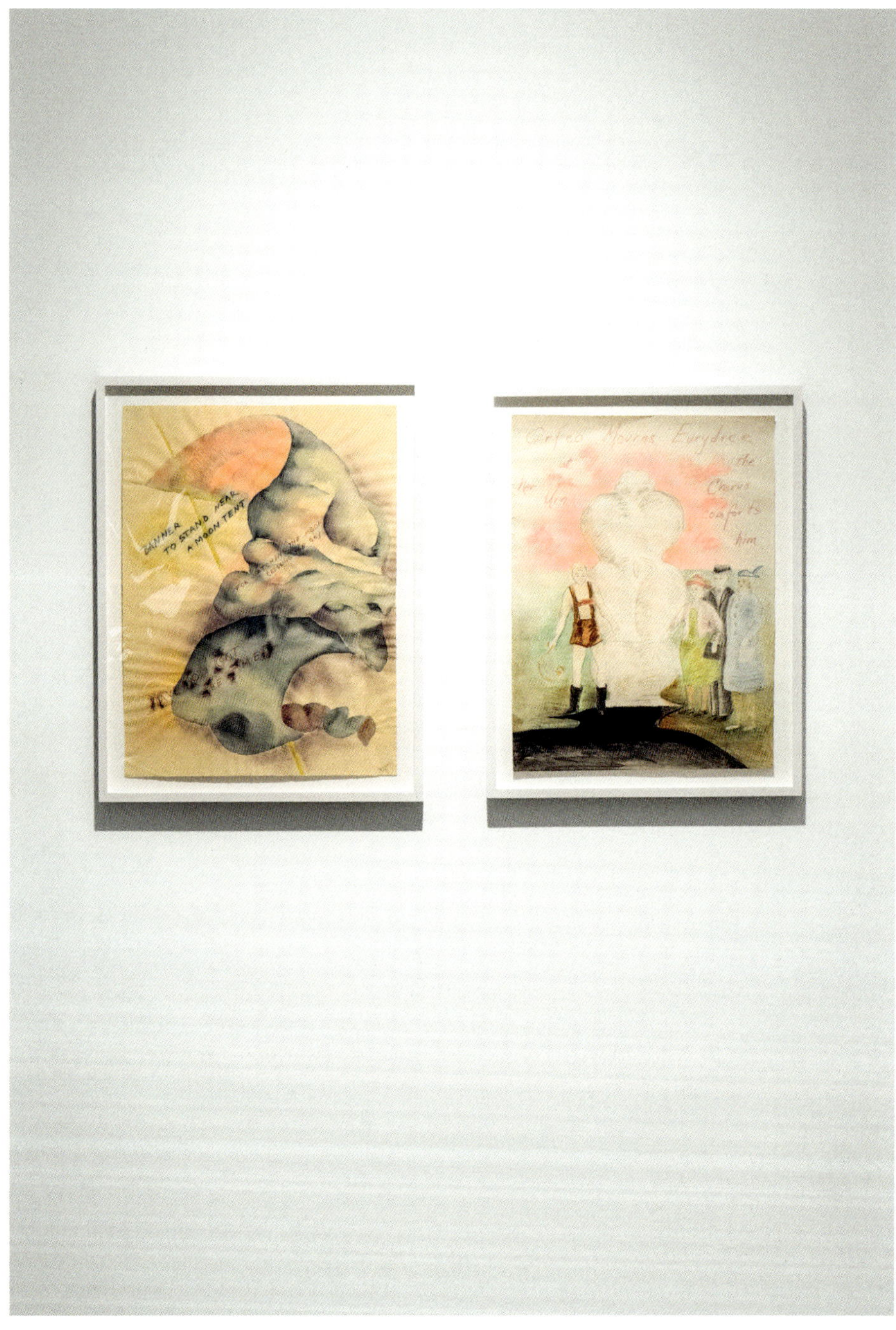

Left: Rosemary Mayer, *Banner to Stand Near Moon Tent*, 1982. Watercolor and colored pencil on paper; 24¾ × 19 inches (62.8 × 48.3 cm)

Right: Rosemary Mayer, *Orfeo Mourns Eurydice at Her Urn, the Chorus Confronts Him*, 1982. Charcoal, pastel, and graphite on paper; 23¾ × 18 inches (60.3 × 45.7 cm)

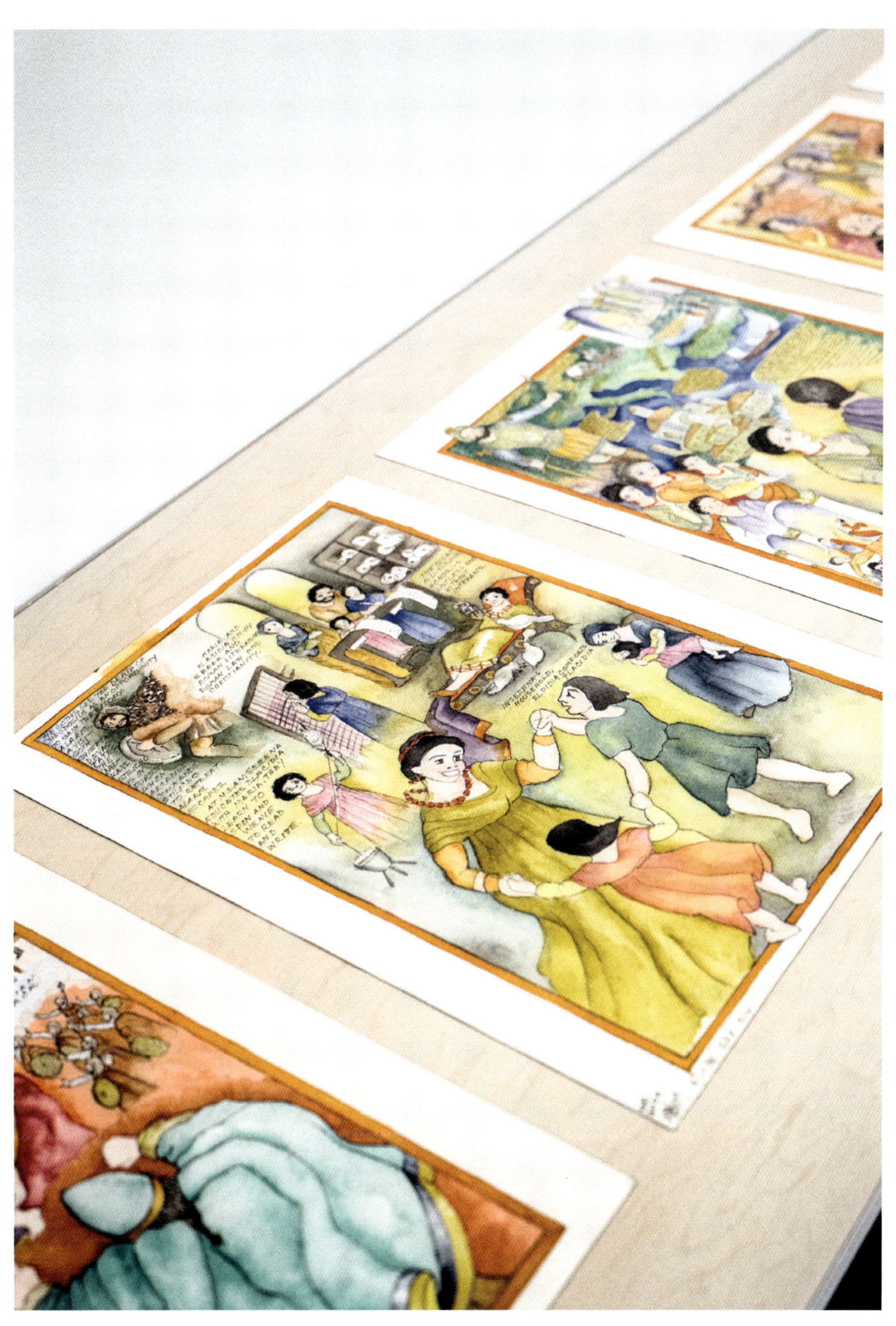

Rosemary Mayer, *100 Years*, 2007–11
(detail). Watercolor and ink on paper;
16¼ × 12¼ inches (41.3 × 31.1 cm) each sheet

Ser Serpas

UNTITLED, 2022

fresh aroused slant hand
in spring motion caress the edge of stairs
slashed me ruined once perfect runaround
sinewy hips rounded back and wallowed these traits we
bear when things get done accidentally how do
they happen to you
jurisprudence for the ones taped down easy a lot of the time to fall in place
    submerged and
play chicken road across the turnpike and feeling
hole ambition training day motions me to stare
undulating cathartic autonomy the shack you cant shake off terror and
    fortitude face of
crestfallen

UNTITLED, 2022

main event this is
main settle score and scary right udder malnutrition is in
eye the beholder thicker yet in praise of other beings sense
    in sensibility
destitute ways to scar yourself straight honestly try and see it my way you
    lose and see
not all is lost in memory wipe shit
stains are more legible the racing around the
block and falling at attention you ask why do you know the things you
    know escape from that final destination
seen of most identification with trees and
branches and highway 666
where we go to play volatile corners of
clubs we forgot up into until now
elvis guesthouse

UNTITLED, 2022

she fell 10 blocks down and around the corner from
desire windfall fell
through glass mirror then she
stalled in that white dress wearing her so
as to be incomplete motion detected in forrest
cafe see mine
forever out of corner eye
defend from graces tale of regret forgetful forever and falling
over yet we trudge to
acknowledge the path lest take me away
you dont get to see it all
reserved for gods and trespassers are you afraid to spy vs spy it cannot
    trouble you for more
than a few the devil on his side i rented my friends apartment
near this foundation and cant get off

UNTITLED, 2022

as it is above so they below
thems the ones who know
gadgets and how to work them stragglers how to tag and bag them dirty
cobwebs in corners dinkus and dinner left
my friends down low sought communion with the furthest thing from me
    someone not cut bleeding trip down the stairs feathered cap
in moonlight just an animal on the upper floor but it frames your hair
the right way as to maintain it in the summer months
turnover is massive hills heavy and have eyes
if there wasnt so much riding on everything all the time i could be
    convinced
not so much as you but convinced punt a circle in my eye but not to stay
    sober and punitive for i am afraid
what got left out of the box could fight its way back in a losing war with
the city and staycation in the north for i am afraid

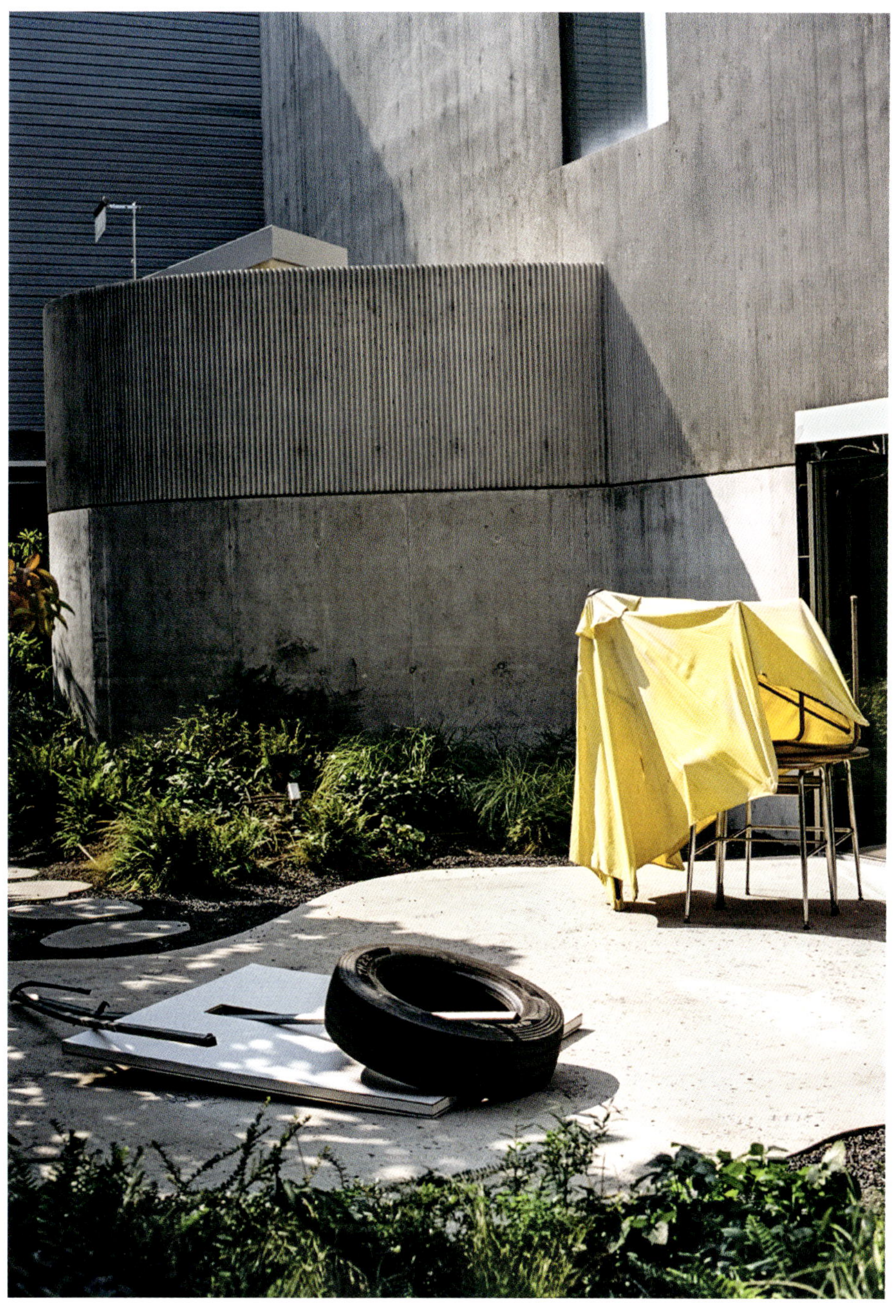

Foreground: Ser Serpas, *the path lest take me away*, 2022. Mixed media of found objects (tire, drywall, metal bar from bookcase), 16 × 107 × 72 inches (40.6 × 271.8 × 182.9 cm)
Background: Ser Serpas, *undulating cathartic autonomy the shack*, 2022. Mixed media of found objects (umbrella and public-school desks); 57 × 80 × 79 inches (144.7 × 203.2 × 200.6 cm)

Liliane Lijn

I had just seen the flash
    the beam
    the ray
    the blast of colour
    one colour at a time one band one frequency narrow and precise
I had seen it clear
    a zone of the flow
    not reflected but passed through
    through and changed within
    transformed
Matter had sent me a message
    had taken the sun's ray transformed it and sent me the result
My emptiness had received it

Until now I had seen indirectly
I had seen the pulse of light
    the captured particle
    a minute of the flow
    flow wrapped in time
    like a bundle
    easier to hold in the hand of the mind
    to catch and hold
    to hold and throw
    time tied
    knotted by seconds
    fixed tightly between past and future

Who put together time? I wondered
    but that was later the wondering
    the asking of that question
    that took time
And once I asked it the question stayed unsatisfied and ate my answers
    lapped them off the surface
First it licked off the icing
    the many small decorations
Then regretfully it went on to eat the next layer
    which was not so easy needing more than the tongue
    the acids went to work dissolving

    the inner liquids of the mouth
        until the second layer was all eaten
But the third was not so pleasant
        even harder
        and the teeth went to work
        and the muscles of the mouth
        but even when this layer had all been eaten the question was not
        satisfied
What is the meaning of time?
        but that was much later the wondering

I saw the pulse quiver
I saw it pass through itself
I saw it become another
I knew what I saw
        but it had no name
I will give it name I thought
        no I will give the name to it
        I will offer name and word to it
        I will make it an offering
        I will give it meaning to play with as it pleases
        as it wills

I took words
I took meanings
I took what we call thought
        and I offered these to the pulse I had seen
        and the pulse was pleased and played with them
        and I looked at its games
        I followed them
        I watched the dance the frolic the play
        and I saw that the words were part of the pulse
        what I called the pulse in my timetied way
        sight tied to time

Then I thought
        I will alter time and free my sight
And again I looked at the game

I saw the soundless sound
        the line of life
I saw it sing
        in lines of land
        in lines of light
        there and not there
        defining the space between
        only with the moment
        a code
        a way of seeing

And that summer before I left the city before I saw the flash
        I had made clear the becoming
        but even then I had not known or seen
        and unaware of what I made I had made it
When I left the city and returned to our house on the hill
        I took what I had made with me
And having seen that a transparent solid sphere a ball of matter through
        which light could pass intensified the light which it received I took
        such a sphere I happened to have and placed it upon what I had made
        to see the beam of white light
        the wide beam
        from red to blue but unrefracted
I saw the beam as I had expected but with it I saw
        what I had not seen before
        that which I knew nothing of
        not having seen what I made
        or having seen only a part thereof
        that which I had wished to see
        having been prepared to see it
        having seen it before
        always wishing for what I knew
        holding change on a lead
        directing it
        keeping it under control so it wouldn't move too fast
        faster than I could and get away
        out of sight

out of hearing
beyond control
But the unexpected brought me delight
I saw the becoming and was glad
the continual trajectory
the constant spin
the crossing
and
the
flash

NOTE ON CROSSING MAP

I wrote *Crossing Map* between 1967 and 1974 to explore the idea that the human mind disposes of a vast supply of untapped energy. What would it be like, I asked myself, to inhabit a world in which humans had become light?

Crossing Map was published in 1983 by Thames & Hudson and produced by Edition Hansjörg Mayer in Stuttgart in two versions. For the deluxe edition, the text was printed as a separate book, and the drawings for each "song," or chapter, were printed as folding leporellos, the whole bound and boxed. In the softback version, the text was printed over the drawings. In order to print the drawings in color, I entered the press and distributed the inks as the press rolled, becoming a part of the machine. The outcome of this was that each of the softback books became unique in its coloring.

Crossing Map is an epic poem and a philosophical monologue, a feminist lament of human greed and fear, exploring relationships in terms of the flow or blockage of energy between people. A woman artist questions the meaning of time and, meeting the last man, is witness to the dematerialization of her society.

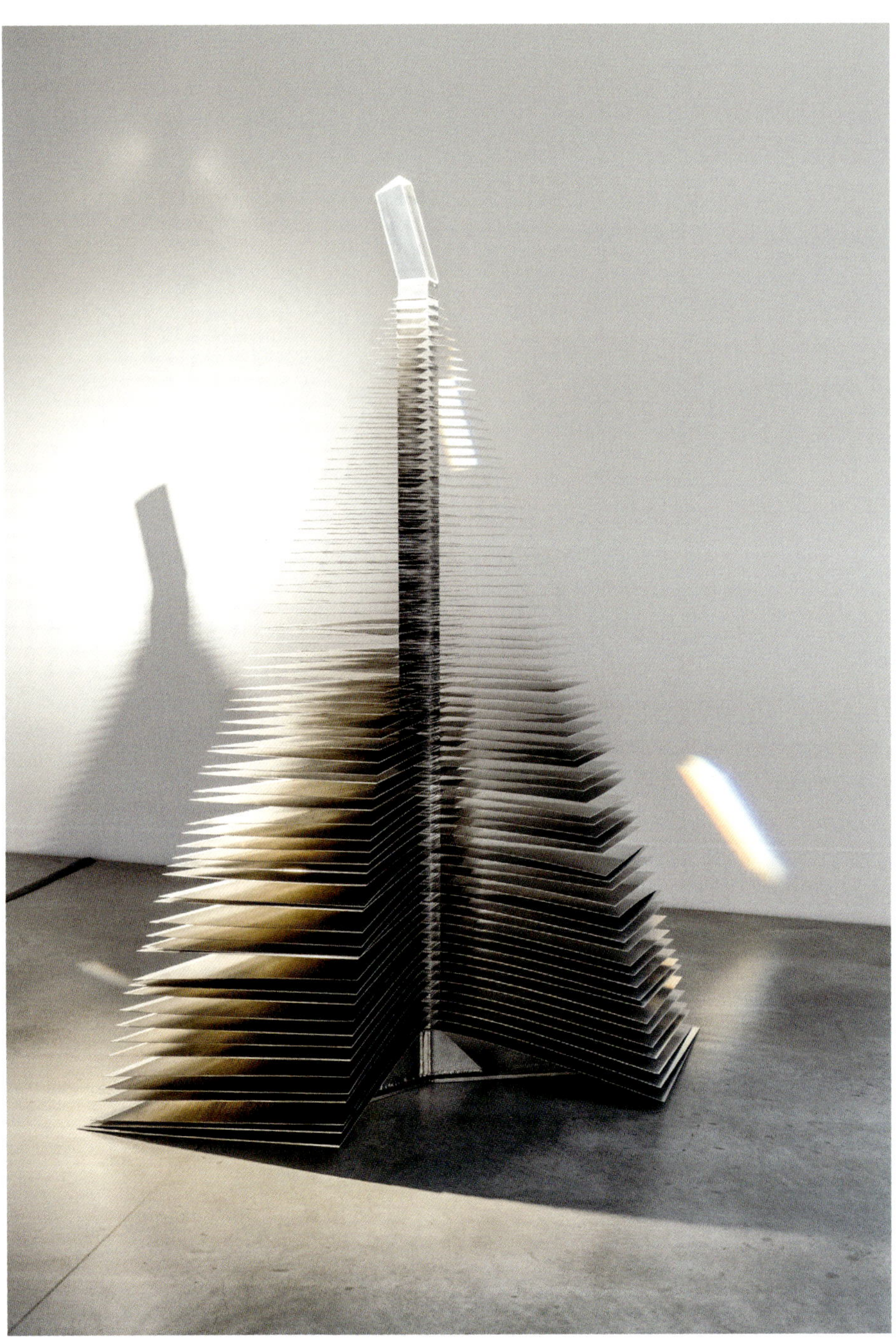

Liliane Lijn, *Queen of Hearts,*
Queen of Diamonds, 1980 (detail).
Optical glass prism and aluminum;
one of two parts: 90 × 73 × 73
inches (227 × 185 × 185 cm), 94 ×
73 × 73 inches (237 × 185 × 185 cm)

172

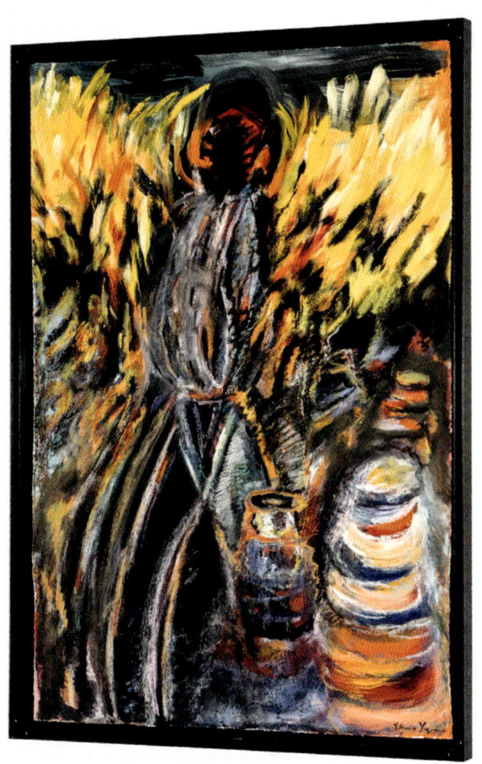

Liliane Lijn, *Woman of War with Koans*, 1987. Acrylic and oil pastel on filter paper; 43¼ × 30 inches (110 × 76 cm), framed

Mayra A. Rodríguez Castro

MIRACULOUS WEAPONS

could be twigs   even

lips

  that blasting

no war   still burn

 the green waters

Mayra A. Rodríguez Castro, *Senti*,
2022. Stainless steel, aluminum
and silver aggregate chimes, and
horsehair string; 43 × 22½ × 14 inches
(109.2 × 57.1 × 35.6 cm)

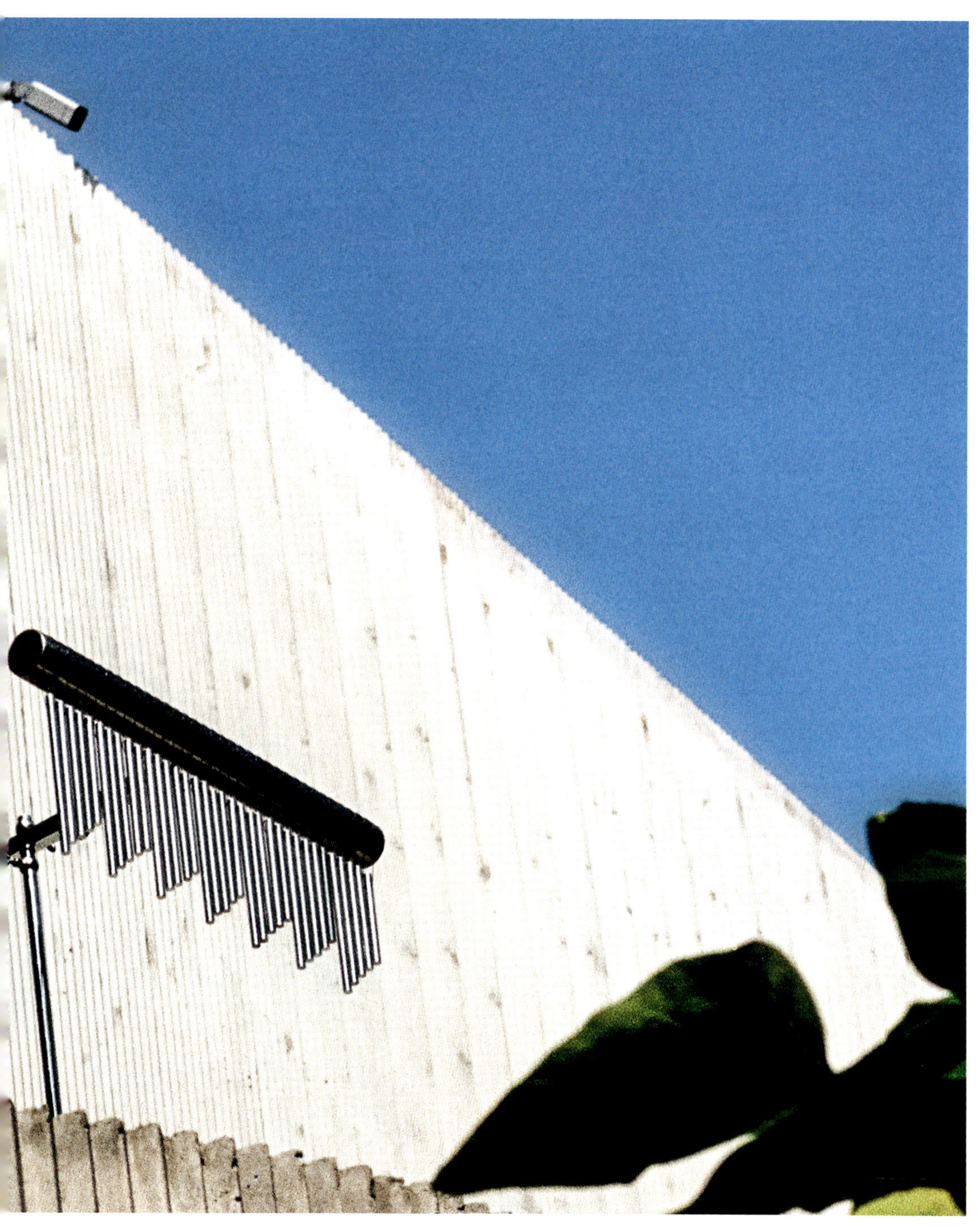

Rivane Neuenschwander

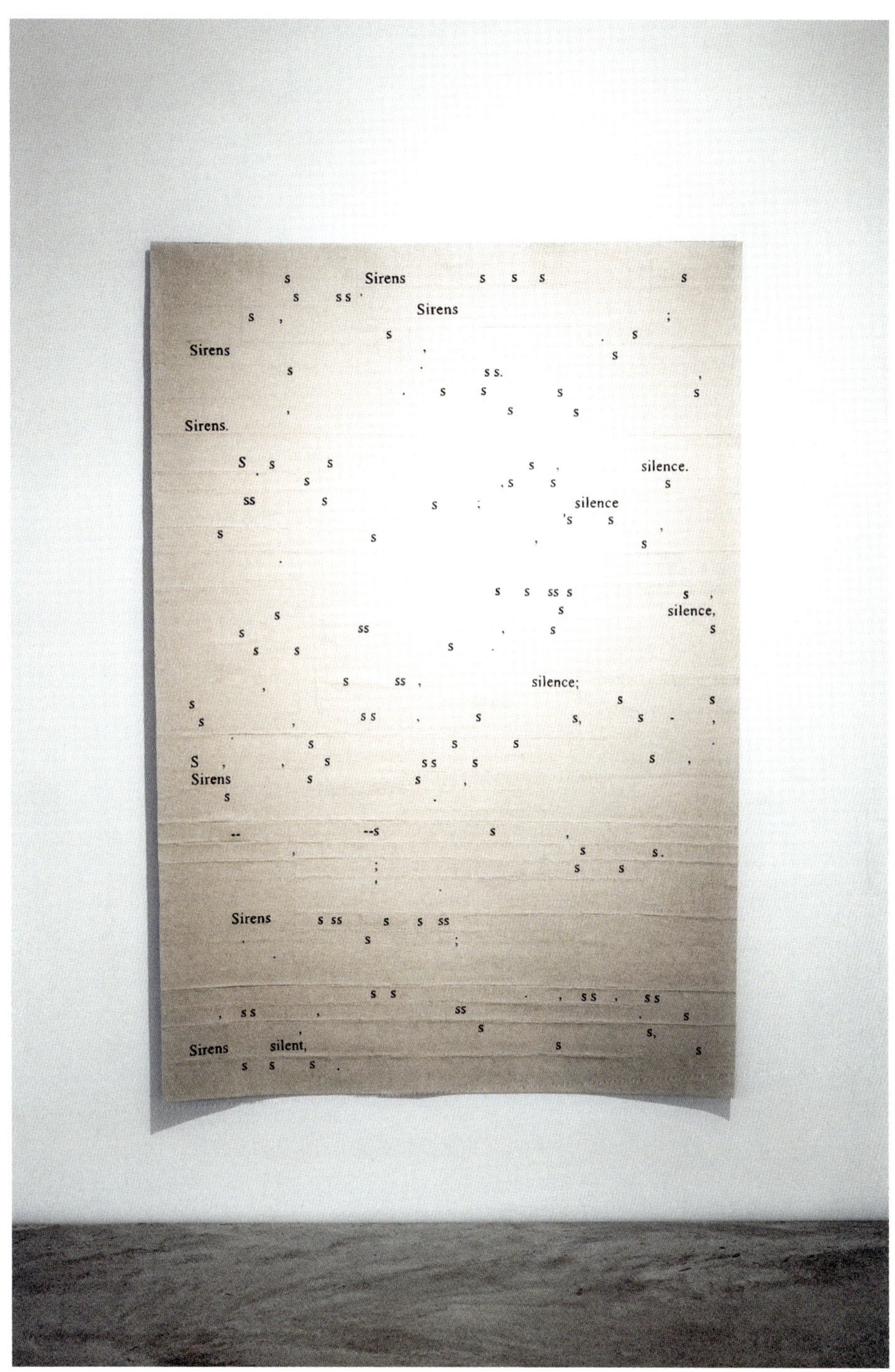

Rivane Neuenschwander, *The Silence of the Sirens*, 2013. Felt, thread, fusible interfacing, and D-ring metal; 51⅛ × 73¼ inches (129.8 × 186 cm)

parables
and
paradoxes

parabeln
und
paradoxe

FRANZ KAFKA

schocken   sb 12

THE SILENCE OF THE SIRENS

Proof that inadequate, even childish measures, may serve to rescue one from peril.

To protect himself from the Sirens Ulysses stopped his ears with wax and had himself bound to the mast of his ship. Naturally any and every traveller before him could have done the same, except those whom the Sirens allured even from a great distance; but it was known to all the world that such things were of no help whatever. The song of the Sirens could pierce through everything, and the longing of those they seduced would have broken far stronger bonds than chains and masts. But Ulysses did not think of that, although he had probably heard of it. He trusted absolutely to his handful of wax and his fathom of chain, and in innocent elation over his little stratagem sailed out to meet the Sirens.

Now the Sirens have a still more fatal weapon than their song, namely their silence. And though admittedly such a thing has never happened, still it is conceivable that someone might possibly have escaped from their singing; but from their silence certainly never. Against the feeling of having triumphed over them by one's own strength, and the consequent exaltation that bears down everything before it, no earthly powers could have remained intact.

And when Ulysses approached them the potent songstresses actually did not sing, whether because they thought that this enemy could be vanquished only by

89

their silence, or because the look of bliss on the face of Ulysses, who was thinking of nothing but his wax and his chains, made them forget their singing.

But Ulysses, if one may so express it, did not hear their silence; he thought they were singing and that he alone did not hear them. For a fleeting moment he saw their throats rising and falling, their breasts lifting, their eyes filled with tears, their lips half-parted, but believed that these were accompaniments to the airs which died unheard around him. Soon, however, all this faded from his sight as he fixed his gaze on the distance, the Sirens literally vanished before his resolution, and at the very moment when they were nearest to him he knew of them no longer.

But they—lovelier than ever—stretched their necks and turned, let their cold hair flutter free in the wind, and forgetting everything clung with their claws to the rocks. They no longer had any desire to allure; all that they wanted was to hold as long as they could the radiance that fell from Ulysses' great eyes.

If the Sirens had possessed consciousness they would have been annihilated at that moment. But they remained as they had been; all that had happened was that Ulysses had escaped them.

A codicil to the foregoing has also been handed down. Ulysses, it is said, was so full of guile, was such a fox, that not even the goddess of fate could pierce his armor. Perhaps he had really noticed, although here the human understanding is beyond its depths, that the Sirens were silent, and opposed the afore-mentioned pretense to them and the gods merely as a sort of shield.

THE SIRENS

These are the seductive voices of the night; the Sirens, too, sang that way. It would be doing them an injustice to think that they wanted to seduce; they knew they had claws and sterile wombs, and they lamented this aloud. They could not help it if their laments sounded so beautiful.

LEOPARDS IN THE TEMPLE

Leopards break into the temple and drink to the dregs what is in the sacrificial pitchers; this is repeated over and over again; finally it can be calculated in advance, and it becomes a part of the ceremony.

Dena Yago

DOLPHINS

O this old world may never change!

A hard wave claps
at the punchline.

Never been a good provider,
    always opting out of the
    add-ons
    upsells
    the extras.

The great layer cake
laid on its side on a plate.

Onlookers share their love for a soft division
wet cream and the sponge that takes it in,
from the sidelines I crowdsource the hot takes.

Good evening everybody, how're we doing tonight?

ZIPPITY DO DA MOTHERFUCKERS

Surround sound says (whisper) rush.

Surrounded by minimum viable icons
    gestural outline indicating
    what breaks a line but hides the cut inside.

Double walled deco
dead on arrival.

I've got a
    soft lap,
she's got a
    clutched purse,
they have a hood of matted hair.

Let's just
    call the whole thing off
let's just
    call it a wash
let's just
    call someone, anyone's supervisor
let's just
    peel back the wild posting
let's just
    lick the sticker with the tenderness accessible only
    by letting all of your tongue muscles go slack.

A flat pressed tongue against the teeth.

A grateful prayer for the continuation of public services,
if even only
by the skin
of their crooked yellow teeth.

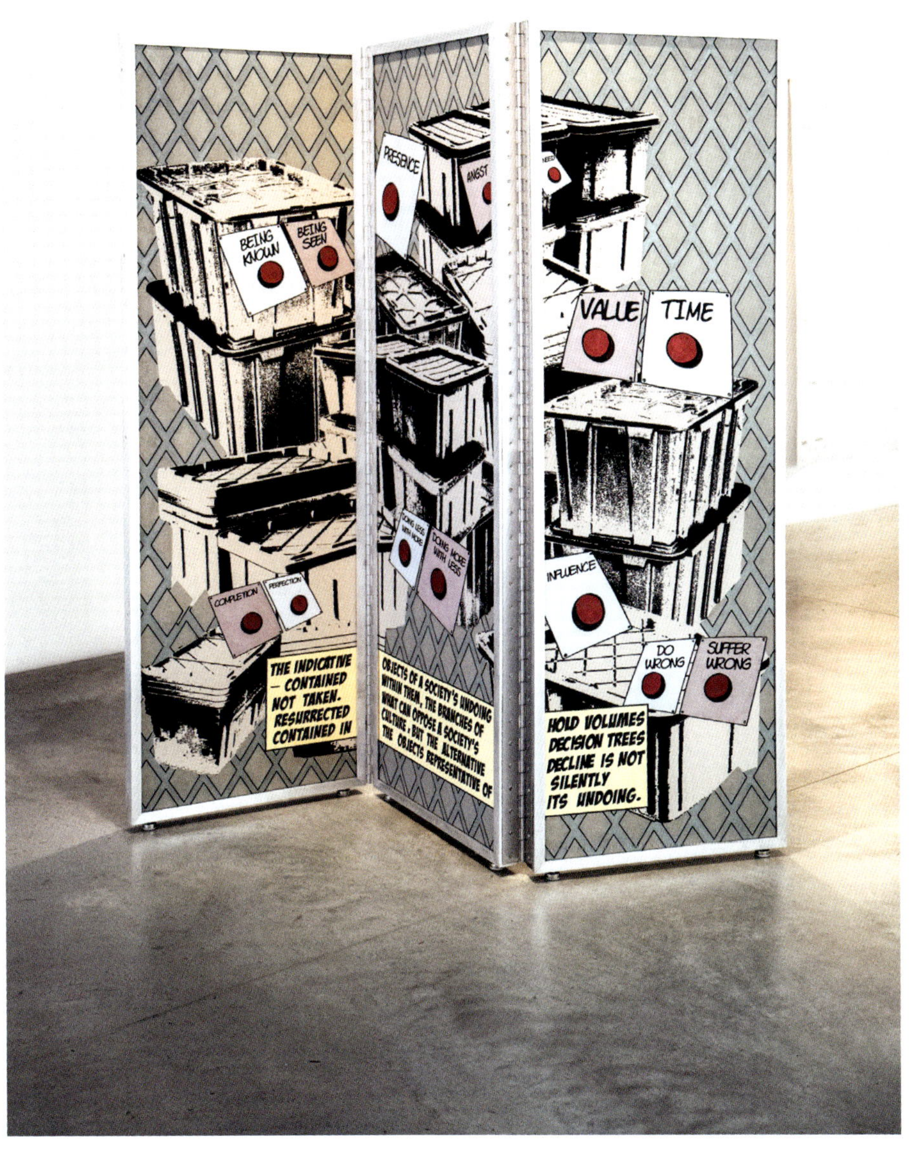

Dena Yago, *The Bins*, 2021. Acrylic
and inkjet on canvas in aluminum and
stainless-steel frame; 73½ × 73 × 3 inches
(186.7 × 185.4 × 7.6 cm) unfolded

ODYSSEUS OR MYTH AND ENLIGHTENMENT

As we have seen, the Sirens episode in the Odyssey combines myth and rational labor. In fact, the poem as a whole bears witness to the dialectic of enlightenment. The epic narrative, especially in the most ancient of its various layers, clearly exhibits its close relation to myth: its component adventures have their origin in popular tradition. The Homeric spirit takes over and "organizes" the myths, but contradicts them in the process. Philosophical criticism shows that the usual identification of epic and myth (refuted, in any case, by modern classical philologists) is wholly illusive. *Epos* and *mythos* are two distinct concepts, and indicate two stages in an historical process which can still be discerned where the disparate elements of the Odyssey have been editorially reconciled. If it does not already presuppose a universality of language, the Homeric narrative effects one; by using an exoteric form of representation, it dissolves the hierarchical order of society in the very process of glorifying it. To celebrate the anger of Achilles and the wanderings of Odysseus is already a wistful stylization of what can no longer be celebrated; and the hero of the adventures shows himself to be a prototype of the bourgeois individual, a notion originating in the consistent self-affirmation which has its ancient pattern in the figure of the protagonist compelled to wander. The epic is the historico-philosophic counterpart to the novel, and eventually displays features approximating those character-

43

istic of the novel. The venerable cosmos of the meaningful Homeric world is shown to be the achievement of regulative reason, which destroys myth by virtue of the same rational order in which it reflects it.

The late German Romantic interpreters of classical antiquity, following on Nietzsche's early writings, stressed the bourgeois Enlightenment element in Homer. Nietzsche was one of the few after Hegel who recognized the dialectic of enlightenment. And it was Nietzsche who expressed its antipathy to domination: "The Enlightenment" should be "taken into the people, so that the priests all become priests with a bad conscience—and the same must be done with regard to the State. That is the task of the Enlightenment: to make princes and statesmen unmistakably aware that everything they do is sheer falsehood . . ."[1] On the other hand, Enlightenment had always been a tool for the "great manipulators of government (Confucius in China, the *Imperium Romanum,* Napoleon, the Papacy when it had turned to power and not only to the world) . . . The way in which the masses are fooled in this respect, for instance in all democracies, is very useful: the reduction and malleability of men are worked for as 'progress'!"[2]

The revelation of these two aspects of the Enlightenment as an historic principle made it possible to trace the notion of enlightenment as progressive thought, back to the beginning of traditional history. Nevertheless, Nietzsche's relation to the Enlightenment, and therefore to Homer, was still discordant. Though he discerned both the universal movement of sovereign Spirit (whose executor he felt himself to be) and a "nihilistic" anti-life force is the enlightenment, his pre-Fascist followers retained only the second aspect and perverted it into an ideology. This ideology becomes blind praise of a blind life subject to the same nexus of action by which everything living is suppressed. This is clear in the attitude of the cultural fascists to Homer. They scent out a democratic spirit, characterize the work as redolent of seafarers and traders, and condemn the Ionian epic as all-too-rational expository narrative and a mere communi-

1. Nietzsche, *Nachlass,* Vol. XIV, p. 206.
2. Nietzsche, *Nachlass,* Vol. XV, p. 235.

DIALECTIC OF ENLIGHTENMENT

MAX HORKHEIMER AND THEODOR W. ADORNO

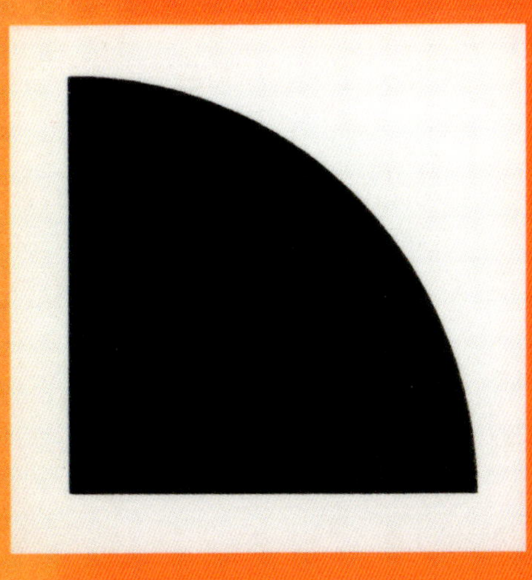

Aura Satz

PREEMPTIVE LISTENING

How to listen ahead, how to hold the future in mind when listening? The siren is the prism through which to refract this notion of *Preemptive Listening*: a complex web of entangled relationships to threat, alert, alarm, a doorway, an exit route, and survival. At its most basic, beyond any learned sound signal, the siren is firstly a *call to attention*, secondly a *call to action*, and lastly, *it faces forward*. It hovers in the split second before future ruins. Wound up into its wail is a bifurcation of time, multiple cascading paths collapsing into disaster, devastation, and everything in between. The siren builds on previous trauma, ostensibly learns from it, and provides a gap before that past can repeat. In the warning's suspended pause, we find possible rescue or refuge, a sound that demarcates a way out from past catastrophe, pointing to the path of survival.

The siren folds into its future tense these unraveling scars, some near and visible, others remote, imperceptible, and buried in the deep future, unimaginable beyond this lifetime. Living across multiple scales of threat, how to disentangle immediate danger from long-term distant danger? But more importantly, how to recalibrate the siren away from the sound of trauma? Toward a sound that allows us to imagine otherwise, toward a future that is not mired in catastrophe.

In the throes of a generalized crisis of attention, the siren's loud wail is nested in this cacophony of things crying out to be heard. Everything is beeping, signaling, a sonified alert of things connecting, disconnecting, near collisions, boundaries reinforced or trespassed. The siren is a mouth, but it is closely wired to a network of eyes and eavesdropping ears, surveillance superstructures and simulations—it benefits and feeds off these to command its sonic obedience. Across the spectrum of sonic commands, there is perhaps a hierarchy of obedience levels, louder calls to collective clustering in shelters from climate disaster or war, as opposed to the more granular dispersion of disobedience, dissent, or rebellion. This latter sound is the noise of friction, turbulence, conflict, revolution, and therefore also change, like waves of warning crashing against the walls we have built. The siren has been weaponized as an acoustic force restraining riots, attempting to crush the perils of an alternative future.

This could be the siren's revolutionary potential, an alarm that can become a call to arms (*all'arme*), holding space for a different thread, a fork in the road. *Preemptive Listening* is attuned to threat, operating according to the logic of emergency, accelerated preemptive measures, often violent clampdowns undertaken in the name of security. But it is also this point of resistance, an attempt to unpack what is meant by *preemptive*, to question the coordinates of what is to be saved, who is to be warned, who is worthy of warning, safety, future. What if we move away from a time-scarce imagination to a longer vision to address slower emergencies? What will we carry forward?

Realign and reorient the siren toward a map. The siren's visual counterpart, the emergency rotating light, is an accelerated strobe flashing for attention, calling out with a breathless pulse. Retune it to a different frequency and think instead of a lighthouse beacon, a slower light that rotates to a different beat, with a wider reach, alerting those in dark seas of treacherous cliffs. Can a warning do more than avert catastrophe? Can it be reconceptualized as a clarion call, a navigational tool, or a guiding light? Shift registers. Recompose the siren. Retune it to navigate differently, toward elsewhere, otherwise.

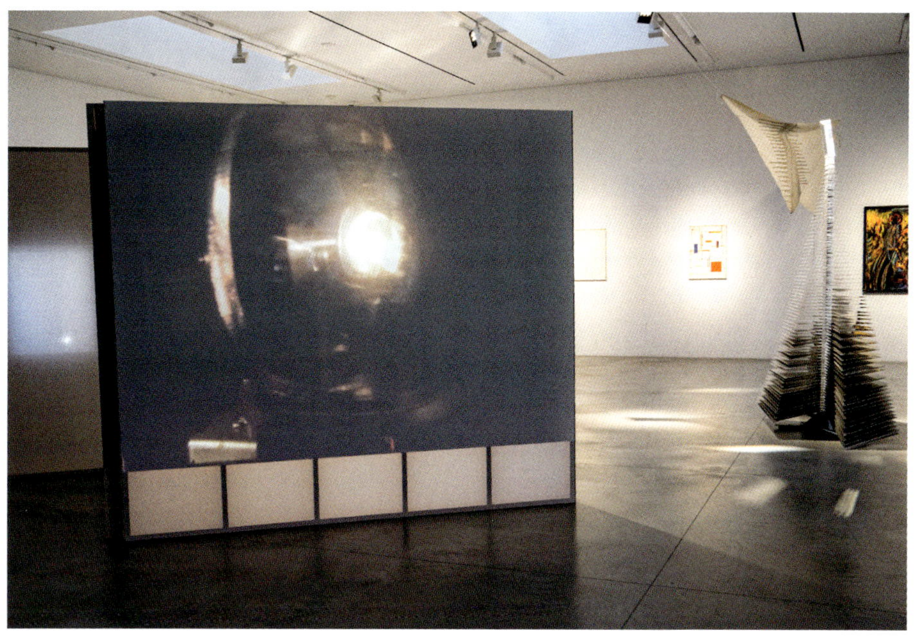

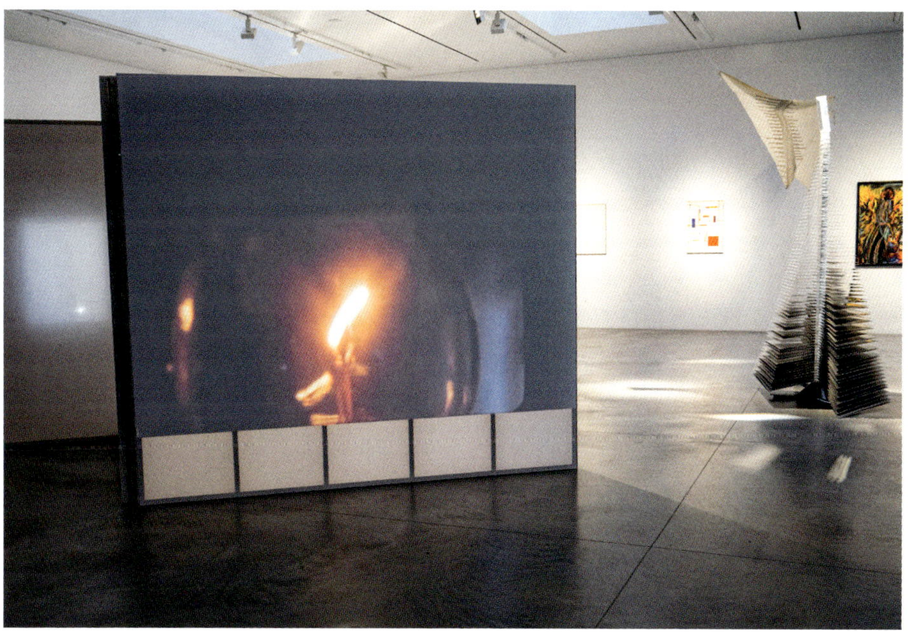

This page and following spread:
Aura Satz, *Preemptive Listening (part 1: The Fork in the Road)*, 2018. 16 mm film transferred to HD video (color, stereo sound, 8:47 min.)

195

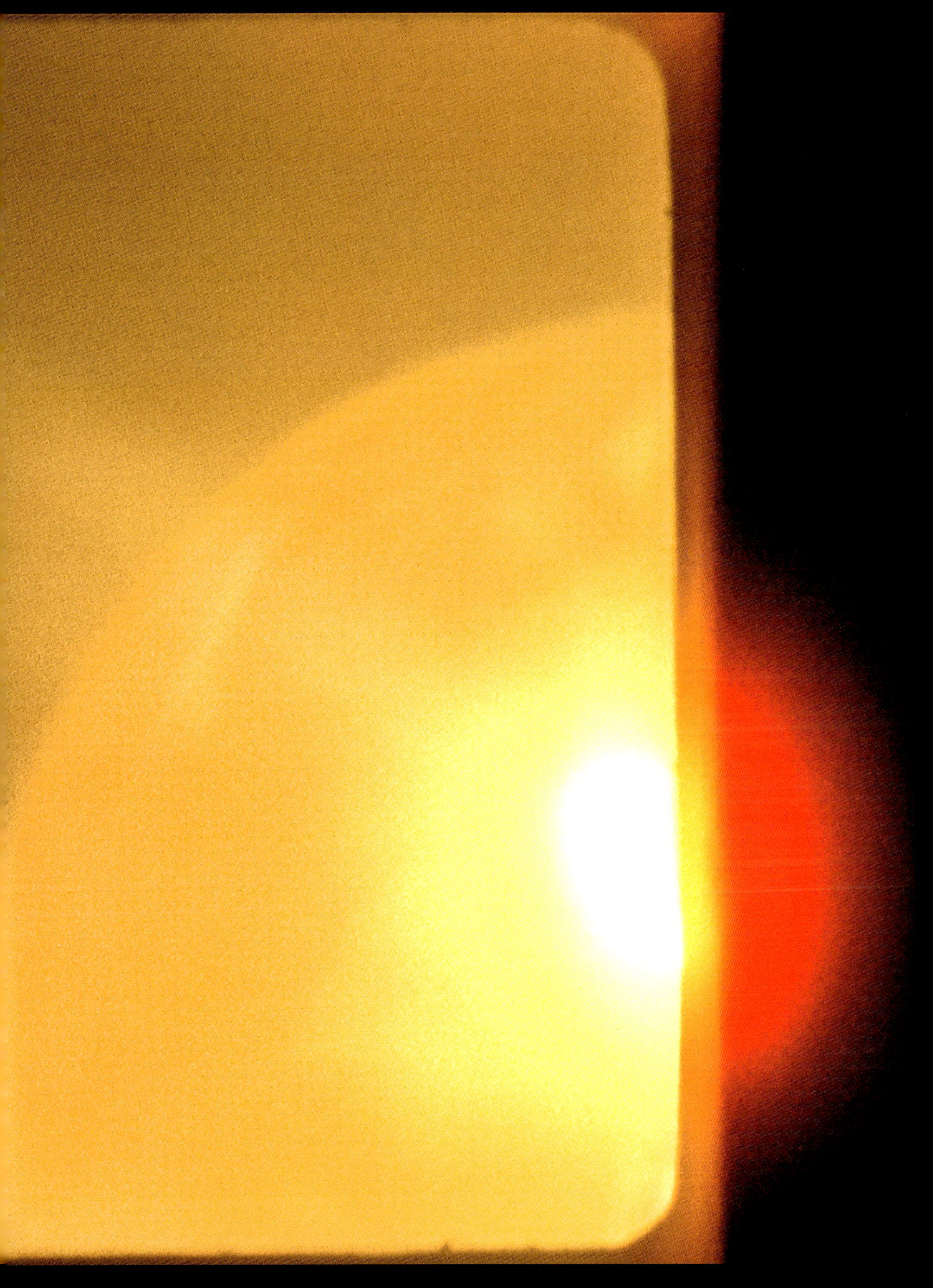

DMZ COLONY

DON
MEE
CHOI

7256

Ahn Hak-sŏp #4

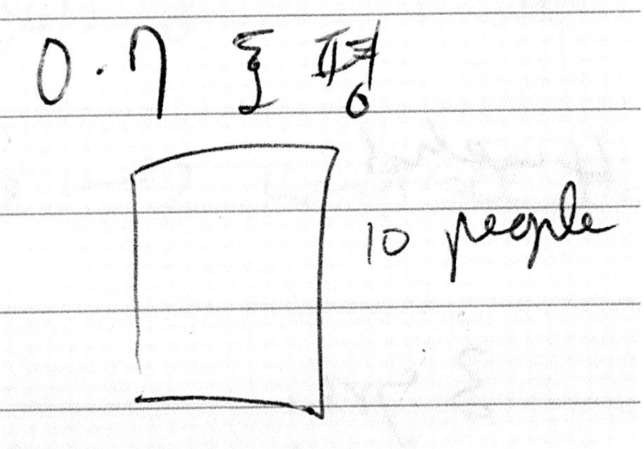

24.9082 square feet

... I'll leave it up to your imagination ... they even shoved 20 people in at one point ... we were beaten when we needed to urinate, defecate ... there was an army lieutenant ... he was arrested for insubordination ... he accidentally came across a certain book and thought ... ah ... world ... could such a world exist? ... he was released but was still under surveillance ... he was captured when he tried to escape to the north ... I mention him because he also refused to change his political view ...

convert ?
change ?
view   ?

. . . it was August . . . he was beaten severely . . . then his blood dried up . . . he was wearing a T-shirt under a uniform . . . he couldn't take them off till his scabs came off . . . he was all skin . . . he still refused to ? ? ? . . . then

water torture
? ? ?
C N C
N V H
V R N
R T G
T ? ?
C H V
H N W
N G ?
G ?

. . . that didn't work either, so the guards tied him up to beat him . . . I endured water torture twice . . . I still didn't budge . . . in winter the guards opened all the windows and doors
of my cell and sprayed water . . . I was stripped . . . . the cell turned into a freezer . . . I could
endure the cold for 6 days . . . I squatted . . . jumped to keep warm . . . I was exhausted in the
morning . . . without food . . . on day 7 I leaned against the ice wall and passed out . . . I heard
a siren . . .

then I heard the vowels from my own mouth
O E
A E
I E
E E E
이 이 이

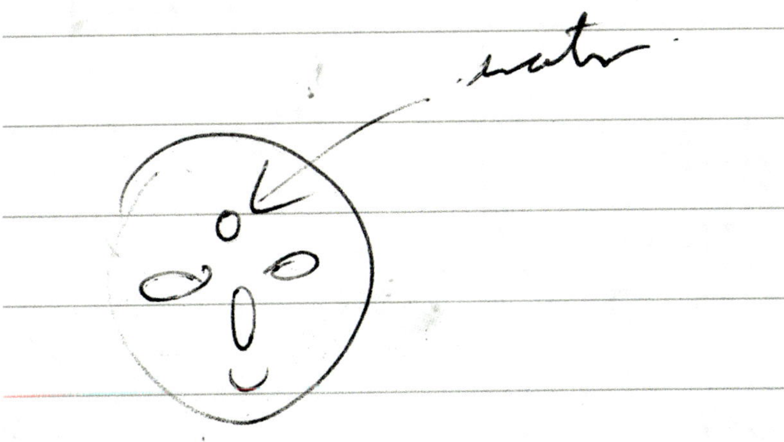

my face

browless

earless

my eyes

my nose

my mouth

moonless

my comet

. . . the guards aimed a jet of cold water at my forehead . . . full force . . . it looks like nothing

yet . . . it felt as if my head was being bashed with a rock . . . my toenails fell off . . . they kept

hitting my toes . . . unbearable pain . . . my toenails fell off . . . twice . . .

a siren

full speed

full orbit

full matter

full toenails

then I heard my vowels

oe

ae

ie

e

e

e

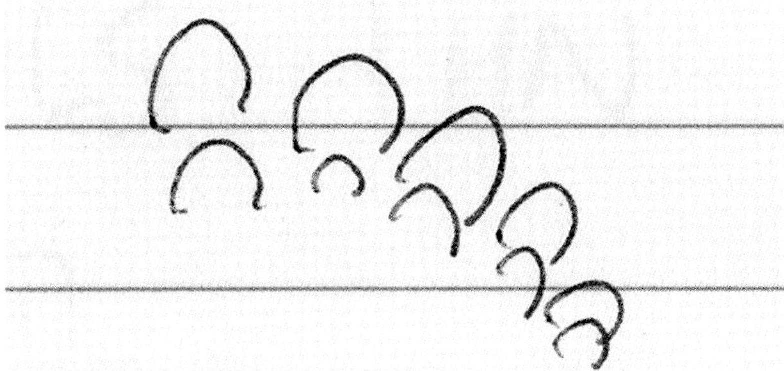

it looks like nothing yet

planets appeared in the sky

○] Mercury

○] Venus

○] Earth

○] Mars

○] Jupiter

○] Saturn

○] Uranus

○] Neptune

○] Pluto

○] Planet Nine

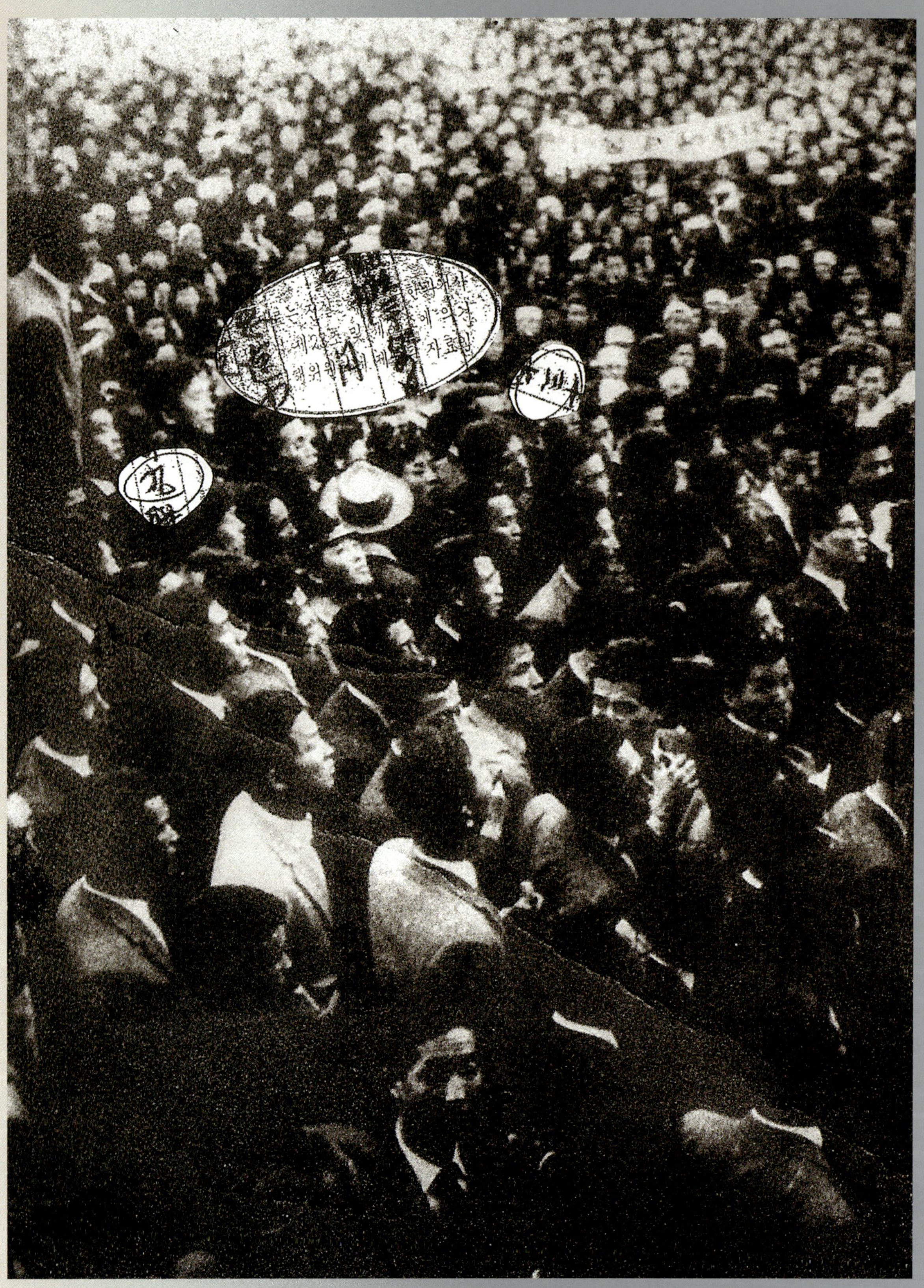

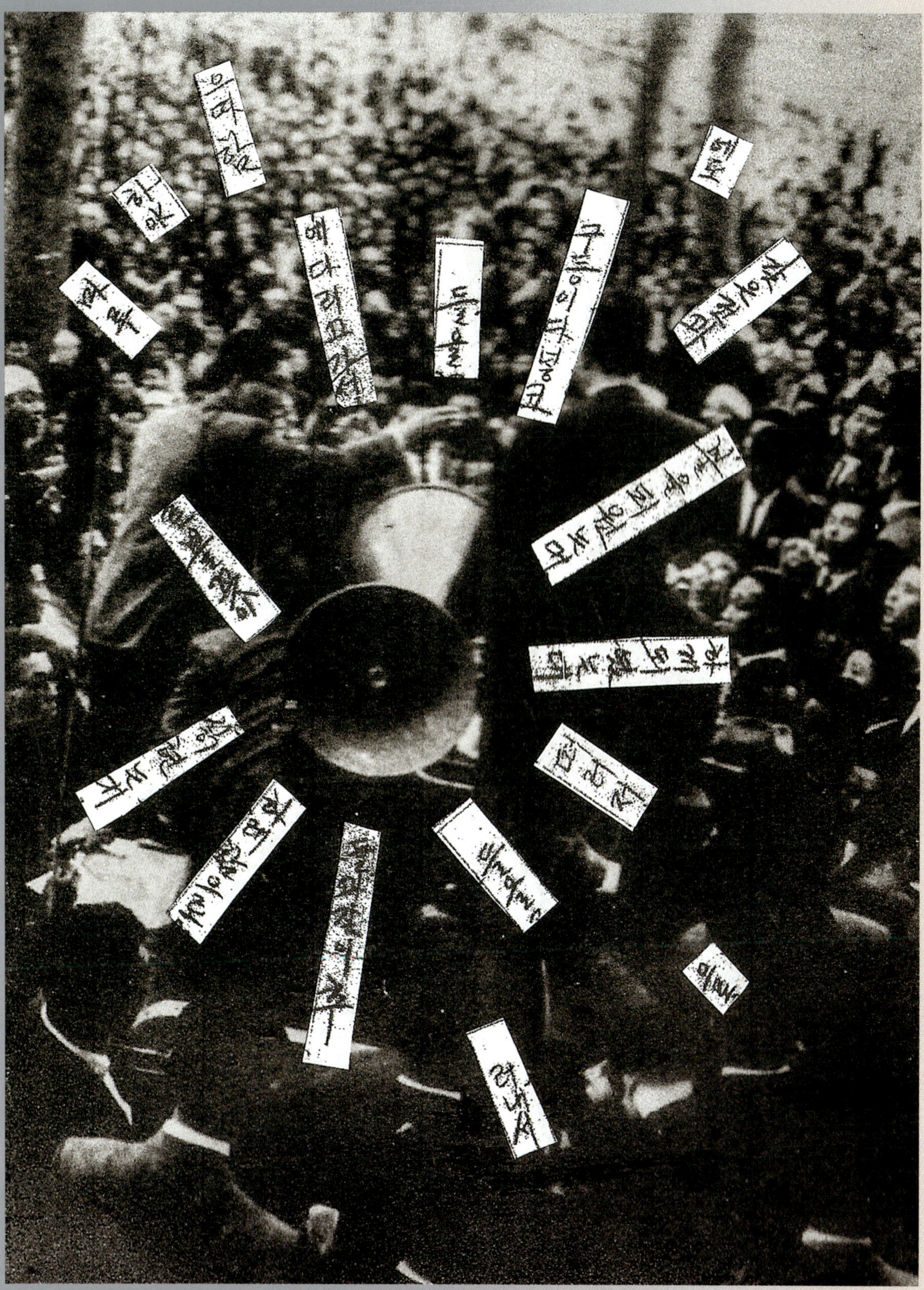

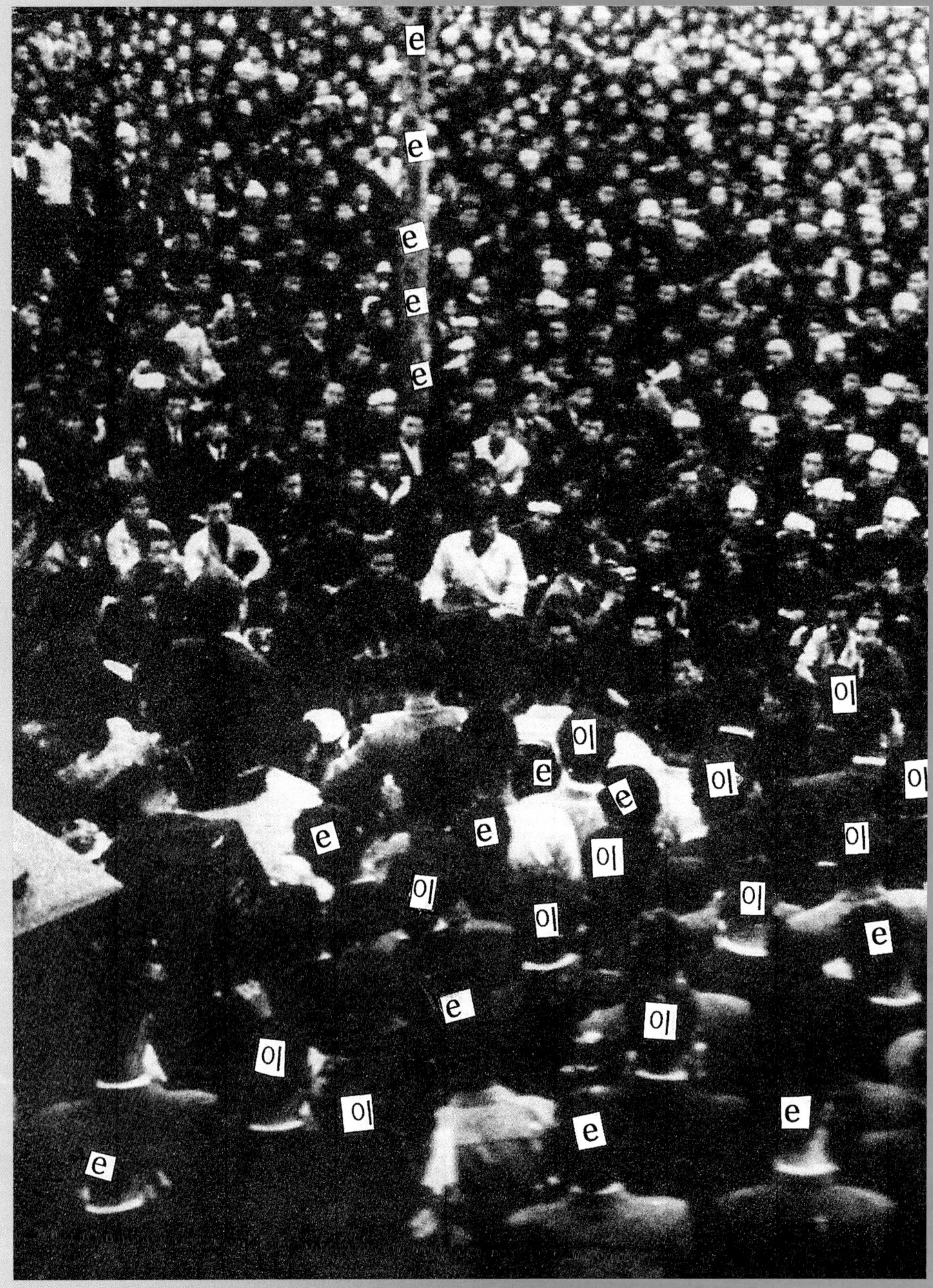

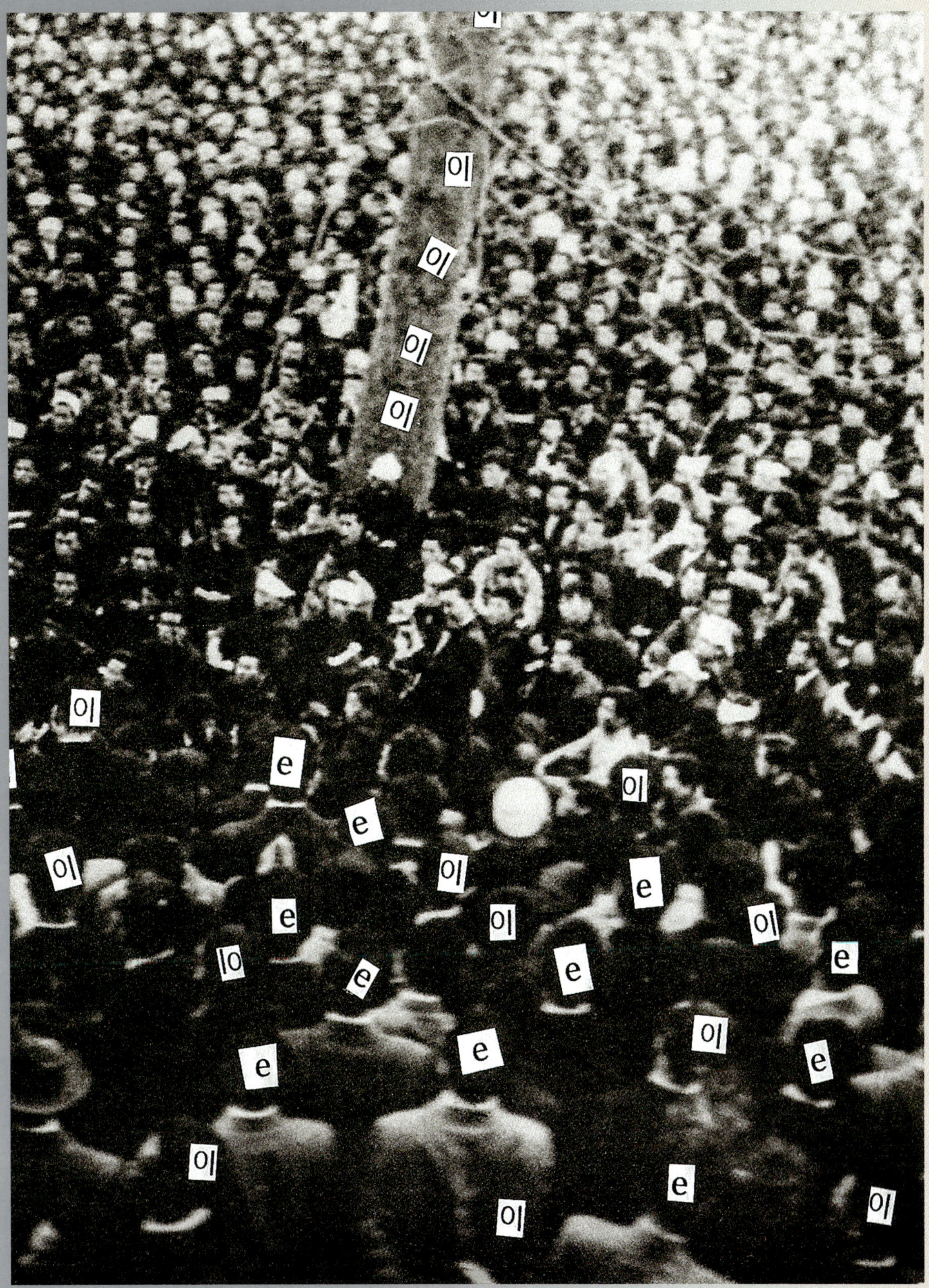

The Figure and the Field, or the Siren and the Ocean: Some Poethical Wagers

Hana Noorali and Lynton Talbot

The noon sirens are tests. In small towns and cities around the world, these civil-defense warnings—installed to alert the public, as well as rescue teams, to the imminent danger of attack or natural disaster— are tested at midday on a daily, weekly, or monthly basis by the relevant authorities. Ensuring the efficacy of the warning system, the tests remind the community that their daily lives can be unexpectedly, and perhaps violently, disrupted. These sirens are rehearsals for living with disaster; the evocative nature of their harsh tone is affectively allied to a sense of struggle. *The Noon Sirens*, our online program and preface to the exhibition *SIREN (some poetics)*, is also a test.[1] Just as the siren brings forth the event, the sirens sounded at noon rehearse that struggle.

Quinn Latimer's curation of *SIREN (some poetics)* at Amant brings together artists who move toward the voicing of language: thinking through the physicality of speech; registering the shape, sound, and poetics of the speaker. The exhibition recognizes the double meaning of the word *siren*, signifying both a mechanical device warning of danger and a mythological figure luring you to danger itself. In doing so, Latimer suggests the siren's song as a perfect expression of a double ontology and paradox. Through speech and language and song (that is, sound and tone and noise and word and refrain), the show reveals to us the siren as a disembodied voice that somehow makes real our own fears, prejudices, and ideologies, as well as our innate desire to project them onto one another. If *SIREN (some poetics)* characterizes voice and language itself as always already political, then *The Noon Sirens* challenges the sites and

1   *The Noon Sirens* is available at https://www.amant.org/publications/5-the-noon-sirens.

territories in which the voice is heard. Just as there is no neutral voice, there is also no neutral space.

When we were first invited to put together a parallel program for the digital infrastructure of Amant, we considered the context carefully. What did it mean to ask artists for whom language (written or spoken) is an essential part of their practice to inscribe their work inside the digital architectures of a nascent New York art institution? How could we confront our shared ambivalence to certain technologies and invite critical participation in such space? While much has been said about the fluidity (if not quite democracy) of digital space, it remains deeply contested water. With the artists, we wanted to anticipate the trouble and find the limits of what could be done beyond a form of extended "publishing."

We began *The Noon Sirens* by asking the artists and writers Anaïs Duplan, Lara Mimosa Montes, and Johanna Hedva to challenge the dominance of any "universal" language. We were interested in resistance to data's absolutization of knowledge, where numbers speak for themselves and regress the violence of accelerated digital communication. In other words, we wanted to know what it means to speak *here*. And how could a critical impulse toward the poetic over the informational disrupt the dominance of digital communication? The siren's affective, cognitive relationship to danger might be tested in many ways, though. For instance, the relationship between sound and a response to it, in the context of politics and poetics, space and appearance, might be thought of as the relationship between noise and resistance. Indeed, we wondered: How might contemporary political struggles be positioned alongside and in dialogue with sound and its discourses? And, in giving expression to this online, how do we contend with our complicity with the infrastructures and institutions that stratify us and hold our dissenting voices?

Such queries became the basic premise of *The Noon Sirens*. Accordingly, our aim has been to think about the appearance of language online; to consider the dominant forms of digital engagement, in particular the ways they increasingly capitulate toward entertainment and the visually spectacular; and to encourage the possibility of performing differently in this very space. Alongside our positioning of sound and its discourses in dialogue with political struggles, we have imagined how one might level a critique against existing modes of engagement in digital space in a manner not inherently conservative. It has seemed important to think about complicity and how we might curatorially "build in" more agential participation.

At the time of writing, two contributions to *The Noon Sirens* have been realized and one is still to come. The first was by the poet, curator, and artist Anaïs Duplan, whose lecture-performance *Out of Dark Noise* was livestreamed on June 6, 2022, at 6 p.m. EST (a kind of 6/6/6). Duplan's narration of a sequence of excavated and abstracted 1990s-era rap videos—often detached from the original audio and isolated as visual media—offered ad hoc commentary filled with a sense of jeopardy and unknowability. Duplan invited the online audience to respond vocally or in the chat function as he attempted to fold their comments into his lecture in a processual and casual way, which at times became uniquely awkward. His precarious and quite autobiographical interaction with seminal rap videos drew on their historic and cultural specificity, while the live feedback from the audience left an openness that felt at odds with ideas of artistic or academic professionalism. This form of reading and being read made space for collectively reading the material for affect and emotion, neither shying away from the uncomfortable nor foreclosing outcomes to ensure success. Duplan's affective reading and performance followed a mode practiced by poet-thinkers such as Édouard Glissant, Fred Moten, and Simone Wright, and considered the additional difficulty of practicing such technique online. Indeed, affect and emotion are perhaps the least considered or studied phenomena of our universal move into online communication as public discourse.

At the same time, many of us have felt encouraged, particularly over the past two years, to become broadcasters of our projects, transmitting them through the smooth cadence of professional hawkers. Our success online—that is, our visibility *and* audibility—seems to depend on our ability to speak without hesitation or pause or stutter. In our new world, voices are singular and detached. Where a cacophony of speech was once invited, dramatic pauses for emphasis "read" as network interference, and time taken to think is confused with radio silence. Online, the professional insistence on perfect delivery renders us all standing spotlit onstage. Convivial speech is mired in the pressure to perform—that is, to offer expertly parceled information with the expectation of establishing ourselves within the group. This has encouraged and garnered, particularly in educational and critical artistic environments, a meritocracy of confidence rather than empathetic arenas for shared discourse.

By removing the original sound from the rap videos, Duplan embraced the possibility of failure to deliver, and his *Out of Dark Noise* prompted a type of live *poethics* uncommon in digital terrains. Used by artists and writers such as Rhea Dillon and Joan Retallack, this term thickens the word *poetics* in order to speak to an aesthetic of complexity and the call to take responsibility for chance. *The Noon Sirens* embraces the poethical framework in offering the possibility that art can be a form of living in the world, potentially rendering the online envelope of the institution as not simply an edifice on which to hang representational gestures or political positions, but a space of consequence that, characteristic of the poethical wager, considers responsibility to and for the other.[2]

Duplan's performance hopefully produced a site of relationality, feeling, and collective resonance while pushing gently against the walls of convention in digital space. The documentation of *Out of Dark Noise* resides on the website of Amant as a mostly visual collage. The source material, used without sound, is offered as a seemingly endless scroll, an opaque field devoid of context or comment. As such, it leaves space for continued reading and collective reflection, an uncommon trace on the website of a cultural institution, where, broadly speaking, the mission is to clearly communicate (and, to an extent, overexplain) the contributions of artists to the public. Thus, *The Noon Sirens* wishes to stir the waters of the digital environment and usurp certain conventions of clear, smooth communication in online participation. To understand the critical impulse of this effort, it might be useful to take a slight detour by considering the recent writing of Byung-Chul Han on new technologies of power and professionalism, and the ways in which they are employed at the expense of ambiguity and relation.

In *Psychopolitics: Neoliberalism and New Technologies of Power* (2017), Han argues that we are living in a society in which negativity has essentially been erased.[3] Concerned with showing only our positive selves and motivated by constant pressure to achieve recognition and success, we are

---

2   See Rhea Dillon's print publication accompanying *Catgut—The Opera*, her performance at the Serpentine Pavilion, London, for the series *Park Nights* in 2021; and Joan Retallack, *The Poethical Wager* (Berkeley: University of California Press, 2003).

3   Byung-Chul Han, *Psychopolitics: Neoliberalism and New Technologies of Power*, trans. Erik Butler (London: Verso, 2017).

becoming increasingly atomized and detached from one another even as we maintain the illusion of connectivity. The world, both online and off, increasingly appears as an infinite landscape of interactions that provide only reflections of ourselves. However, if social media is concerned with presenting these opportunities as perfect images without ambiguity, Han suggests it is precisely in ambiguity and confrontation that we are most able to connect, because in more complex spaces we are not afraid of negativity and we relate to the other.

Franco Berardi has likewise written extensively on the ever-increasing concern for direct communication, clear language, and the expeditious conveyance of information by connected means rather than conjunctive, messy forms.[4] If this tends to find expression in our cultural sectors and public-facing institutions in the insistence on over-explanation and perfect contextualization, it does so in the conviction that confusion or ambiguity or opacity is a problem to overcome not a potential state for transformation or deeper understanding. The imperative for clarity in speech attracts Han's attention, too. In his celebrated critique of "smoothness," Han notes that we no longer find the beauty in difference, in the difficulty and messiness of the other. Instead, smoothness embodies today's society of positivity. What is smooth does not complicate, harm, hesitate, or offer resistance. Liking something is easy, and our cultural spaces (again, both online and off) increasingly need likes. The fervor for positivity has initiated a paradigmatic shift in the function of the art institution, where a symbiotic relationship of constant affirmation now drives the culture. The smooth is looking for likes; its smoothness negates what is against it. Any negativity must be removed.

It is not difficult to connect the digital landscape, and its many forms of visual and textual media, to the imperative of smoothness and the appeasement of subjects who are encouraged only to respond positively. Instagram and other media offer little more than a recursive look at ourselves, or what Han would call "the smooth space of the same."[5] As we have moved from the disciplinary society into the achievement society—as Han's reading of Michel Foucault goes—the panopticon as a technology of oppressive surveillance no longer holds. Now, as we digitally submit

---

4 Franco "Bifo" Berardi, *The Uprising: On Poetry and Finance*, Semiotext(e) Intervention Series (Los Angeles: Semiotext(e), 2012).

5 Ibid., 83.

and perform ourselves in hypervisible terms, offering every facet of our data and/or personhood willingly to corporations, we are continually building and maintaining our own all-pervasive panopticon. Google, alongside those social networks that present themselves as spaces of freedom and self-expression, assumes total panoptic form. We collaborate in the panoptic gaze by exhibiting ourselves. Even when we feel we are speaking up and out and against something, we are, in fact, simply (re)producing and (re)enforcing our own corporate confinement. We commodify ourselves so as to achieve success and sell ourselves as entrepreneurs. And our sales pitch is increasingly dependent on perfect images, perfect performances, smooth linguistic delivery, and clearly articulated outcomes that can be received and liked.

Our collaboration with Latimer predates *The Noon Sirens* and in fact began with her participation in our own project platform, *parrhesiades*, which takes its name from Foucault's lectures on problematization and *parrhesia*.[6] The multiplatform nature of the *parrhesiades* project space attempts to disrupt smooth exhibitionary and corporate modes of address by introducing diffraction into the reading of single artworks, thereby offering multiple positions to the viewer. Neither the work, the audience, nor the project itself can be objectified in this loose matrix of interstitial spaces, and outcomes are neither perfect nor knowable.

Parrhesia is defined by Foucault as a speech act instituted in an action that interjects explosively into a conversation where someone clearly holds more power. The interjection balances the playing field and levels the stakes, but only by exposing both the listener and the speaker to a field of dangers—the consequence being that both are exposed to unknowable outcomes. For example, an employee who asks his employer about employment rights thereby shifts the frame through which the conversation must be pulled. By derailing the employer's rhetoric that would inevitably lead to a planned outcome (that only the employer knows), the employee regains equal status in a discussion where neither party knows the end point.

An art institution's inherent desire to increase and develop audiences, and its reliance on engagement-dependent funding, intersects with the compulsion to please the achievement subject. While *The Noon Sirens* is not a criticism of institutional complicity in this situation—after all, the

---

6   See https://parrhesiades.com.

violence of neoliberalism's infrastructural operations is always enveloped in a certain smoothness—it is a modest attempt to think through multiple complicities. We all have to confront the central paradox of our cultural institutions: that while they may be spaces to voice dissent, participation in them as curators, artists, cultural workers, or audience members reifies the problems the artwork may intend to critique, from unfair pay and unpaid labor, to racism and misogyny, to problematic funding structures and corporate partnerships.

In commissioning Duplan, Montes, and Hedva to contribute to *The Noon Sirens*, we hoped that a certain matrix of interconnected forms and modes of address across time and space would produce a cacophony rather than singular objects to contend with. To that end, we have wanted *The Noon Sirens* to be a field; or perhaps more appropriately, an ocean. And a noisy ocean at that. When so much of digital life is concerned with the signal, what does it mean to be noise, neither singular nor repeated nor clarion? Here we might go to the poet Lisa Robertson's characterization of noise as a kind of poetic politics:

> Noise is a confusion of figure and field. It presents no discernible figure of meaning. It's not silence's opposite, but an outside, mutating term. In a way it is the double of silence, with this difference: Silence's indiscernibility is more often institutionally codified and mystified as value—whether spiritual, punitive or economic. Money, Justice and Gods buy silence. The objects of exchangeability and value can then appear as figure on silence's supporting field, and exchangeability has also its correspondent, communicative sound-objects. From the perspective of these systems of value and meaning, noise belongs to poverty and the failure of value. Noise is pollutant, a sign of the wasteful expenditure of unused energy. Noise is inefficient. Like garbage, it has no meaning at the same time that it signifies an excess of signification; meaning become so dense and continuous that it transforms into field, having previously functioned as figure.[7]

---

7   Lisa Robertson, "Disquiet," in *Nilling: Prose Essays on Noise, Pornography, the Codex, Melancholy, Lucretius, Folds, Cities and Related Aporias* (Toronto: Book*hug Press, 2012), 63.

Perhaps the siren of *SIREN (some poetics)* and those of *The Noon Sirens* are figure and field, respectively. And their noise is a problematization to meaning. Noise as poetry. Poetry as politics. For as Robertson writes, "Noise exceeds its own identity. It is the extreme of difference. Noise is the non-knowledge of meaning, the by-product of economies."[8]

At the moment, works by Duplan and Montes for *The Noon Sirens* are silently occupying space inside the Amant website, as persistent and perhaps parrhesiastic presences. This space engenders a kind of participation not dependent on explanation, knowable outcome, or reaffirmation of something already known. It is a central hope of *The Noon Sirens* that the works, their appearance, their interaction with publics, their legacy and situation inside the contested waters of digital space, all continue to problematize and offer some diffractive quality to the encounter with art online.

Han's critique of surveillance can at times feel judgmental and punitive in its position toward the user, and it does not fully account for all the truly interesting and radical positionalities and works that currently exist online. The organization Trust is one such example. A network of critically engaged users and educators working together, Trust moves toward decentralized online institutions that are financed, owned, and governed by their members. Trust has outlined their "moving castles concept" as a kind of constitutive metaphor and "real-time media type" that combines collective agency and public participation in "miniverses" that are modular, portable, and multiplayer.[9] Trust makes clear that there are a growing number of subcultures, digital communities, and guilds that have turned away from ad-supported social media. Instead, they are migrating their social and cultural activities into semiprivate digital spaces, chat rooms, and Discord servers that aim to be interconnected with ever-changing infrastructure that resists capture.

Yet our concern with *The Noon Sirens* has been with existing cultural territories and how participation online cannot always (or ever) truly escape capital's capture, its grip. We have wanted to test how we might confront, as curators collaborating with poets and artists, our complicity *here*. Not to refuse it but to offer a state of unknowing, or of

---

8   Ibid., 57.

9   "Moving Castles: Modular and Portable Multiplayer Miniverses," Trust website, accessed September 1, 2022, https://trust.support/feed/moving-castles.

the possibility of discomfort, misunderstanding, and problematization. Not as an obstacle to overcome or as a failure of the institution to explain but as a valuable space for transformative experience, a set of lived encounters that prompt a different kind of engagement. Indeed, as we stated from the outset to the artists invited and in the text that announced our program, *The Noon Sirens* is not an attempt to rise above complicity but instead an effort to forge a radical one by recognizing the disposition of the terrain in order to occupy it more fugitively than before, together. We are: testing, waiting, living through, and contending with the siren. Its song at once noise and silence and smoothness and discomfort and danger and ambiguity and, perhaps, solidarity.

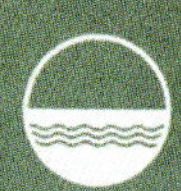

BLACKSPACE:
On the Poetics of an Afrofuture

Anaïs Duplan

Tony Cokes, *No Sell Out*, 1995, 6:20

Fade to Black   a text from popular
culture   but also in riot
                 or otherwise I'm not your
commodity————Cokes as capitalism
                             as a spider
that,
        him in his web. He: am I
        the real thing? We

invent, he submits, the real
thing come up again and again as

images and text,
as the basis, the visual fabric.

Tony Cokes, *Ad Vice*, 1999, 6:36

We've all got opinion   life
is a sport   What's the idea
         of "swipe country"?

do you get down or high

certainly the most typographical

rather an image
behind the text,

through screens of various colors
and conflicting

         the main substance of
the film,
THE IDEAL COPY——   (Andrews
    also retained a concern for the copy,

for imitation throughout) which
         took him away from
                  the computer
         this, getting farther
away from quotations
using color   and I will be
an example of this
                  to influence
and strike me
         to cut and   once or twice
to signal a later sonic

Exhibition
Guide

Katja Aufleger, Patricia L. Boyd,
Bia Davou, Sky Hopinka,
Liliane Lijn, Bernadette Mayer,
Rosemary Mayer, Nour Mobarak,
Senga Nengudi,
Rivane Neuenschwander,
Mayra A. Rodríguez Castro,
Aura Satz, Ser Serpas,
Shanzhai Lyric, Jenna Sutela,
Iris Touliatou, and Dena Yago

Curated by Quinn Latimer

SIREN

(some poetics)

September 15, 2022 –
March 5, 2023

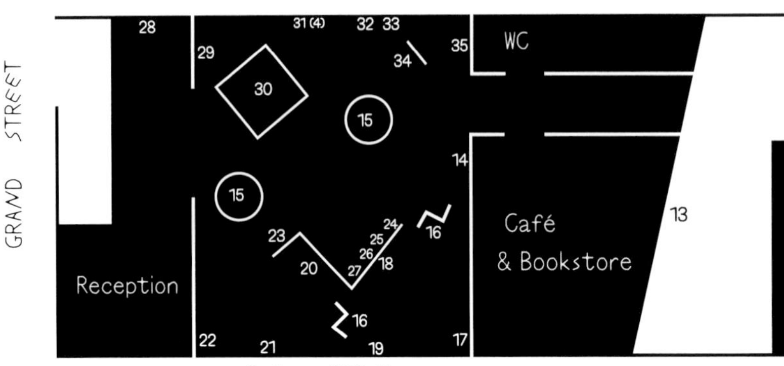

LIST OF WORKS

Gallery 315

1. Liliane Lijn
Study for Woman of War III, 1984

2. Nour Mobarak
Fugue I and *Fugue II*, 2019

3. Senga Nengudi
R.S.V.P. Reverie–Combat Fatigue, 1977-2011

4. Bia Davou
Untitled, 1980s

5. Bia Davou
Untitled (If, Yes, No, Impossible, Stop), 1973

6. Dena Yago
Rope and Lead, 2018

7. Jenna Sutela
nimiia cétii, 2018

8. Rosemary Mayer
Banner to Stand Near a Moon Tent, 1982

9. Rosemary Mayer
Orfeo Mourns Eurydice at Her Urn, the Chorus Comforts Him, 1982

10. Sky Hopinka
I think of my home tonight..., 2020

The clouds are too dull this time of year..., 2020

The mountains are growing..., 2020

11. Bia Davou
Untitled (Odyssey), 1980s

12. (a, b, c, d)
Patricia L. Boyd
Borrowed Time I-IX, 2022

Café and Bookstore

13. Nour Mobarak
Dafne Phos, 2022

Gallery 932

14. Rosemary Mayer
City Roof Tent on Wheels, 1980

15. Liliane Lijn
Queen of Hearts, Queen of Diamonds, 1980

16. Dena Yago
The Bins, 2021
The Announcement, 2021

17. Katja Aufleger
Condition 7.3 5pm (Al Wakra), 2019

18. Aura Satz
Preemptive Listening (part 1: The Fork in the Road), 2018

19. Liliane Lijn
Study for Woman of War V, 1984

20. Sky Hopinka
Fainting Spells, 2018

21. Rivane Neuenschwander
The Silence of the Sirens, 2013

22. Sky Hopinka
Here and after, never knowing what came before..., 2020

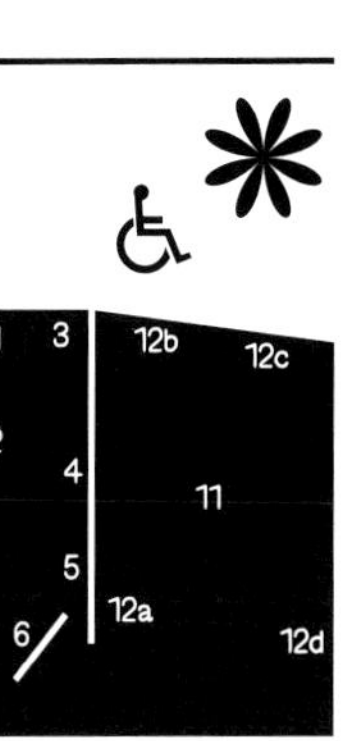

23. Bernadette Mayer
Untitled (index of letters
with their corresponding
colors), originally published in
Proper Name, 1996

24. Bia Davou
Untitled, 1980s

25. Rosemary Mayer
Festive Tent with Lanterns,
1975

26. Rosemary Mayer
In Time Order (Day Lily),
1978

27. Sky Hopinka
*Free me from this body, my
voice can carry only so
far....*, 2020

28. Jenna Sutela
Gut-Machine Poetry, 2017

29. Bernadette Mayer
"Sardines," originally published
in *Works and Days*, 2016

30. Katja Aufleger
Sirens (Al Wakra Vol.III), 2019

31. Bia Davou
Untitled, 1974-1978 (4)

32. Liliane Lijn
Woman of War with Koans,
1987

33. Rosemary Mayer
Marie's Banners, 1982

34. Bia Davou
*Untitled (Serial
Structures)*, 1970s

35. Iris Touliatou
*HAPPINESS, 2018 to 2022
(to Laurie), Vol. III*, 2022

Courtyard 306

36. Ser Serpas
*undulating cathartic
autonomy the shack*, 2022
the path lest take me away,
2022

37. Mayra A. Rodríguez
Castro
Senti, 2022

Gallery 306-
Reading Room

38. Shanzhai Lyric
The Incomplete Poem, 2015-

39. Shanzhai Lyric
*Untitled (Portrait of a
Siren)*, 2022

40. Rosemary Mayer
100 Years (selection),
2007-2011

41. Patricia L. Boyd
*Wastebook (excerpt: M
to S)*, 2022

42. Documentation, books,
and printed poems

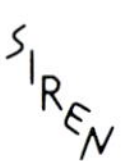

GALLERY 315

1. Liliane Lijn
Study for Woman of War III, 1984
Oil pastels, ink, self-adhesive velvet,
and mirror on filter paper

2. Nour Mobarak
Fugue I and *Fugue II*, 2019
Trametes versicolor mycelium, wood
pellets, and speakers

Language is a material that the
artist Nour Mobarak relies on for
its intersensory potential, at once
memorial and generative (is there
a difference). The vessels of her
embedded sound sculptures are made
with a medicinal saprophytic mycelia,
a fungi with its own intelligent
network that reproduces itself by
eating dead matter. She feeds the
works with wood pellets to cultivate
their growth; mushrooms, the
fruiting bodies of mycelia, write and
wreath their surface, giving ancient
form and legibility to decreation.
Form figured by decay echoes the
sound compositions the sculptures
emit. One sound component offers
phonetic utterances and acapella
songs; the other, conversations
with the artist's late father,
Jean Mobarak, a polyglot with a
30-second (and decaying) memory.
Here, Nour and her father speak in
French, English, Arabic, and Italian,
about cars, soccer, cities, and love.
They speak in song, in rhyme, as play.
Their echoing refrains and melodic
conversations constantly circle
back, reprised like the motifs of
Baroque fugues. A fugue connotes
a lapse in memory and awareness,
as well as a musical structure of
repeated contrapuntal motifs.
Absence and repetition, sign-making
and singing. The elder Mobarak
passed away in the mountains of

Lebanon in the summer of 2022. This
work is shown in his memory.

3. Senga Nengudi
R.S.V.P. Reverie–Combat Fatigue,
1977-2011
Nylon, mesh, and sand

Senga Nengudi's artistic name
signals a sounding. "Senga" means
listen or *hear* in the Duala
language, while "Nengudi" translates
to "a woman who comes to power
as a traditional healer." If her
practice has long centered the
abstract language of materials,
it also emphasizes their virtuosic
performances and ritualistic
resonance with the limits and
conditions of the body. Nengudi
has described her "R.S.V.P." series of
soft, sculptural works of knotted
nylon appendages, weighted
with sand, as fabric spirits and
"abstracted reflections of used
bodies." Whose body, though? Her
works—articulating embodiment,
elasticity, and time while examining
sculptural mores like form, space,
volume, line, and gravity—suggest
such heavy, metaphysical questions.
The "R.S.V.P" series emerged
from Nengudi's experience of
pregnancy and motherhood and
the transformations (corporeal,
ecstatic or otherwise) that
occurred with it. It also reflects on
the history of Black wet-nurses,
which the artist notes suckled
"child after child, their own as well
as those of others, until their
breasts rested on their knees." If
her series title invokes a familiar
French acronym for an expected
response, it is attended to in this
work by the rhyming dichotomy
of reverie and fatigue. A dancer
and performer influenced by
Gutai during her studies in Japan,
Nengudi meant her nylon works to

be manipulated and performed, by collaborators like Maren Hassinger, Ulysses Jenkins, or herself. Thus, the works initially offer stillness and silence but also the inevitability of movement. That said, Nengudi is also a poet, writing under the persona of the pointedly named Lily Bea Moor, whose poems can be found elsewhere in the exhibition.

4. Bia Davou
Untitled, 1980s
Fifteen pages; marker, pencil on tracing, and graph paper

5. Bia Davou
Untitled (If, Yes, No, Impossible, Stop), 1973
Ink, pencil, and marker on watercolor paper

The artistic oeuvre of Bia Davou (1932–1996) was devoted, in part, to the poetics of communication and the ideological and serial structures of language, from myth to math, epic poetry to the Fibonacci sequence. From the 1970s on, the Athens-based artist experimented with scientific models, information technologies, and ancient literary inheritance, translating them into visual artworks that often suggest technologies both ancient (weaving and writing) and recent (coding). Despite her devotion to serialism, however, her work remained lucidly expressive and handmade, evoking musical notation and the early avant-garde. In *Untitled (If, Yes, No, Impossible, Stop)*, 1973, the titular words in Greek are overlaid, like some instructive and yet ambiguous palimpsest, over a circuit board-like ground. The work also evokes a sign of protest, with all the desire and ambivalence such resistance holds. It was made the

year of the Athens Polytechnic student uprising in Greece against the military junta of 1967–1974. The student protests began in November 1973, and effectively brought the Greek dictatorship to an end the following year. Davou's works often explored the Homeric dialectical ideas of *nostos* and *thanatos*, that is longing for return and renown, and death. Both find resonance, in some sidelong way, here.

6. Dena Yago
Rope and Lead, 2018
Pressed wool, hand embroidery, pewter charms, and steel

7. Jenna Sutela
nimiia cétii, 2018
HD video, sound, color, 19 minutes

Jenna Sutela employs words, sounds, bacterium, and other living materials in her installations, performances, and videos that channel precarious social moments entangled with technology. She often casts the computer as medium—as a new alien—able to conduit messages from entities that we usually cannot hear or understand. Inspired by experiments in interspecies communication, in *nimiia cétii* she documents the relations of a neural network, audio recordings of a Martian language, and footage of extremophilic bacteria—a kind of bacterial chorus or glossolalia results. The work uses machine learning to generate a new written and spoken language based on the computer's interpretation of a Martian tongue from the late 1800s, originally channeled and written down by the Swiss spiritualist and artist Hélène Smith, while simultaneously recording the movements of *Bacillus subtilis,* which, according to recent spaceflight experiments, might survive on Mars. Smith, who said she received the Martian language in her trances, claimed to be a reincarnation of both Marie Antoinette and a Hindu deity named Simandini, and was known as the muse of automatic writing by the Surrealists. Smith's Martian language was said to be a kind of speaking in tongues. So might be Sutela's, though her tongue is also a computer, and a bacterium.

8. Rosemary Mayer
Banner to Stand Near a Moon Tent, 1982
Watercolor and colored pencil on paper

From the late 1970s to the early 1980s, New York-based artist Rosemary Mayer (1943-2014) created luminous and witty drawings of tents that she envisioned as sites for celebration that would echo the ancient Greek festivals linked to women and the changing of the seasons, as well as to Chinese moon celebrations. Mayer often situated her tents on New York City rooftops, where one might watch the spectral full moon rise. "To let the moon be seen, a moon tent can't have a roof," she wrote. "And its supports have to float, suggest the draped figures who would have been holding them up, caryatids and the dancing women who held the moon." Alongside her tents, she envisioned banners and lanterns (that which holds writing or light) for these occasions, and she often drew them. Her tent drawings include repeated written refrains in her inimitable slant and cursive hand: chatty asides to viewers to participate. "Anyone can build one," some drawings declare.

Others ask: "Have you got the time?" and: "Can you stay up late?" The drawings mostly remained unrealized performances, but in 1982 Mayer created *Moon Tent*, an installation on the roof of art historian Robert Hobbs's home. The work was installed for one night, during the October full moon, as people played music and ate moon-shaped food. In one of her notebooks, Mayer queried her own motivations. "What kind of pleasures am I suggesting with my tents," she asked, before listing: "Sex, lying about in softness, contemplation of transitory forms." Pleasure, then, was paramount.

9. Rosemary Mayer
Orfeo Mourns Eurydice at Her Urn, the Chorus Comforts Him, 1982
Charcoal, pastel, and graphite on paper

Mayer had a longtime fascination with the Greco-Roman world, and the gendered myths and historiography it both did and did not relinquish. Among her many works that gleaned Greek mythology and the histories of Roman women were Mayer's series of *Orfeo and Eurydice* drawings, made in 1982 for *Drawings for Productions*, an exhibition at the Soho Baroque Opera Company, an alternative space in a harpsichord factory on West Broadway run by Robert Bueker. Mayer's drawings depict scenes from the titular early 1762 Italian opera, based on the myth of Orpheus, composed by Christoph Willibald Gluck. The vessel depicted in Mayer's drawing is a funeral urn, around which mourners, including Orfeo, might dance. The myth of Orpheus and Eurydice has long inspired composers, artists, dancers, filmmakers, and, most famously, poets. In an ancient world, Orpheus was considered the father of poetry, of music, and the art of writing itself. Mayer's own investment in writing, poetics, and the classics was deep and considered, yet her take on the Orpheus and Eurydice myth, which is often approached with grave seriousness (see Apollinaire, Rilke, H.D., Cocteau, Sartre, Senghor, Glück, Valentine, Hayes, et al.) is, instead, light and strange and urbane and a bit fetish.

10. Sky Hopinka
I think of my home tonight. I don't have any resolutions, but I've felt so much through these streets, these neighborhoods. This land and this Land hold so much, and this pain and this Pain call for salves we already have, still needing to be wrapped and poulticed., 2020
Inkjet print, etching

The clouds are too dull this time of year. It's late June and I'm full of anger and hate. They think we're trash, they think we're as useless as our garbage buried in their fields turned up under plow, exposed in heavy rain. It makes me angry to think about that. To feel like that. Under plow and over plowed and plowed over by machines dredging and weeding through the hills and the fields and my family and my home., 2020
Inkjet print, etching

The mountains are growing and you're over there looking at me like that. These Breathings are begging's, these Breathings are asking for anything having to do with direction. Wrapped in blankets made of clouds, Morning Star got up and pointed the way. We were too tired and too weak to

proceed, but still the gesture is still in the east at a certain time of year., 2020
Inkjet print, etching

11. Bia Davou
Untitled (Odyssey), 1980s
Ink, fabric, and thread on linen (set of four sails comprising one installation): small black sail; large sail with brown fabric; sail with black fabric and blue lettering; sail with gray lettering

Bia Davou's series of "Sails," large-scale textile works embroidered with Homeric verse and Fibonacci's golden spiral sequence, conflate technologies both ancient—Greek epic poetry—with those more recent: the language of cybernetics. This relationship between text and textile, song and poem, the oral and the written, epic and code—and the serial structures and operating technologies that weave them together—was a long preoccupation of the artist, whose works in various media evoke the seriality and circulation of language and meaning in radically different ways. Her textile works assume and take space in a pointedly material manner indicative of the late-century art historical moment in which they were conceived and produced, from the text/textile practices of women's work and feminist art to serialism and the feminized labor of early circuit board manufacture. In Davou's late set of "Sails" on view here, lines from the *Odyssey* are embroidered on fabric whose form and title suggest the sails of ships that both did and did not take Odysseus, famously, home. They also invoke the labor of Penelope's dazzling weaving (suggesting those who wove the sails of those ancient ships), and which epic poetry often conflated with the weaving of tales, that is, poetry and renown itself. One of the "Sails" is scripted with the defining Homeric dialectical ideas of *nostos* and *thanatos*. The latter is a figure of death (and its drives). Per the poet Hesiod's *Theogony*, Thanatos is the son of night and the brother of sleep. *Nostos*, meanwhile, is the operating trope of ancient Greek literature, in which an epic hero returns home after a long journey at sea, beset by challenges, and is granted fame. *Nostos* suggests a longing for return and renown. Odysseus's most famous challenge to getting home was the *Sirens*, whose female, not-quite-human voices, and all the knowledge their entrancing sound imparted, would, if heard, bring stasis, exile, death, no fame at all.

12. Patricia L. Boyd
Borrowed Time I, 2022
Borrowed Time II, III, IV, V, 2022
Borrowed Time VI, VII, 2022
Borrowed Time VIII, 2022
Borrowed Time IX, 2022
Used restaurant grease, wax, and damar resin

Serial structures of communication, with their signs, silences, and thresholds—what is held and what is withheld—also define Patricia L. Boyd's "Wall Pieces" (2017–). Embedded high up on the wall, or placed at eye level, Boyd's cast objects—soft, amber forms of some illumined opacity—can appear like votives, like relics, like icons, like fragments of memory and language, both image and sculpture, sign and signified. For them, the artist makes negative casts of small precision consumer objects—here the appendages of a Herman Miller 'Aeron' office chair and a Technic turntable,

both of which Boyd bought at liquidation auction—and embeds them into institutional walls. These readable yet gnomic objects concern calibration and ergonomics, cognitive labor and office work. As a lexicon of forms recessed in the wall, they can suggest the room-as-stanza—that is, the basic unit of poetry and its pale architectonic page. Their citational structure, meanwhile, invokes memory and its medium, language. The abject materiality of the casts—made of food, grease, leftover biological matter—implicate a soiled softness, lucid with light, into the hard, clean, white drywall in which they are embedded. The works are, in a sense, double negatives, receptive forms: negative casts then embedded into recesses in the walls. How far, one wonders, do they need to go? What eroticism of negation, and its sister, abjection, is this? If the abject is that which is "cast off," per Julia Kristeva, and that whom we first discard is our mother, how might we read Boyd's negative casts of signs signaling to us, silently, from these walls?

Amant Café and Bookstore

13. Nour Mobarak
Dafne Phos, 2022
Etched colored glass

*Nour Mobarak's newly commissioned piece is a work of concrete poetry made out of light and shadows, color and language. It emerges from the libretto of *La Dafne*, the first opera from 1598. Like so many Greco-Roman mythic female figures, Dafne was physically transformed into a nonhuman figure under threat of a god's violence: she was transmogrified into a laurel tree to escape Apollo. To that end,

(some poetics)

Mobarak's work plays with language vis a vis the transformation of peoples and power. Here, she selects one word from Dafne's opening lines in the opera—*footprint*—and translates it into six languages; these words are then etched into colored glass panes. *Del fugitivo cervo / quest'è pur orma impressa: / fusse almen qui vicin la fera stessa*, Dafne begins. "Of the fugitive deer / this is the very footprint impressed: / if only the beast itself was here nearby." Beside the original Italian and Latin, the languages Mobarak uses here are the most phonetically complex still in existence. A wide range of sounds, both language tones and clicks, are signified but not heard by the colored panes, then. Etymologically, "footprint" leaves both a light and heavy trace: in Latin, it means vestige, moment, and instant, as well as footprint.

 orma (Italian)
 vestigium (Latin)
 huella (Spanish for *Silbo Gomero* whistling language)
 aиьma (Abkhaz)
 nǂang (!Xoon)
 jyaqᶠslaqᴶ (Eastern Chatino)

932 GALLERY

14. Rosemary Mayer
City Roof Tent on Wheels, 1980
Watercolor and colored pencil on paper

15. Liliane Lijn
Queen of Hearts, Queen of Diamonds, 1980
Two sculptures; optical glass prism and aluminum

The Queens—one of muscular organs, one of solid carbon minerals—are twins. Based on the idea that structure is born from the interaction of negative and positive elements, the sculptures are many-layered, conical, and derived from the radiating reflective facets of a prism. The aluminum plates that make up the two sculptures were originally intended to form one sculpture. This proved too dense, and Lijn split the work into two equal and opposite figures. An optical glass tank prism served as the artist's starting point, whose three facets were then extended out horizontally and vertically in space through a progression of triangular aluminum plates. At once material and immaterial, the Queens emerge from Lijn's long-held interest in pre-patriarchal female archetypes and goddess figures, Greek, Hindu, Indigenous or otherwise. Her various series of vertical prismatic sculptural figures are both mythic and speculative, their technologies of gender, history, and fabulation a corrective to the western trope of divinity as a male principle. "Spirit was claimed by man," she writes, "and woman was left with the burden of a body." What to do with it then. How to build it anew.

16. Dena Yago
The Bins, 2021
The Announcement, 2021
Acrylic and inkjet on canvas in aluminum, and stainless steel frame

The artist and poet Dena Yago's allegorical screens issue queries and posit concerns at once epistemological, aesthetic, and economic. Suggesting both graphic novels and visual essays, each screen narrates the myriad ways in which language shadows and divides and clothes us, using the virtuosic text-image visual grammar of cartoons, while partitioning and channeling art viewers through the very space in which they are placed. As figurative assessments of current cultural issues and their ideological underpinnings, the paravents question labor, meaning, productivity, compensation, temporality, and language itself. One painted screen offers stacked Amazon delivery bins punctuated by cartoon buttons presenting rhetorical refrains and idiomatic equivalencies like "Value and Time." The riff is both philosophical and slapstick, but it also evokes a global precarious workforce of temporary contracts and the recent attempts to unionize such manual and cognitive laborers (from Amazon employees to art museum workers in New York, for example). On another screen, a group of puppies from Disney's *101 Dalmatians* (1961) is informed by an off-screen speaker that "the franchise is dead." If some puppies seem relieved, one is animated by alarm; how will her career pan out now? Her life, like ours, depends on some sequel, that is, an artistic industry shaped by capital and returns, which casts and builds bodies around a certain voice, before disposing of them, and moving onto the next thing.

17. Katja Aufleger
Condition 7.3 5pm (Al Wakra), 2019
HD video, no sound, color, 10 minutes and 15 seconds

Katja Aufleger's work considers the phenomenon of sound as a visual, material, experiential, and narrative medium, one heard or remembered, audible or silent, offered by another or originated in the speaker/ receiver. With its glitchy aesthetic and auditory resistance, her silent video of a Qatari dune as wind imperceptibly alters its pyramidal, granular form, takes as its starting point the so-called singing dunes of the Al Wakra desert. The phenomena of singing dunes—not myth but fact—in which the dune's sheer, granular faces become speakers, and the avalanche of their grains, sound waves, suggests that wall of sound we often talk about in music. Here it is the face of the dune, as avalanches of grains move down its surface. If synchronized in their fall, a humming sound emerges; as grains collide with each other, audible booms are emitted. The size of the sand grains determine the tone, thus each dune offers a different song. In a late, fragmented poem, Paul Celan wrote: *Keine Sandkunst mehr, kein Sandbuch.* That is: "No more sand art, no sand book." The "sand" of his poem is often read as an invocation of the desert, of the Holy Land, and of the book as the holy book—both of which the poet negates. Neither art nor language, he suggests, nor the ability to create coherent meaning through them. Yet Celan's double negation, his line's shifting ground of sand, might today widen, encompassing more than the specific destruction of life and language during Europe's mid-century horrors to contemporary issues of war and its acoustic experience, ecological violence and state misogyny, and all of their soundscapes.

18. Aura Satz
Preemptive Listening (part 1: The Fork in the Road), 2018
Film, stereo, color, sound, 8 minutes and 47 seconds

Aura Satz's ongoing research project on sonic obedience and disobedience is here explored through the trope of the siren. Her short 16mm film, *Preemptive Listening (part 1: The Fork in the Road)*, proposes the siren's glissando wail as a "conditioned and learned signal, one that can potentially be perceptually and musically rewired." In the film, actor and activist Khalid Abdalla narrates his experience of sirens in Egypt during a moment in the Arab Spring, offering them up as the emblematic sound of resistance, oppression, and lost futures. His voice becomes a beacon, activating emergency rotating lights that spin across the film according to the cadence of his speech, suggesting histories of experimental structural cinema as well as structural political violence. Meanwhile, Lebanese trumpet improviser Mazen Kerbaj plays a composition using circular breathing, citing a previous experience striated by sirens, when, in July 2006, he stood on a balcony in Beirut and played his trumpet to the sound of Israeli bombs falling in the distance. "How to listen ahead?" Satz has asked, reflecting on her work. "How to hold the future in mind when listening? The siren is the prism through which to refract this notion of *Preemptive Listening*."

19. Liliane Lijn
Study for Woman of War V, 1984

20. Sky Hopinka
Fainting Spells, 2018
HD video, stereo, color, sound, 9 minutes and 45 seconds

Sky Hopinka's film is an imagined myth for the Xąwiṣka, or the Indian Pipe Plant, a medicinal plant used by the Ho-Chunk to revive those who have fainted. It is narrated through recollections of Ho-Chunk youth, learning, lore, and ideas of departure and arrival. Language in his film is offered in its many guises: as spectral song, ancestral story, handwritten subtitles, poetic script, mythological fabulation, and trancelike oral narrative. The layering of image, subtitle, and voiceover is kaleidoscopic, showing the manifold ways in which communication can be cast and offered and weighed. Language situates Hopinka's practice as an artist, filmmaker, and poet who often works with images, both moving and still. He has taught *chinuk wawa*, a language indigenous to the Lower Columbia River Basin, and his works posit personal positions of Indigenous homeland and landscape while considering language as a container of culture expressed through personal, documentary, and nonfiction forms.

21. Rivane Neuenschwander
The Silence of the Sirens, 2013
Felt, thread, fusible interfacing, and D-ring metal

"Now the Sirens have a still more fatal weapon than their song, namely their silence," writes Kafka in his parable, "The Silence of the Sirens." It is to this he attributes Odysseus's survival, not the wax with which his crew closed their ears, or the rope with which they bound Odysseus to a mast. Rivane Neuenschwander's hanging fabric work takes Kafka's thesis and casts it as both conceptual poem—see the small and large S's of "silence" and "Sirens" stud her pale fabric field like some piece of paper—and as weaving-as-literary-analysis. Odysseus's wife was, of course, Penelope, the expert weaver who kept her suiters away by weaving and unweaving the same shroud every night. Weaving and

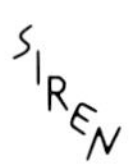

epic poetry were often made analogous in ancient Greek texts, their technologies conflated. If Neuenschwander's larger practice pursues an "ethereal materialism," as she calls it, it is one in which issues of language, materiality, temporality, geography, inheritance, and the social world are stitched together to create aesthetic experiences as expertly layered and tightly woven as a poem or parable itself.

22. Sky Hopinka
Here and after, never knowing what came before or comes next, they sit and watch the ocean thinking of the sand and what's buried underneath. I heard a long time ago that there's a village somewhere near here. Under the sand, overgrown by trees, restless and quiet., 2020
Inkjet print, etching

23. Bernadette Mayer
Untitled (index of letters with their corresponding colors), originally published in *Proper Name*, 1996
Poem projected on screen

Bernadette Mayer's wall poems on view correspond to a synesthetic index that she created in the 1990s based on how she sees letters, in which each letter of the Modern English alphabet corresponds to a different hue. The poems themselves come from her books *Works and Days* (2016) and *A Bernadette Mayer Reader* (1992). An experimental poet, writer, and artist, Mayer has long pursued epic, diaristic, and durational literary projects and constraint-based works of poetry, as well as conceptual artworks that she has called "emotional science experiments." Her more than thirty books include *Midwinter Day*

(1982), an epic poem devoted to the quotidian—writing, mothering, cooking, thinking, reading, sleeping, dancing, working, cleaning, loving, surviving—that narrates a single December day in 1978. (The book-length poem also includes an index of various forms of visual art practice written by her sister Rosemary Mayer.) Other epics of poetics include *Memory* (2020), which collects in book form a July 1971 project in which she produced more than 1100 photographs, and two hundred pages of text, in her examination of the nature of memory, as well as the collections *Eating the Colors of a Lineup of Words: The Early Books of Bernadette Mayer* (2015), and *The Helens of Troy* (2013). As co-editor of the experimental magazine *0 To 9*, with Vito Acconci, and *United Artists*, with Lewis Warsh, Mayer has long fused poetry and visual art practice, and the conceptual, critical, and narrative methodologies that so often attempt to demarcate them. A book of her correspondence with her sister was recently published as *The Letters of Rosemary & Bernadette Mayer, 1976–1980* (2022).

24. Bia Davou
Untitled, 1980s
Ballpoint pen on graph paper

25. Rosemary Mayer
Festive Tent with Lanterns, 1975
Colored pencil and pastel on paper

26. Rosemary Mayer
In Time Order (Day Lily), 1978
Ink, oil crayon, and photograph on paper

27. Sky Hopinka
Free me from this body, my voice can carry only so far. Free me from this body, as I lay on the grass it feels heavy and I can't move. Free me from this body, the color burns brown with dark limbs so tired and missing the weightless breadth of above., 2020
Inkjet print, etching

28. Jenna Sutela
Gut-Machine Poetry, 2017
HD video, sound, color, 19 minutes and 1 second

Jenna Sutela often attempts to interfere with language and its symbolic systems, trying on other forms of language-making through the employ of bacterium, computational processes, and slime molds (in her performance *Many-Headed Reading*, for example). As she reflects on all the ways in which humans interface with technology, she is inspired by "wetware," the idea of a machine with organic, living innards and the potential for biological computing. In *Gut-Machine Poetry*, she examines embodied intelligence, inserting a gut into a computer via a kombucha ferment that works as a number generator. The work proposes a biological computer system in which the chaotic activity of micro-organisms contributes to the creation of a new type of poetry. As the video portrays the evolution of a symbiotic kombucha colony, where yeast and bacteria together produce a stream of words that constitute a new language, the database it interacts with is fed texts glossing the complexities of language and self-replicating machines and code laws. On the basis of biochemical cues from the colony, an algorithm creates new combinations of poetic fragments: a new kind of computer poetry, one that might be inside us already.

29. Bernadette Mayer
"Sardines," originally published in *Works and Days,* 2016
Vinyl cut

30. Katja Aufleger
Sirens (Al Wakra Vol.III), 2019
Seven glass organ pipes, engine, wood, silicone hose, and aluminum

Katja Aufleger's *Sirens (Al Wakra Vol.III)* are constituted, both materially and conceptually, from Qatar's desert and its so-called singing dunes. At once sculptures and instruments designed to echo those dune's tones, her work comprises a series of glass organ pipes connected to an engine and tubes of oscillating air. The sounds the glass pipes emit are the kinds of evocative, almost haptic drones familiar to listeners of new music. The instruments themselves are delicately beautiful translucent organ pipes made from quartz and Al Wakra desert sand. If we all know that glass is made of sand, still the transformation from rough grain to translucent material remains miraculous, and as strange as a dune that might sing to those who approach it. Yet if the artworks begin with the dunes of Al Wakra, they depart from there, going in disparate directions, like grains of sand dispersed by wind. Here, Aufleger's glass pipes rest horizontal, in a series of seven. Their forms evoke transparent Cycladic funerary figures or gleaming medical instruments or the series of scars such instruments might attend to. Each minimalist 'volume' suggests a kind of formal art-historical analogy gleaned from the history of contemporary sculpture, as air pumps through its pipes, creating soundtracks that evoke the mythic drones of the desert, its acoustic experience and immaterial facts.

31. Bia Davou
Untitled, 1974–1978
Four works: Ink, pencil, dry pastel on watercolor paper

32. Liliane Lijn
Woman of War with Koans, 1987
Acrylic and oil pastel on filter paper

The virtuosic sculptures of Liliane Lijn often offer technological bodies—all surface, sound, smoke, prisms, poems, and lasers—gleaned equally from pre-patriarchal myth and speculative science fiction, poetry and sculpture, archeology and ecology, as well as the burden of bearing a female-hewing body. Her painting *Woman of War with Koans* depicts some of her common sculptural forms, from her rotating "Koans" and "Poem Machines" of the early 1970s to her later giant goddess figures of the 1980s. In this work, we see an image of her *Woman of War*, her female archetype allegorizing the creative impulse (in which creation remains a battle, and the artist a warrior), standing alongside a "Koan." In these latter sculptures of large conelike forms, often irregularly slatted tetrahedrons that revolve slowly in place, Lijn attempts to dematerialize volume and accept ambiguity. A koan, one could note, is a question without an answer. *So might be this work.*

33. Rosemary Mayer
Marie's Banners, 1982
Charcoal and pencil on paper

34. Bia Davou
Untitled (Serial Structures), 1970s
Ink on linen and rope

35. Iris Touliatou
HAPPINESS, 2018 to 2022 (to Laurie), Vol. III
i. on accents and arousals, in vivo and in vitro
ii. on middle age in the islands
iii. on the sleep of mothers and the refusal of paternal legacies
iv. on spoilers and the bottom line,
2022
Unread email inbox, subscriptions, alerts, software, counters, verses, 7" LCD screen, carton, magnets, and eggs

Iris Touliatou's *HAPPINESS, 2018 to 2022 (to Laurie)* is the third volume of a series of works that survey the way language, both oral and written, scores and scripts lives inflected by gender, age, islands, ideology, economy, attachments, architecture, consumption, cities, poverty, ambition, disappointment, family, hormones, friendship, literature, climate collapse, geography, war, labor, desire, infrastructure, both maternal and paternal legacies. A small screen, held in place on the wall by the frame of an egg carton, offers a nonlinear narrative of textual fragments, statements, and non-sequiturs that appear, disappear, and are replaced against an unchanging dark digital ground. The pace of the captions' appearance onscreen—sometimes slow, sometimes fast—is set by custom-made software regulated by the speed of the incoming notifications from an entirely unread Gmail inbox. The inbox receives job alerts, astrological newsletters, weather predictions, travel opportunities, news headlines, and various spam and subscriptions, all of which remain unopened and unread. As the unread emails pile up, the screen's own fragmented narrative fails to progress toward any resolution. The artist herself has written: "It is like lip-singing to the rhythm of one's selfcare, and to the attachments, attractions, and experiences of precarious living imposed by architectural, social, and economic structures." *HAPPINESS* is dedicated to Laurie Parsons, as is the unread email account.

COURTYARD 306

36. Ser Serpas
undulating cathartic autonomy
the shack, 2022
Mixed media of found objects (umbrella, public school desks)
the path lest take me away, 2022
Mixed media of found objects (tire, wall, metal bar from bookcase)

Ser Serpas is an artist-poet who, like Senga Nengudi, found her artistic and activist voice in Los Angeles, and likewise assembles quotidian and found material—from industrial and domestic detritus to gifted fabrics ands gleaned fragments of language—into shapes we might call, in some dry shorthand, sculpture and poetry. Her works labor the line between value and meaning, material and form, volume and line, title and poem, furniture and garbage, inside and out. For Amant's courtyard she has created two new sculptural works, whose ingredients—neither completely raw nor cooked—come from the streets around the industrial East Williamsburg neighborhood of warehouses, family homes, and small storefronts where the art foundation is situated, and which the artist spent the summer canvassing for ideas and discarded

objects. The resulting installation features what the artist calls her "assisted readymades," in which she sources her materials from the surrounding environs of the exhibition space, then produces them on site. The assembly of the work, and its titling, is its own performance, as Duchamp (also a poet) once taught us. The animating silence of Serpas's sculpture—here as light and ludic as a collapsed yellow umbrella, and as heavy as a piece of drywall—arises perhaps from its materiality and breadth, and its deft consideration of volume, weight, line, and object. But it does not preclude Serpas's investment in language, which is there, and which we might grasp, if only we could understand it.

37. Mayra A. Rodríguez Castro
Senti, 2022
Stainless steel, aluminum and silver aggregate chimes, horsehair string

Issues of sound, narration, translation, poetic inheritance, and language both embodied and disembodied are integral to the work of poet, translator, and artist Mayra A. Rodríguez Castro. Her disparate oeuvre is situated in a long lineage of diasporic Black feminist narrative poetics and conceptual art practices. She has translated written works by Adrian Piper and recently edited a collection of Audre Lorde's lectures, writings, and seminars in Europe. For the exhibition, Rodríguez Castro contributes a commissioned sound sculpture composed of wind bells made in Colombia to approximate the poet's own tonal register. The bells borrow from passing wind currents, "making a song in standing," as she notes. Their bells might be said to sound

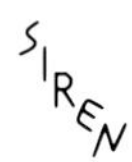

the alarm of wind, of weather, of airy disturbance, but their tone is anything but alarming. An instrument made of consecutive, hollow, metal bars, which play by clinking as they react to air draughts, the bars are tuned to the musical key of her voice. As she writes: "The low notes are obtained by vocalizing until the voice is nearly imperceptible. The high notes mark wherever the voice strains. Other vocal features are nonreplicable in the instrument because the voice is shaped internally by water, bone, and muscle. The brightness of the voice, a quality produced by vocal folds and intermittent spaces in the vocal tract, cannot be replicated in rigid metal. Every curve draws a sonic quality." Over the course of the exhibition, Rodríguez Castro accompanies her bells in a series of unplanned readings for two voices, or one.

Gallery 306: Reading Room

38. Shanzhai Lyric
The Incomplete Poem, 2015-ongoing
Poetry-garments, mixed media, dimensions variable

Shanzhai Lyric considers their ongoing *Incomplete Poem* (2015–) project to be one long poem moving across bodies and landscapes (like many ancient epics themselves). Indeed, the exhibition's thread of text and textile, and the oracular, bootlegged line as a kind of urbane geopolitical poetics, is woven through Shanzhai Lyric's body of work, from their archive of garments featuring poetic fragments to their recent work exploring gendered theft and counterfeit goods. The artistic duo's name shares certain resonances and rhymes with epics of ancient literatures and shipping societies, "Shanzhai Lyric" being an anonymously and collectively authored ongoing poem emerging out of the detritus of empire and consumerism and a trade-ridden oral-to-text culture. Meanwhile, what they call their "Poetic Research and Archival Unit" acts as a roving set of apparatuses for linguistic transmission, evoking questions of mistranslation—and the idea of translation as an anti-neocolonial mode, per the poet and translator Don Mee Choi (whose own works on the coloniality and violence of language are on view nearby as well). For *SIREN (some poetics)*, Shanzhai Lyric present a new iteration of *Incomplete Poem*, their shifting archive of *shanzhai* t-shirts they source in cities from Hong Kong to New York. Their purpose-built reading apparatuses, meanwhile, reference structures where text and textile trouble the borders of public and private space: laundry lines, newspaper racks, billboards, runways, and trash heaps. Here they inaugurate a new system, repurposing anti-theft security tags as a poetic tagging system for a growing archive of poetry-garments. Alongside the archive, accumulating reading materials explore the poetics of bootlegging, shoplifting as subversion, and the archetype of the thief.

39. Shanzhai Lyric
Untitled (Portrait of a Siren), 2022
50 pounds plastic anti-theft security tags, modified anti-theft security panels, six-channel audio

Created in collaboration with artists Natalie Galpern and Yuhan Shen

Six tall panels are arranged in a circle, forming a siren chorus, of a kind. The work's sculptural form suggests a ritualistic circle of slight standing stones in particularly silver and slender manufacture, or more contemporary minimalist environmental sculpture. It is composed, though, of anti-theft panels designed to secure consumer goods and discourage the thief (whoever she may be). The sculpture's alarms are activated when viewers to the exhibition slip through the panels with the security tags that trigger the sirens (one of our contemporary rituals). The work emerges from the artists' interest in theories of gendered theft—that is, shoplifting—and the auditory experience and specific policing that accompanies it. Visitors are invited to steal the security tags and pass through the panels, which have been reprogrammed to emit a haunting and layered sonic landscape that evokes alarm, yes, but also something else. Composed of distorted siren sounds, their soundscape transforms instruments of punishment into instruments of song. Inspired by the mythical Sirens, whose subversive singing and total knowledge lured ancient sailors away from trade and conquest and into stasis—or so it was told and then written down, *as poetry*—the artwork asks us to rethink ideas of property, and to perhaps even celebrate the liberatory, redistributive aspirations of those who resist such notions of possession. Created by *Shanzhai Lyric* in collaboration with artists *Natalie Galpern* and *Yuhan Shen*, the work is accompanied by a publication produced in conversation with feminist shoplifting theorist *Silvia Bombardini*. The publication considers

"shui huo," (水货), a Chinese phrase that means smuggled contraband but translates literally to "water goods," referring to those un-declared commodities often cast-off ships in harbors to avoid taxes. What else do we cast off to avoid getting caught?

40. Rosemary Mayer
100 Years (selection), 2007-2011
Six works; watercolor and ink on paper

Rosemary Mayer's *100 Years* series of watercolors narrate the lives of elite Roman and Byzantine political women between the fifth and sixth centuries in the form of a particularly painterly and color-struck graphic novel format. Like one of her most well-known fabric sculptures, *Galla Placidia*, Mayer's *100 Years* series of works paper consider powerful women figures like the titular daughter of the Roman emperor Theodosius I, Galla, a mother, tutor, and advisor to emperor Valentinian III herself. The works on view here narrate the entangled and often related lives of Roman royalty, including Justina, an empress married to Valentinian I, as well as Juliana, a princess and daughter of Anicius Olybrius, one of the last of the Western Roman emperors. Along with their marrying and mothering and politicking—the women bred emperors then raised and advised them—they also did scholarly work. Around 515 BC Juliana commissioned a codex known as the Vienna Dioscorides, an illuminated scientific manuscript that features more than 400 pictures of animals and plants rendered in a naturalistic style. In later centuries it was used as a textbook in the imperial hospital of Constantinople; it is now called the Juliana Anicia Codex. The full forms and luminous colors of Mayer's watercolors here—toeing the line of illustration but not quite crossing it—resonate with the multihued volumes of her fabric sculptures, which almost feel like abstractions of these very images. Mayer was interested in the graphic novel format and taught it at LaGuardia Community College in New York. Along with her work on Greco-Roman women, she would also illustrate the epic poems *Beowulf* and *The Epic of Gilgamesh*, perhaps the world's oldest long poem. Here, though, in *100 Years*, the frames of Mayer's images are crammed with color and text and line—there is little of the articulated empty space that the grammar of cartoons usually relies on. Instead, a rush of visual and textual information attempts to fill in the lives of these women, so integral to history's machinations and continuance, and yet often disappeared in its historical record.

41. Patricia L. Boyd
Wastebook (excerpt: M to S), 2022
Ink on office paper

42.
Documents, books, and poems

Courtesies:

Katja Aufleger: Galerie Conradi, Hamburg and Galerie Stampa, Basel
Bia Davou: Radio Athènes and Melas Martinos, Athens
Liliane Lijn and Iris Touliatou: Rodeo, London/Piraeus
Rosemary Mayer: Estate of Rosemary Mayer and Gordon Robichaux, New York
Senga Nengudi: Lonti Ebers Collection
Rivane Neuenschwander: Deedie Rose Collection

All the works in the exhibition are courtesy of the artists.

Thanks to Max and Marie Warsh; Zafos Xagoraris, Katerina Stefanidaki, Helena Papadopoulos, and Andreas Melas; Sylvia Kouvali; and all the artists and poets.

All programs are supported by Amant.

Texts by Quinn Latimer.

Amant

315 Maujer St. Brooklyn, NY 11206
amant.org
@amant.arts

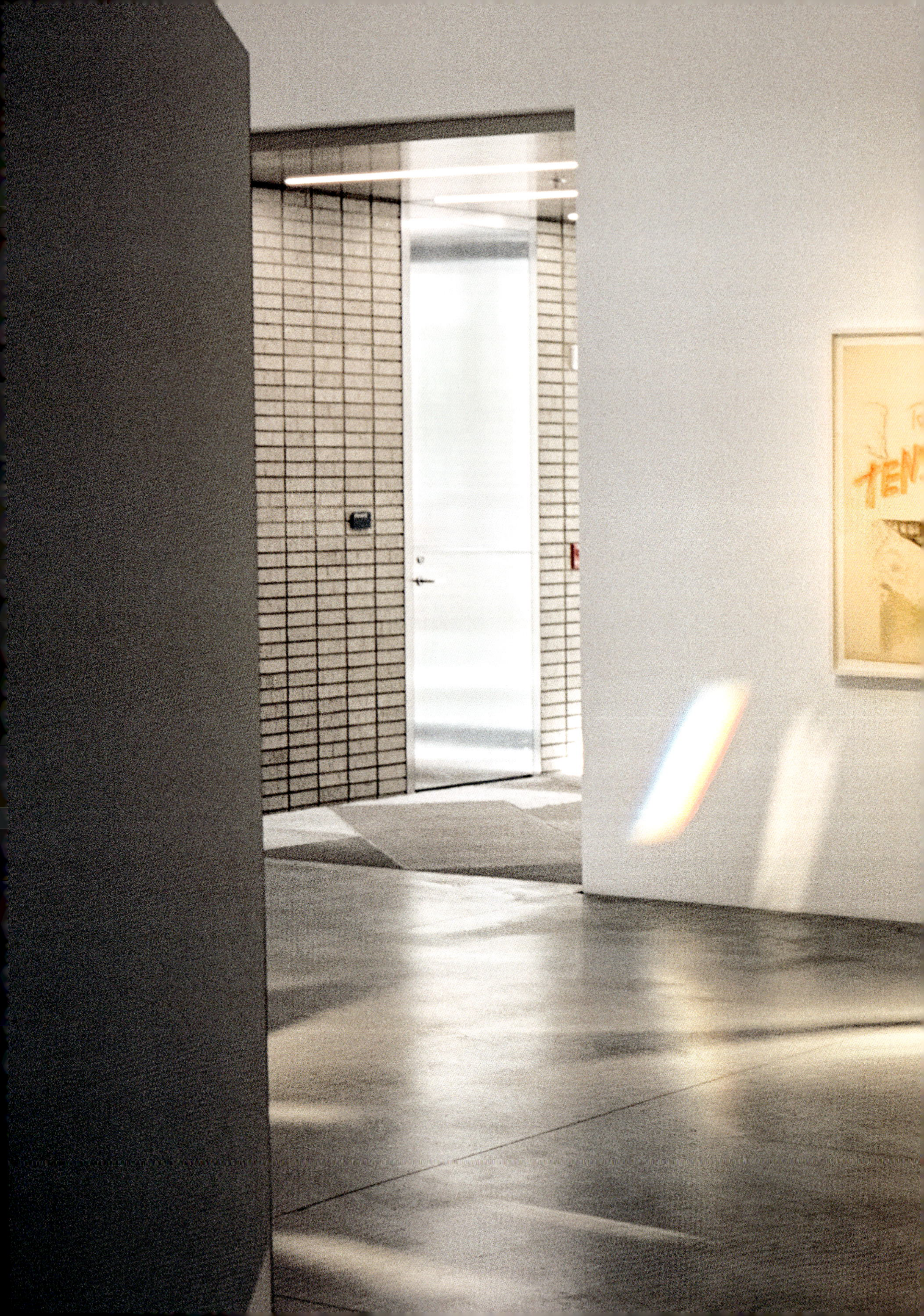

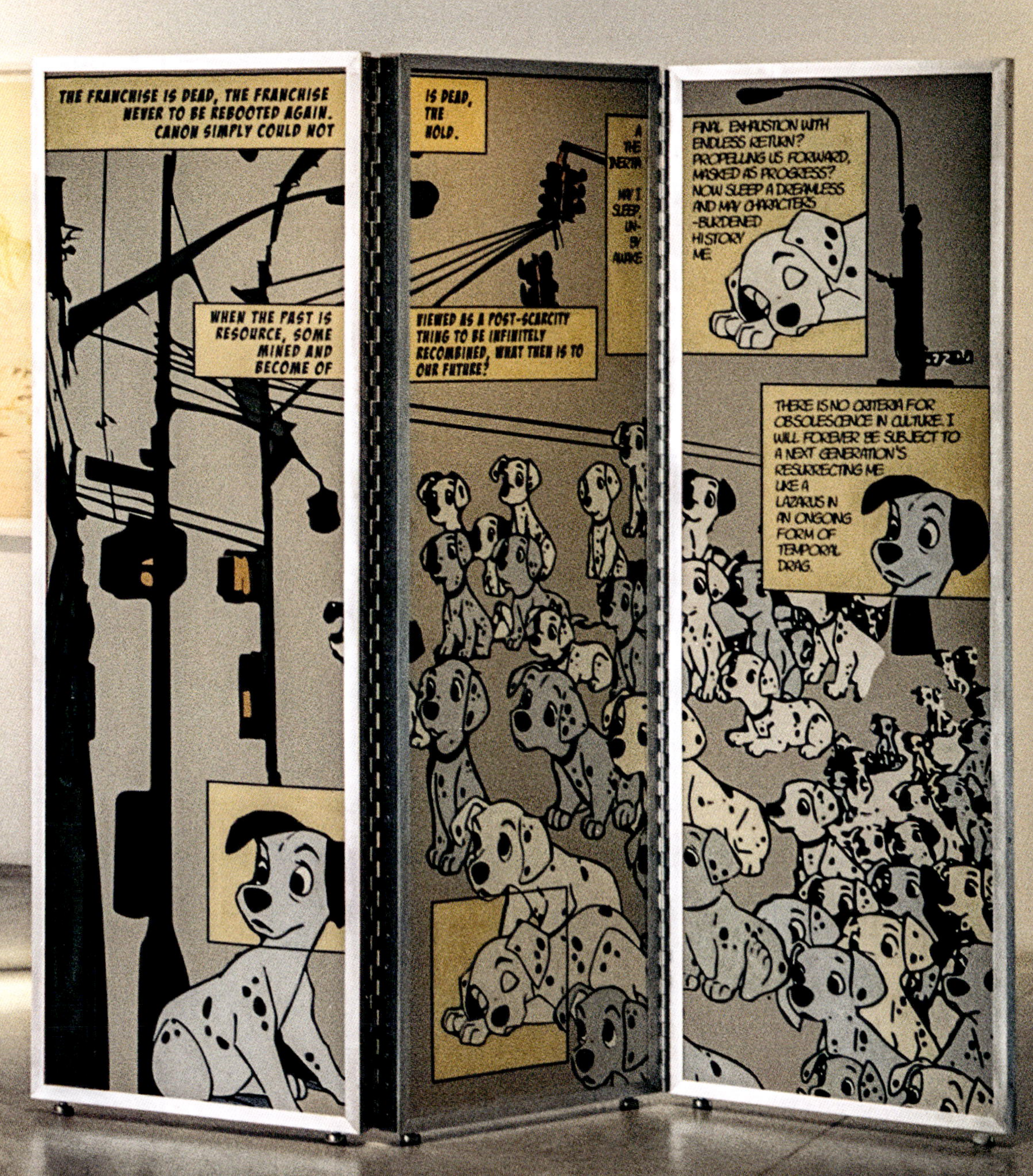

THE FRANCHISE IS DEAD, THE FRANCHISE NEVER TO BE REBOOTED AGAIN. CANON SIMPLY COULD NOT
WHEN THE PAST IS RESOURCE, SOME MINED AND BECOME OF
IS DEAD, THE HOLD.
VIEWED AS A POST-SCARCITY THING TO BE INFINITELY RECOMBINED, WHAT THEN IS TO OUR FUTURE?
FINAL EXHAUSTION WITH ENDLESS RETURN? PROPELLING US FORWARD, MASKED AS PROGRESS? NOW SLEEP A DREAMLESS AND MAY CHARACTERS -BURDENED HISTORY ME.
THERE IS NO CRITERIA FOR OBSOLESCENCE IN CULTURE. I WILL FOREVER BE SUBJECT TO A NEXT GENERATION'S RESURRECTING ME LIKE A LAZARUS IN AN ONGOING FORM OF TEMPORAL DRAG.

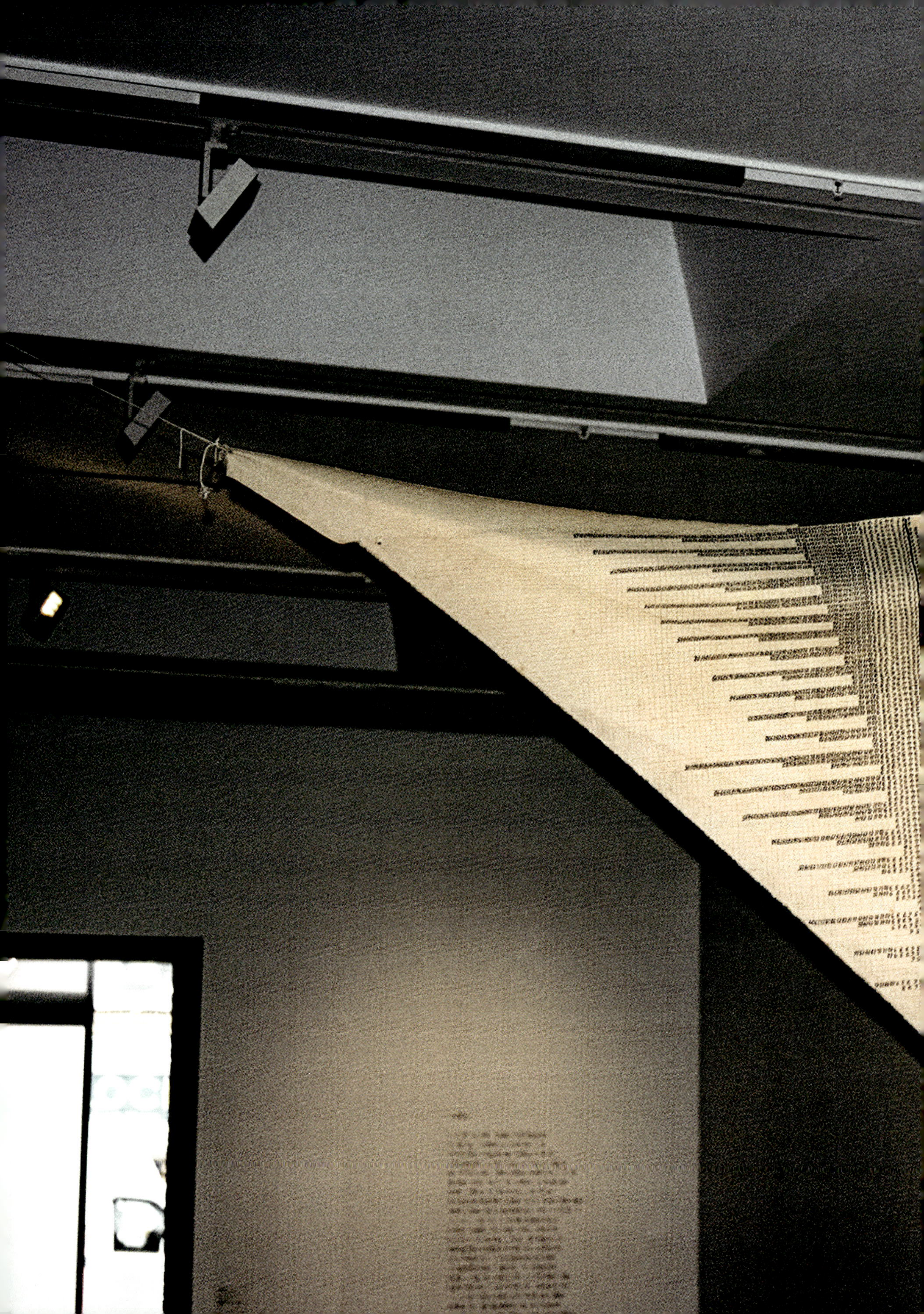

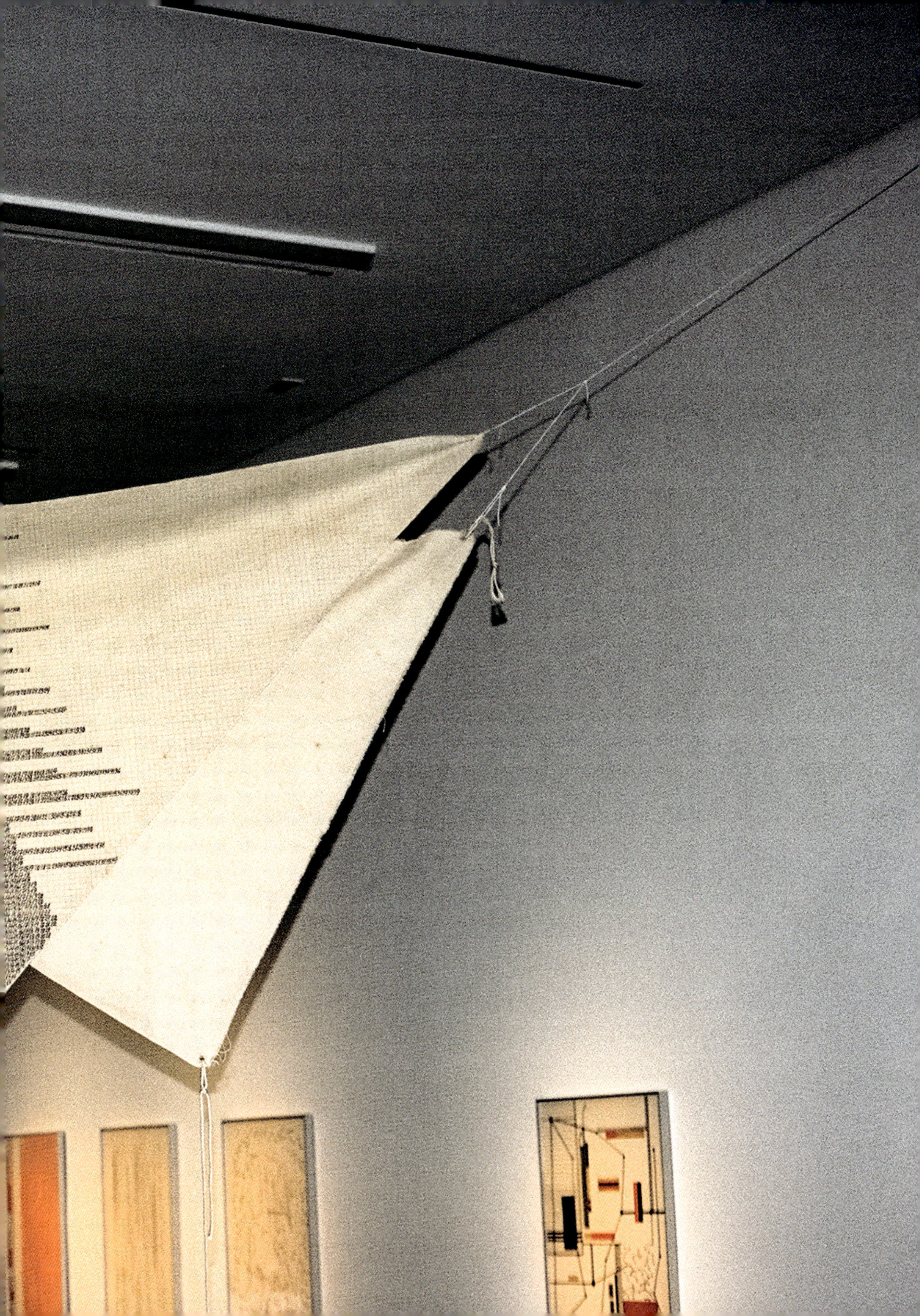

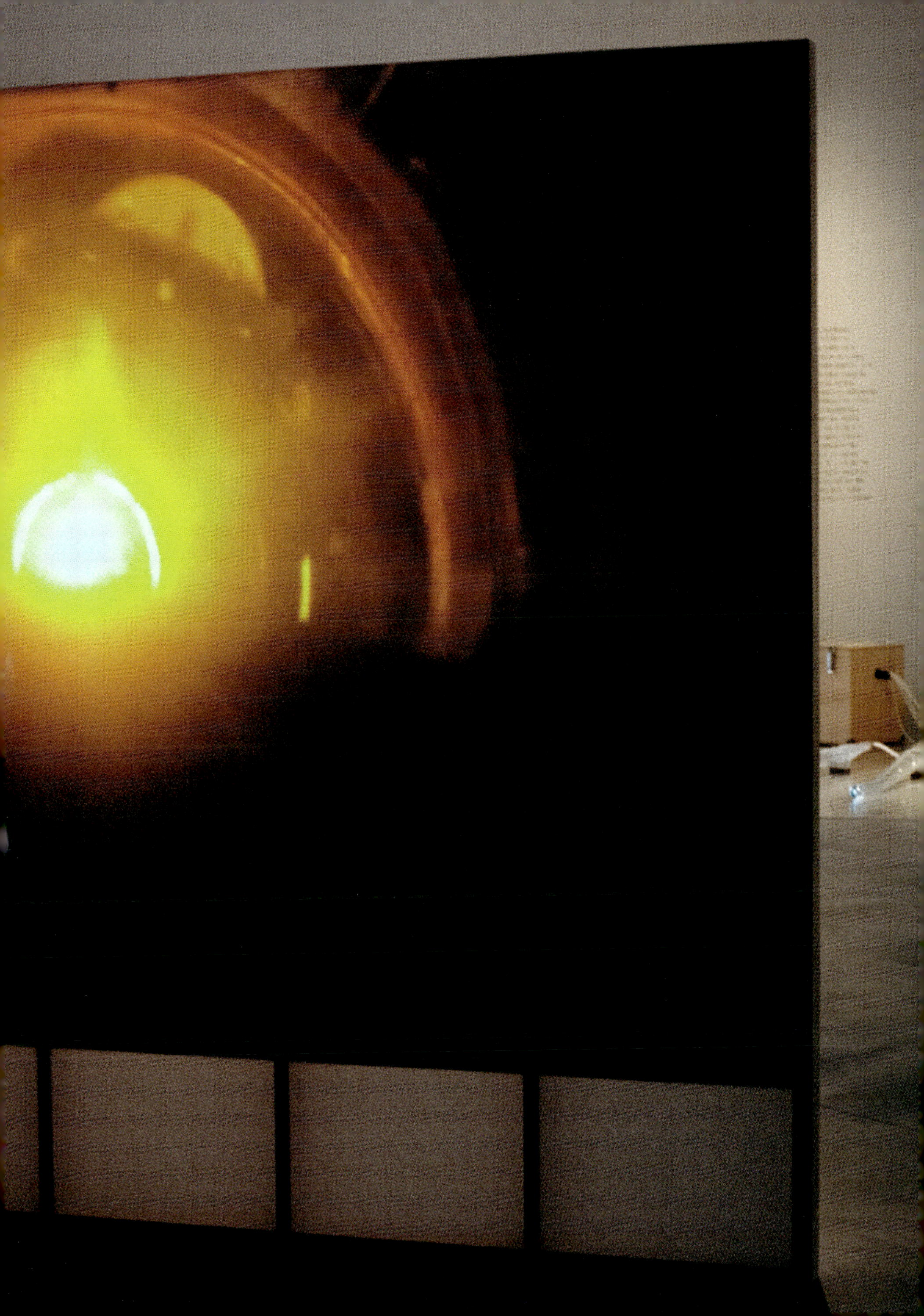

Reprint Permissions, in order of appearance:

Excerpt and cover design from *Cassandra: A Novel and Four Essays* by Christa Wolf, translated by Jan van Heurck. Text: translation copyright renewed © 1984 by Farrar, Straus and Giroux, Inc. Cover design © 1984 by Jacqueline Schuman. Used by permission of Farrar, Straus and Giroux

Édouard Glissant, "Concerning the Poem's Information," from *Poetics of Relation* (University of Michigan Press, 1997). Reproduced with the permission of the University of Michigan Press

Bia Davou, "Serial Structures," from *The Serial Structures of Bia Davou, Space + Arts Issues* [Θέματα Χώρου + Τεχνών II] magazine. Reprinted in *Bia Davou* (Paratiritis Art Gallery, 1992). Newly commissioned English translation by Vassilis Douvitsas. Courtesy Radio Athènes

Bia Davou, "Serial Structures 2. *The Odyssey*: A Brief Summary" (Desmos Art Gallery, 1981). Newly commissioned English translation by Vassilis Douvitsas. Courtesy Radio Athènes

Lilia Bea Moor (Senga Nengudi), "Lilies of the Valley Unite! Or Not," 1998/2023. Courtesy the artist and Sprüth Magers

Nour Mobarak, "Recital" (2019), from *Father Fugue Libretto*. Courtesy Recital (Sean Mc Cann)

Bernadette Mayer, "Section 6," from *Midwinter Day* (New Directions, 1982), 110–19. Reprinted with the permission of New Directions

Rosemary Mayer, cover of *Bernadette Mayer Poetry* (The Kulcher Foundation, 1976). Reproduced with the permission of the estate of Rosemary and Bernadette Mayer

Cover of *The Letters of Rosemary and Bernadette Mayer* (Lenbachhaus, Ludwig Forum, Foundation, Spike Island, and Swiss Institute, 2022). Courtesy Swiss Institute, New York

Rosemary Mayer, "Passing Thoughts," 1998. Reproduced with the permission of the estate of Rosemary Mayer

Liliane Lijn, "Song 7: What I Saw," from *Crossing Map* (Thames & Hudson, 1984). Reproduced with the permission of Hansjörg Mayer

Franz Kafka, "The Silence of the Sirens," from *Parables and Paradoxes* (bilingual edition), edited by Nahum N. Glatzer (Schocken Books, 1946). Reproduced with the permission of Schocken Books, an imprint of Knopf Doubleday Publishing Group, a division of Penguin Random House LLC. All rights reserved

Max Horkheimer and Theodor W. Adorno, "Odysseus or Myth and Enlightenment," in *The Dialectic of Enlightenment* (Continuum US, 1969). Reproduced with the permission of Continuum US, an imprint of Bloomsbury Publishing

Don Mee Choi, "Ahn Hak-sŏp #4," from *DMZ Colony* (Wave Books, 2020). Reproduced with the permission of the artist and Wave Books

Anaïs Duplan, "Tony Cokes, *No Sell Out*, 1995, 6:20" and "Tony Cokes, *Ad Vice*, 1999, 6:36," from *Blackspace: On the Poetics of an Afrofuture* (Black Ocean, 2020). Reproduced with the permission of Black Ocean

SIREN (some poetics), exhibition brochure. Courtesy Amant

List of Works, installation views at
Amant, September 15, 2022–March 5,
2023

pp. 6–7
Aura Satz, *Preemptive Listening (part 1:
The Fork in the Road)*, 2018. 16 mm film
transferred to HD video (color, stereo
sound, 8:47 min.)

pp. 8–9 (from left)
Iris Touliatou, *HAPPINESS, 2018 to
2022 (to Laurie), Vol. III
i. on accents and arousals, in vivo
and in vitro
ii. on middle age in the islands
iii. on the sleep of mothers and the refusal
of paternal legacies
iv. on spoilers and the bottom line*, 2022;
Liliane Lijn, *Queen of Hearts, Queen of
Diamonds*, 1980; Rosemary Mayer, *City
Roof Tent on Wheels*, 1980

pp. 10–11
Dena Yago, *Rope and Lead*, 2018
(detail). Pressed wool, hand embroidery,
pewter charms, and steel; 105 × 57 ×
2 inches (266.7 × 144.8 × 5.1 cm)

pp. 42–43 (from left)
Liliane Lijn, *Queen of Hearts, Queen
of Diamonds*, 1980; Katja Aufleger,
Sirens (Al Wakra Vol. III), 2019; Bia
Davou, *Untitled*, 1974–78; Sky Hopinka,
Fainting Spells, 2018

pp. 44–45
Liliane Lijn, *Queen of Hearts, Queen of
Diamonds*, 1980. Optical glass prism
and aluminum; two parts: 90 × 73 ×
73 inches (227 × 185 × 185 cm), 94 × 73 ×
73 inches (237 × 185 × 185 cm)

pp. 46–59
Shanzhai Lyric, *Untitled (Portrait of
a Siren)*, 2022 (detail). Fifty pounds
of plastic anti-theft security tags,
modified anti-theft security panels,
and six-channel audio; 63 × 77 ×
77 inches (160 × 195.6 × 195.6 cm)

pp. 50–51
Shanzhai Lyric, *The Incomplete Poem*,
2015–ongoing (detail). Poetry garments
and mixed media; dimensions variable

p. 52
Bia Davou, *Untitled (Odyssey)*, 1980s
(detail). Ink, fabric, and thread on
linen; four parts: 45¼ × 31½ × 30¾
inches (115 × 80 × 78 cm), 145⅝ × 173¼ ×
96½ inches (370 × 440 × 245 cm), 131⅛ ×
133⅞ × 74¾ inches (333 × 340 × 190 cm),
129⅞ × 114⅛ × 59 inches (290 × 330 ×
150 cm)

p. 53
Liliane Lijn, *Crossing Map*, published by
Thames & Hudson by arrangement with
Editions Hansjörg Mayer, 1984

p. 54
Bia Davou, *Untitled*, 1980s (detail).
Marker and pencil on tracing and graph
paper; 15 sheets: 6 × 4½ inches (15.5 ×
11.5 cm) each

p. 55
Patricia L. Boyd, *Borrowed Time IV,
V, VI*, 2022. Used restaurant grease,
damar resin, and beeswax; three parts:
4⅜ × 12¼ × 2⅜ inches (11 × 31 × 6 cm),
3½ × 2¼ × 2¼ inches (9 × 6 × 6 cm),
12¼ × 9 × 1½ inches (31 × 23 × 4 cm)

p. 56
Nour Mobarak, *Dafne Phos*, 2022.
Etched colored glass; 1 part: 12 ×
12 inches (30.5 × 30.5 cm), 4 of
12 parts: 8 × 12 inches (20.3 × 30.5 cm)

p. 57 (from foreground)
Katja Aufleger, *Sirens (Al Wakra Vol.
III)*, 2019; Bia Davou, *Untitled*, 1974–78

pp. 122–23
Entrance to Géza at Amant, 306 Maujer
Street, Brooklyn, New York

pp. 124–25 (from left)
Rivane Neuenschwander, *The Silence
of the Sirens*, 2013; Shanzhai Lyric,
Untitled (Portrait of a Siren), 2022;

Sky Hopinka, *Here and after, never
knowing what came before or comes next,
they sit and watch the ocean thinking of
the sand and what's buried underneath. I
heard a long time ago that there's a village
somewhere near here. Under the sand,
overgrown by trees, restless and quiet.*,
2020

pp. 126–27 (from left)
Aura Satz, *Preemptive Listening (part 1:
The Fork in the Road)*, 2018; Bia Davou,
Untitled, 1974–78; Bia Davou, *Untitled
(Serial Structures)*, 1970s; Liliane Lijn,
Queen of Hearts, Queen of Diamonds,
1980; Liliane Lijn, *Woman of War with
Koans*, 1987; Rosemary Mayer, *Marie's
Banners*, 1982

pp. 128–29
Shanzhai Lyric, *The Incomplete Poem*,
2015–ongoing (detail). Poetry garments
and mixed media; dimensions variable

pp.130–31
Ser Serpas, *undulating cathartic
autonomy the shack*, 2022 (detail).
Mixed media of found objects (umbrella
and public-school desks); 57 × 80 ×
79 inches (144.7 × 203.2 × 200.6 cm)

pp. 240–42 (from left)
Rosemary Mayer, *City Roof Tent
on Wheels*, 1980; Dena Yago, *The
Announcement*, 2021

pp. 242–43 (from left)
Bernadette Mayer, "Sardines," first
published in 2016; Bia Davou, *Untitled
(Serial Structures)*, 1970s; Bia Davou,
Untitled, 1974–78

pp. 244–45
Aura Satz, *Preemptive Listening (part 1:
The Fork in the Road)*, 2018. 16 mm film
transferred to HD video (color, stereo
sound, 8:47 min.)

p. 248
Entrance to Géza at Amant, 306 Maujer
Street, Brooklyn, New York

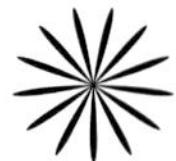

Amant

315 Maujer Street
Brooklyn, NY 11206
amant.org

Lonti Ebers, Founder and CEO
Nicholas Pilato, Executive Director
Isabella Nimmo, Associate Curator
Patricia Hernández, Associate Curator of Learning
Maggie Bamberg, Production Manager
Hannah Marks, Executive Assistant
Eda Li, Design and Communications Coordinator
Melissa Rodríguez, Visitor Engagement Manager
Anthony Limauro, Head of Installations